You *&your* *ADD* Child

You & your ADD Child

practical strategies for coping with everyday problems

Ian Wallace

HarperCollins*Publishers*

HarperCollins*Publishers*

First published in Australia in 1996
Reprinted in 1997, 1998 (twice)
by HarperCollins*Publishers* Pty Limited
ACN 009 913 517
A member of the HarperCollins*Publishers* (Australia) Pty Limited Group
http://www.harpercollins.com.au

HarperCollins*Publishers*
25 Ryde Road, Pymble, Sydney, NSW 2073, Australia
31 View Road, Glenfield, Auckland 10, New Zealand
77-85 Fulham Palace Road, London W6 8JB, United Kingdom
Hazelton Lanes, 55 Avenue Road, Suite 2900, Toronto, Ontario M5R 3L2
and 1995 Markham Road, Scarborough, Ontario M1B 5M8, Canada
10 East 53rd Street, New York NY 10032, USA

National Library of Australia Cataloguing-in-Publication data:

Wallace, Ian, 1958–   .
You and your ADD child: Practical strategies for coping with
everyday problems.
Includes index
ISBN 0 7322 5686 0.
1. Attention-deficit hyperactivity disorder – Treatment.
2. Attention-deficit-disordered children – Rehabilitation-Education.
I. Title. II. You and your attention deficit disordered child.
618.92858906

Cover illustration by Scott Rigney
Printed in Australia by Griffin Press Pty Ltd on 79gsm Bulky Paperback

9 8 7 6 5 4   98 99 00 01

CONTENTS

▲ *Contents* ▲

FOREWORD

In the mid eighties I believed that the behavioural techniques I was promoting worked well for children with Attention Deficit Disorder (ADD). But, despite my best efforts, parents in my practice reported remarkably little success. When I rethought my way of working there were much greater gains, but the real turnaround came when I discovered the teachings of Ian Wallace.

Ian had come down the same behavioural path and had also found that the classic behaviour and psychological theories he knew were relatively ineffective with these children. He saw that special ways were needed to manage a child who was inattentive, forgetful, disorganised and acted without proper thought. When Ian tried the usual rewards to motivate, the ADD child would demand another and then another. If he resorted to reasoned debate, they would argue to the death.

The first time I heard Ian speak I liked his commonsense approach. But more impressive was the feedback from parents who saw their lives had been helped through this man's intervention. There is no doubt that Ian is a militant behaviouralist, but he is also a humanist and a realist. He is highly supportive of parents and he sees the ADD child as exciting, challenging and full of life.

Ian is knowledgeable about all possible therapies for ADD and believes that these children need a combination of the best that is available. He accepts the place of stimulant medication, which often helps a child focus and then enables his behaviour programs to work.

Ian is honest about what he can achieve. In this book he claims no quick cures, on offer is a slow, step-wise way to turn around behaviour and move parents to a position of control. His ideas are practical and based on immense hands-on experience.

This is an optimistic book in which the author sees the drive, enthusiasm and creativity of the ADD child as a great talent. *You and your ADD child* may have been written for parents, but professionals will also find it fascinating, certainly I did. This must be one of the best books ever written on behaviour management and I am proud to be part of it.

Dr Christopher Green,
Paediatrician, Child Care Author,
Head, Child Development Unit,
New Children's Hospital, Sydney

PREFACE

ADD is an extremely complex disorder. No one book can cover all the separate aspects of managing an ADD child. In this book I have tried to concentrate on practical strategies. Many parents and teachers I have met Australia-wide suggest that they now understand what ADD is and how medication is used. The most typical comment made is that they are not sure what to do next. In fact when first planning this book I had in my mind a title of 'Pills, what next?' It is this issue that now demands the greatest attention.

As ADD is such a complex disorder this book tends to make some generalisations. It is always important to discuss any strategies you are to implement with the professionals helping your ADD child.

I have not addressed the issues of individual treatment for learning difficulties, and adults with ADD, as I believe each of these subjects could make up a separate book. Skimming over such important topics would not be justified. Instead I have tried to concentrate on answering those questions I am most often asked in regard to managing ADD kids' difficult and demanding behaviour.

I would like to thank the many ADD kids and their parents for inspiring me to write this book. Their encouragement in clinic sessions and seminars kept me motivated. Their willingness to trial techniques and strategies has benefited many other ADD kids. I would also like to thank my professional colleagues, not only for their support but for their encouragement in developing unique strategies for ADD kids rather than relying on traditional behaviour techniques. My special thanks to Dr Chris Green in this regard. I am extremely grateful to Jenny for not only putting up with my long clinic hours but typing my never-ending thoughts that eventually formed this book.

Above all, I cannot express enough gratitude to my wife, Denise, and my children, Ben and Hayley for love, support and their belief in me. Their willingness to put up with my hyperactive behaviour in working on this book over long hours was incredible.

ABOUT THE AUTHOR

Ian is the owner of and consultant psychologist with Forestway Psychology Centre (Sydney); where he specialises in working with families with ADHD and ADD kids. He regularly presents talks and seminars on ADD and other topics for television, radio, universities, schools and parent support groups around Australia. Ian provides consultant services to many well-known paediatricians, psychiatrists, doctors and professionals in different cities, as well as for parents. He is completing university research on the differential diagnosis of ADHD and Conduct and Oppositional Disorders. He co-authored, with Dr John Irvine, the popular book, *Coping With School*. He is also on the editorial board for *Practical Parenting* magazine.

$\mathcal{I}$NTRODUCTION
—— chapter ①——

I want to emphasise here at the beginning that while ADD kids are difficult, many turn out to be delightful and successful adults. I often comment that if we can get them from six years to eighteen years of age then they will be successful. Many of the ADD kids referred to in this book have been successes, turning out to be some of the best and most creative adults I know. While I paint a dim picture at times, ADD kids can be most loveable, caring, sensitive, innovative and lively characters. They truly have hearts of gold.

I am often reminded of this aspect of ADD when mothers describe their ADD kid. He might have been suspended from school, but he is the only kid to pick up the injured bird, bring it home and care for it. It is this side of the ADD child that I am sure often leads to an individual's success. They are certainly some of the most warm, caring and affectionate children I have met. We need to acknowledge the positive side of ADD. Many of the ADD kids I have seen show exceptional strengths, creativity and unique ability. I have had many success stories to prove that we can build the best in ADD kids. They have unique potential to better the world.

In this book I am expressing my own opinion, based mostly on practical experience rather than theory books. Much of the content is also based on clinic work, research findings, anecdotal records and collaboration with colleagues. I do not present these ideas as absolute fact or faultless strategies. I too have made errors in treating ADD kids. I trust that readers will take from the book what they need and adapt it to their own knowledge, understanding and common sense. ADD parents are often experts with their own children. Combine my strategies with your own expertise.

In presenting this text I recognise the contribution of parents of ADD kids. Parents have helped me more than any other group. Many of the strategies included in this book were in fact refined on ADD kids by ADD adults. It is only through their help, guidance and flexibility that we came up with many creative strategies. Often my suggestions were slightly altered by parents and this led to a greater success. I am also indebted to my colleagues who have supported me, particularly when I have gone out on a limb. More recently, I am thankful to the flexible and innovative teachers all around Australia who were bold enough to try the strategies I suggested in class and resist the criticism that ADD was merely 'flavour of the month'. Their support and willingness have led to better lives for many ADD kids.

▶ *PILLS, BUT WHAT NEXT?*

So your little dynamo Daniel has been diagnosed with ADD, and the specialist has given you a prescription for Ritalin. Perhaps you left the office thinking there has to be more to this than just a pill. Perhaps you thought you had the solution, but then found that your attempts to reason with 'dynamo Dan' still failed. How come reasoning works with 'sensible Sally', Dan's sister, but not with Dan? Where do you go to next?

The aim of this book is to fill in the gaps for ADD sufferers and parents. Too often, in my work in clinics and seminars around Australia, have I spoken to parents who are unsure about how to manage their ADD children. They have seen their children improve with medication, such as Ritalin or Dexamphetamine, but are not sure what to do next. Some helpful paediatricians have given brief guidance, but many parents still feel very confused and bewildered by the complex problems of dealing with ADD. This book answers some of those questions at a practical level. It aims to provide more help by means of a multi-modal treatment plan that deals with a broad range of your ADD child's needs. It also aims to show that ADD kids, adolescents and adults have great strengths and loveable features and can be very successful and delightful people, despite driving you to near-insanity.

► LET'S NOT BLAME THE PARENTS

When I left university as a new graduate with no training in ADD, I came across a lovely family with a very disruptive son. The mum was very fatigued and mildly depressed. I referred the family to a professional in the field. Mum came back to see me with a script for Valium and an understanding that her son's problems were the result of her depression. However, as Mum took her pills, her son did not improve. Then I referred the family to a well-known ADD specialist in Sydney. This time Mum returned with a script for Ritalin for her son and a plan for some remedial help. Not only did her son improve but Mum's depression lifted. Powerful stuff, that Ritalin!

While this is a simplistic description and today we would aim to provide a broader multi-modal plan it illustrates that ADD is not primarily a parenting problem. There are no doubt parents who need help, who yell and smack, but *the first problem is the child's ADD condition.* The problem often begins with the ADD child's demanding and difficult behaviour, not with poor parenting. We should not begin treating ADD by blaming parents. Most parents of ADD kids are very well-intentioned, well-motivated and interested people who are faced with a bewildering condition. ADD does not respond to many normal behavioural strategies. Parents end up feeling defeated, frustrated and often confused. In my work I have always aimed at providing parents or ADD sufferers with practical ideas that really work, rather than blaming. Similarly, we shouldn't blame teachers, but help them to understand ADD and find class strategies that work.

When I first encountered ADD kids over a decade ago, I too tried traditional strategies. It was like forcing a square peg in a round hole, trying to make the unique features of the ADD child fit the behaviour strategy. I realised I needed to change the strategies to suit the very different and unique features of ADD kids. The strategies I have learnt, worked with, accumulated and refined over the past decade or more have been tried almost solely on ADD kids. They are not always appropriate for more typical kids.

I reason that ADD children are neither traditional nor typical kids. I have found them to be some of the most confusing, challenging and difficult children that I have encountered. While they may be loveable rogues, they certainly can test the patience of their parents and teachers and the professionals dealing with them.

▶ UNIQUE PROBLEMS OF ADD

The very uniqueness of ADD causes most problems for parents. Many traditional behaviour strategies that work well with other kids fail with ADD kids, because they don't allow that ADD kids are different. In my clinic practice I have found that behavioural modification, star charts, play therapy, etc. that help many kids do not work as successfully in managing ADD children.

Let us look, for example, at the ADD child put on a star chart for good behaviour. The child must concentrate for hours or days on end to get a single reward. ADD kids often have a concentration span of only ten or fifteen minutes. Is it surprising then that the ADD child cannot remember that he is working for a star until the few minutes before he is due to be rewarded? He then behaves and expects the reward, but does not receive it because of his poor behaviour over the past two hours. Even worse, he remembers only the last ten minutes and thus can't understand why he isn't receiving the star, so he throws a tantrum. The problem here is that ADD kids cannot concentrate on long-term rewards. Unfortunately, behavioural experts may tell parents the failure on the star chart proves they are poor parents, rather than recognising the fault in the system itself.

Many parents have tried to reason with their ADD kids, as they have successfully reasoned with their other children. One of the advantages of ADD is lateral thinking and the average ADD child is extremely good at arguing. The result is that this child will end up winning the argument or taking Mum so far off-track that no final answer is found. How often I have seen this situation:

'John, can you get in the bath?'
'In just a minute.'
'John, can you get in the bath please, now?'
'Stop hassling me, I just want to watch this.'
'John, don't ignore me!'
'I'm not, why are you always hassling me, it's not fair.'
'I am not hassling you, I'm trying to be fair.'
'See, you are always yelling at me. This sucks.'
'John, I am not yelling at you.'
'Now you're really angry at me. I know no-one loves me.'
'John, I do love you.'
'You do not love me, you suck. You always hate me. You like Ben better.'
'John, this is silly.'

'See, I told you, you think I'm stupid.'
'John, you are not stupid. I have told you lots of times that you are a bright boy.'
'No you don't, you think I am dumb like everyone at school thinks I am dumb.'
'John, you are not dumb.'

And so it goes on — do you remember where we started? Although the original argument was about getting into the bath the ADD child has brilliantly moved Mum to discuss whether or not he is stupid, an argument that Mum is never going to win. Like many ADD kids, John is able to destroy a reasoned argument and turn it into absolute nonsense. Rarely does reasoning work with ADD kids.

You can send your eight-year-old girl to her bedroom to do three tasks, which she can complete successfully, but your ten-year-old ADD boy cannot do two jobs successfully. This contrast in ability shows that we need to follow unique strategies with ADD kids. The ADD child may be ten years old, but he is going on six maturity-wise, and thus needs special management even at this seemingly simple level. The ADD child is not being deliberately naughty: he simply can't avoid distractions and remember instructions over time.

I have seen parents who, through lack of understanding, have been struggling with their ADD kids. They are angry when their ADD child fails to complete three tasks, such as putting their pyjamas under the pillow, cleaning their teeth and getting their bag ready to go to school. With understanding we know the child can't handle three directions as he can often remember only one thing at a time. The aim of this book is to present a very commonsense and practical approach to parenting. Is it the parents' fault that they send the child to follow three complex directions? Any typical child could easily follow three instructions. However, the ADD kid, with high distractibility and low attention span, has extreme difficulty. He will either make it a third of the way to his bedroom but be distracted by the bright red toy on the ground, or get to his room and do one of the tasks and then forget what the other two tasks were, screaming for Mum at the top of his voice. We need to look at even the simple strategies such as telling parents to send the child on only one task at a time. When we are sure they can handle one instruction parents can add a second direction. As they mature, and the ADD symptoms are less pervasive, perhaps then parents can send them with three directions.

If we are ever to realise success with ADD children, we must apply methods that actually cater to their disorder and recognise the weaknesses and strengths of ADD. Only through this method of giving parents very practical and relevant help will we gain success with ADD kids.

► SPARE A THOUGHT FOR THE PARENTS

When I first became aware of ADD, there was an intense, negative and confronting attitude to parents and ADD specialists. Professional misunderstanding of ADD, the denial of ADD symptoms for many years and the criticism and attacks on parents were very damaging to many ADD kids — not to mention the parents. Unfortunately there is still controversy over acceptance of ADD and even of treatments. Parents are still too often being ridiculed for placing children on drugs and 'zonking them out', and being blamed, wrongly, for their children's ADD behaviour. We need to work to develop practical solutions for fatigued parents and teachers, to extend sympathy and support, not to attribute blame.

The capable sad sisters

I wonder if we have ever recognised how difficult it is to grow up in an ADD family. This point was never more startlingly brought home to me than in a recent talk on ADD I gave at a school. I had discussed with the audience the suffering that brothers or sisters of ADD kids underwent. At the conclusion of the night there was the typical long trail of parents who lined up with questions. Right at the end of the queue were two young women. As they finally approached me, one of them very quickly became distressed and tearful. She explained that no-one had ever recognised or accepted how difficult it was growing up with an ADD brother. She thanked me profusely for accepting her difficult childhood.

Although she was a successful medical undergraduate she found it very difficult to be assertive, to cope with aggression from her boyfriend or deal with difficult professors. The other young woman described how she often felt depressed. The level of their distress was such that I sat with both the sisters for an hour at the end of a long night, discussing their feelings. They were both highly intelligent, capable and reasonable women whose lives had been clearly changed because they had both grown up in an ADD family. Hopefully we can alleviate this situation more in the future.

The 'hidden handicap'

I am reminded of a parent who came to see me having both a Down's syndrome child and an ADD child. From day one her Down's syndrome child, Gabby, was identified as being different. Gabby's handicap was not hidden. She was immediately afforded special care in hospital, therapy from a young age, and support from professionals as well as government care and funding. Rarely did Gabby's mother have to establish whether or not Gabby had a special condition or to justify the use of a particular treatment.

Mum's attempts to help her ADD son Jake, however, met a very different response. As the late and very respected Dr Gordon Serfontein said, ADD is a 'hidden handicap' and because of this, Jake was not recognised as having needs. He did not receive any special help or early intervention at school or from professional health bodies. Jake's mum had to constantly fight for acceptance of Jake's disorder and problems. In fact she and her husband had to defend their style of parenting. For these reasons, parents have my sympathy.

Constancy

ADD tends to be unique because the constancy of the ADD child's behaviour wears parents down and causes more problems than would occasional severe outbursts. I often use this analogy: having an ADD kid is like spending days with someone walking behind you all day poking you in the back every five minutes. One poke is not so severe, but constant pokes all day are torture. It is this constant provocation that causes so much stress for parents of ADD children.

Is this inconsistent parenting or a different child?

When I first began to work with unruly, active and disruptive children, I often saw parents who had been told that it was their fault that their child was behaving badly. However, their parenting skills worked well with their twelve-year-old son but seemingly failed completely with their eight-year-old boy (not yet diagnosed with ADD). Further, they again had very adequate parenting skills with their six-year-old daughter. It amazed me how they could presumably have the skills one minute and not the next. It was through seeing many highly motivated and otherwise successful parents struggling with only one of their children that led many professionals to accept ADD, despite our formal training.

▶ *ADD* AS A DISORDER

It is my strong intention that we should accept ADD as a disorder, as it is indeed labelled. ADD is still treated by some as a whimsical notion of certain therapists or doctors, rather than as an accepted condition. I wonder if we were to compare it to diabetes, would critics debate so vigorously the need to give a child insulin. If we in fact treated ADD as we treat diabetes, I believe there would be far more positive outcomes. The severity of the disorder is assessed and a decision made as to the need for medication. Not only do we provide the diabetic child with medication, we also immediately begin training the parents in appropriate management styles. We talk to the parents about issues such as mood swings, diet needs, individual needs and medical support. There are support groups to help parents and children. We also teach the children that they can be successful if they manage their condition well.

▶ *MULTI-MODAL TREATMENT*

Would you plan a holiday trip to a beach resort by only booking the air flights while ignoring accommodation, transport, tours, meals, the spending money? The holiday would surely be unsuccessful. Similarly, treating ADD with only medication is likely to be just as unsuccessful. A holiday becomes successful through planning a good package. Similarly ADD needs a multi-modal treatment package.

Just as with diabetes, we need to follow the trend of these conditions or disorders. Never do we recommend sole dependency on drugs as treatment. It is my intention to promote as intensively as possible multi-modal treatment (see Chapter 15 for a discussion of multi-modal management). We aim to provide parents with behavioural guidelines that work and provide parent management strategies that have relevance to ADD. We need to:

▶ use medication where it is appropriate

▶ teach schools support techniques, so that teachers, often untrained in dealing with ADD, have the appropriate tools to deal with it

▶ build ADD kids' self-esteem and confidence

► address social skill problems
► be reasonable and not use ADD as an excuse
► provide whatever else is necessary to give the ADD child the skills necessary to cope with what must be a very difficult world for them.

Working together on multi-modal plans

The failure of ADD treatment has not been due to medication being ineffective, but rather to the absence of a multi-modal treatment plan. A significant part of this treatment is in training not only parents but also those professionals who work with ADD children, including psychiatrists, psychologists, social workers, guidance officers, counsellors and especially teachers. Many professionals were not trained any better than parents were in dealing with ADD. Through a team approach much more will be achieved with ADD kids. The only professionals who deserve criticism are those who refuse to accept ADD and continue to blame parents.

► *DIAGNOSIS*

ADD does exist. It is a neurological disorder that involves a form of 'faulty wiring in the brain'. There are a multitude of well-accepted, research-based diagnostic measures that can lead to a reliable and valid diagnosis. The greatest risk to the acceptance of ADD now is brief, unreliable diagnosis. It is critical that diagnosis be made from a broad, multi-modal basis.

The need for adequate and thorough diagnosis is critical. I believe that many of the problems with ADD, for example adverse reactions to medication or kids developing strange behaviours, has not resulted from using medication or other treatments but rather from inappropriate diagnosis. There are a very few cases I have seen where the behaviour was due in fact to the child never having been set boundaries. Similarly, I have seen a very small number of kids who had a problem that wasn't ADD. While this has made up only a very small minority of all children with ADD, it has certainly been disturbing. I can never reiterate strongly enough how important it is to gain an adequate diagnosis.

Co-existing conditions or Co-morbidity

Co-morbidity refers to the probability that many ADD children will present with more than one disorder at the same time. For example, a child might have ADD as well as oppositional or anxious behaviour. This book will look at Co-morbidity and the different strategies to manage these children. ADD kids need unique treatments, but each of these groups needs its own slightly different management strategies.

► THE LONG HAUL

It is essential that ADD parents realise that ADD is a very difficult condition, and that there are no simple solutions. Parents should beware the new glossy brochure that promises that someone has 'The answer to ADD'. Parents and teachers need to understand that it is going to take a great deal of time to solve ADD problems. In fact it may take months or years to overcome many of the problems of ADD. Parents who expect a quick cure will often end up defeated and self-critical, believing failure is their fault. You can take only little steps one at a time, day by day, and realise little successes. Often I tell parents not to expect to be perfect with the program that I give them. I suggest they return for the next therapy session having improved by ten per cent.

Expect to make some mistakes

Parents also need to recognise that they are human and are going to make mistakes. It is a reality that the parents of an ADD kid will at times yell. While we need to reduce yelling to a minimum, we should try to build skills so that parents don't feel the need to yell as often. It is important that parents understand that they will at times become frustrated, act inappropriately or, in simple terms, lose their cool. Remember our comments about how constant ADD kids can be? I'd scream at Chinese water torture, too. Our aim should be to help parents build up the number of good days against the bad days. Often ADD parents will tell me that they have six and a half bad days for one hour's peace. Our aim should be to gradually improve this until we have six and a half good days for half a bad day. Even with the most successful ADD kid, I have seen bad times. Parents should not beat themselves up over these but celebrate and build on the gains they make at any time with an ADD kid.

It might be worthwhile to close with a story of my own 'human' error. On this particular day, I had already seen seven very active little ADD kids. As the eighth entered my room, and I tried to manage the eighth hour straight of dealing with ADD, my sympathy for ADD parents grew. As this little delight entered, in a typical impulsive ADD manner, he grabbed a precious baseball figurine my wife had patiently made me and threw it in the air to catch. Needless to say, I roared 'Put that down! Don't ...'

See, even therapists yell sometimes.

In this book I often refer to either ADD kids or ADD children. In fact I am referring to ADD infants, children and teenagers as a group. Perhaps because I see most ADD kids as immature, I still think of them all as kids. Occasionally I refer to adults although treating adults is not within the scope of this book. At times I refer to specific strategies for the very young or for teenagers, as special strategies are appropriate.

There are many cases in this book where I refer to individual ADD kids by name. All these kids are patients of mine, but I have changed their names to protect confidentiality.

Often I use 'we', as in 'we have tried to help by ... '. In these instances I am referring to the parents I am working with and myself.

I see the parents and myself as a team and 'we' are working to help troubled but delightful ADD kids.

In summary:

▶ ADD is clinical disorder that needs special treatment.

▶ ADD needs to be treated with unique strategies, not traditional methods.

▶ Use multi-modal treatment, not just one cure.

▶ The constancy of ADD kids' behaviour wears parents down.

▶ Most gains are made when parents, professionals and teachers work together.

▶ ADD is not caused by poor parenting or teaching.

▶ ADD kids may have co-existing conditions which need more specialised treatment.

▶ Expect to make gradual gains, don't expect miracle cures.

*E*XPLAINING *ADD*

—— chapter (2) ——

*I*f you have been fortunate enough to have your problems listened to and an early diagnosis made, your next difficulty is explaining, to your child, family, school and others, the many issues about ADD. All ADD kids need understanding. ADD teenagers have particular concerns and explaining to the family can be a nightmare.

▶ *MUM, WHAT IS ADD?*

Most kids' first question is 'What is ADD?' How much and what is told to ADD kids very much depends on the child's age and the style and opinions of specialists. There is no absolute rule regarding when to explain ADD fully to a child. The one definite rule is your child has some right to know what is happening to him or her, and why.

Explaining to the very young

I am reluctant to use the label Attention Deficit Disorder with young kids, particularly those in pre-school or infants school. Some very young kids may appear to have ADD but eventually don't present with it. For example, I believe some 30–40 per cent of all boys aged three or four would meet some criteria for ADD. Obviously very few of these boys will actually end up having it.

Often with very young ADD kids I refer to symptoms, rather than the ADD title itself. For example, I might refer to 'the problem you have with keeping still, thinking before you act and doing what you are told'. I might then abbreviate this to 'the problem keeping still, thinking and doing'. If your child then needs to see a counsellor, you might say 'We are going to see this lady to help with keeping still, thinking and doing.' If you were taking your child to speech therapy you might say 'We are seeing this lady so people can understand you better.'

Try to make sure young ADD kids have a reasonable understanding of what will happen. They fear new and unknown situations. Where possible try to avoid talking in front of your child. Promising a reward for behaving well in the office is acceptable — but be careful you don't reward too much so that they are perfect and the professional doesn't believe you! If your very young ADD child is to begin medication a very helpful book is *Shelley, the Hyperactive Turtle* by Deborah Moss (Woodbine Publishers).

Explaining to the young

Once ADD kids are a little older, and certainly if they begin on medication, they need further explanation. From the age of seven or eight years I often begin to use the term Attention Deficit Disorder, but rarely do I refer to ADD as I first begin to explain the problem. Normally I would explain through an analogy from the child's world. For example, if the child likes music I might ask what would happen if we had a good Walkman, but its batteries were running out. To make it work as well as it could we would need to charge the batteries. Having ADD is a little like a Walkman with nearly flat batteries. It is a good Walkman, but needs to have one little bit fixed so it can work well. I have used many similar analogies, such as a remote-control car where the controller was broken, a netball or football team with no coach, or a bike with no brakes to stop it crashing.

Once I've reached this stage I explain the 'proper name' for the problem. There are two books I have most often recommended to parents to assist explanation at this age. *Jumpin' Johnny, Get Back to Work* by Michael Gordon (GSI Publications) is a good book that emphasises multi-modal treatment. *Putting on the Brakes* by Quinn and Stern (Magination Press) gives a brief explanation for parents and upper primary school kids. There are, however, many other excellent guides.

Explaining to teenagers

Explaining ADD to teenage sufferers can involve many complexities. Not only do teenagers need to understand ADD itself, more often they need reassurance, help in understanding the effect of learning difficulties, affirmation that they are not crazy and awareness of the strengths of having ADD. Younger kids need this too, but not to the same level.

I often prefer to explain ADD to teenagers through an analogy, but using more sophisticated examples. For example, we might look at a prestige car. We look at the strengths of such a car, that it can go fast and look good. Then we discuss what might happen if we removed the brakes. It still looks good but gets into trouble when it needs to brake through tight corners.

Similarly, we might look at a skateboard with one wobbly wheel. We would not throw it out but we would work out how to make it work better as it is too good a product to dispose of. Again I have recommended *Putting on the Brakes* for teenagers. *I Would If I Could* by Michael Gordon is a rather more humorous look at ADD.

Explaining to brothers and sisters

The life of a brother or sister of an ADD kid is very difficult. In most cases I believe they need to be informed, supported and allowed to help. Encourage them to come and talk to you about issues as they arise. Don't expect them just to be the good kid who always copes. Try also to avoid placing an expectation on them that because their ADD brother is so bad, they always have to be good and responsible. Every kid needs to test the boundaries once in a while.

Siblings also need to be very firmly told that teasing their ADD brother or sister is totally unacceptable and will be punished. Helpful books include *My Brother's a World Class Pain* by Michael Gordon, which explains ADD to siblings and shows how they can help, and *I'm Somebody Too!* by Jeanne Gehret, a novel with a sympathetic approach by the sister of an ADD boy.

▶ EXPLAINING OUTSIDE THE IMMEDIATE FAMILY

How much you explain to grandparents, aunties, uncles, neighbours, friends and others depends on their understanding and acceptance. I do not recommend telling too many others until you and your kid have had time to work through basic understanding and acceptance yourselves. If relatives are likely to be understanding I recommend telling them, as you will need support and help caring for your child as well as understanding.

If your relatives don't accept ADD don't waste too much energy on a crusade. Some people are not yet ready to be convinced. It is wiser to provide reading material rather than trying to convince them yourself. I also feel it is unwise to inform too many friends or others until the general public is more accepting. Your child probably deserves a more discreet approach.

► *TELLING THE SCHOOL*

Many years ago I was reluctant to tell many schools a pupil had ADD and was on medication for fear parents would be criticised and challenged unfairly. Now I believe we are becoming more enlightened and the majority of teachers are accepting ADD. It is a fact that a well-coordinated and consistent home, school and professional team approach leads to greater success. Developing such a team approach should be a major aim over the next few years as ADD awareness develops. There are exceptions to this suggestion such as the few schools who remain totally opposed to ADD. Exposing your child to ignorant criticism can be very damaging to their already low self-esteem and poor self-image.

I believe parents should tell a school only when they have had a thorough diagnosis made and can present the school with written reports regarding the level of problems their kid has and what plans are being put into place for management.

► *WE CAN OWN IT AND FIX IT*

From the very start we need to help ADD kids to see they can own their problems, work on them and gradually overcome them. Try to avoid allowing ADD to become an excuse. A very important part of this is explaining that an ADD kid is not all bad, but is basically good, with just one or two small parts we need to fix up. Again analogies can be helpful. For example, I might say we don't throw away a great Walkman because the batteries are run down. We work out how to charge them up and keep them charged up.

You mean my brain is not crazy?

Hundreds of ADD kids and teenagers actually feel weird at times because their brains are too active, confused, bouncing with too many ideas and forgetful of things they really want to recall. It is very important to reassure ADD teenagers that they are not crazy or weird. They need to be shown that ADD is not abnormal. ADD kids do what everyone else does, they just do it more frequently and more intensely than everyone else does. Everyone fidgets, they just fidget more; everyone gets bored, they get bored more easily and more often, and so on.

With all ADD sufferers, but particularly teenagers, it is important to reassure them by looking at ADD sufferers who were successful people in history. Many professionals believe Winston Churchill, Edison, Einstein, Mozart, Yeats, Agatha Christie and many others had ADD. Dustin Hoffman and ADD pioneer Dr Gordon Serfontein are further success stories.

Try to enlighten them as to some of the strengths in ADD that will help them achieve. Many ADD kids

▶   are the creative, innovative or inventive minds of the world

▶   are the people who look at things differently and change the world

▶   often have great lateral thinking skills

▶   have energy to keep going when others are tired

▶   have enthusiasm and spirit

▶   have a great ability to relate to others not their own age, either the younger or the older

▶   can debate and argue with great success (as mums know well!).

In summary, ADD kids have skills others don't have. I believe there is a seesaw effect with ADD kids. For what they missed out on they got other strengths and unique abilities. Many adults with ADD have commented that once they learnt to control their ADD they wouldn't dare to wish to be without it.

▶ *ADD IS EVERYONE'S PROBLEM*

It is not just your ADD child who has a problem. Everyone in the family must learn to deal with ADD problems. Parents who expect to just change their ADD kid tend to have greater ongoing problems.

Even as a therapist I had to learn that I couldn't altogether change ADD kids. Rather, I needed to adapt my approach to help them while they gradually changed.

Similarly, don't concentrate all therapy on your ADD child or teenager. For example, if you are seeing a counsellor, explain to your child that it is to help him control his ADD but also it is for you to learn how to be better parents and to manage problems. Often a simple statement such as 'I need to learn not to scream so much' can help greatly to spread responsibility.

Accepting the disorder and coping — parents

Most ADD families look on diagnosis as a great relief, helping them to understand why managing their child has been difficult. However, occasionally I come across a parent who struggles to accept the problem. Most often this is the father, particularly of boys. This could be due to the pressure put on dads to produce a big 'macho' son, or because Dad sees less of the problem as he is not at home as much, or for other reasons. Interestingly, fathers generally are not as good at accepting any disorder in their kids. It is traditionally mothers who most often seek out professional help and answers to problems.

If both parents can accept the disorder and work consistently together the likelihood of a positive outcome is greatly increased.

While finding out why your kid has been difficult and having a label for it can be a relief, it can also spark a grief reaction. Parents all hope for a perfectly healthy, well and complete baby. There can be a slight sense of loss, coupled with anger, fear, hurt, even guilt or other feelings when a child is diagnosed. This is a completely normal reaction. Many parents ask why did I get this problem, and why isn't there a cure? They feel it is not fair, they worry about long-term futures, are angry at professionals and express similar emotions. This is part of a natural grieving process. It is helped by good family support, understanding and open discussion. Sometimes professional help is needed just to get past this stage.

What is normal?

Recently I assessed a kid whose mum thought he was normal, but someone else thought he had ADD. In fact, the kid was completely normal. The assessment was strange as I didn't have to work hard to keep him on task, fight for his attention, keep up constant praise and overcome negativity. I realised at this time what it must be like for a mum of an ADD kid sitting having coffee, trying to control her hyperactive toddler. As she looks around she sees toddlers happily and quietly sitting in their strollers while other mums drink their coffee in peace. It is very difficult, in the midst of battles of managing ADD, for a mum to realise what normal is and thus not to blame herself.

▶ HAVE YOU TAKEN YOUR PILL?

This is a very unfair statement that some parents or siblings throw at ADD kids. When Johnny is at his worst someone accusingly says 'Haven't you taken your pill?' Countless ADD kids over the years have complained that 'It makes me feel that there is something really wrong with me'; 'It's like they're saying I'm crazy if I don't take it'; 'It's like a bat they belt me over the head with every time I muck up, like I'm some psycho.'

Try to develop a regular checking routine to ensure tablets are taken on time. Don't rely on your forgetful ADD kid to remember. For example, try to tie it into lunch-time, set an extra alarm clock to go off at the necessary time in the afternoon after school and on weekends or purchase a week-long medication dispenser and remind your child discreetly by tapping your watch.

Taking medication at school

The rules and procedures regarding taking medication at school vary from state to state and school to school. In general having a school staff or ancillary member supervise medication is the best system. However, this is not always possible due to recent industrial action in some states. If possible, it is advisable for staff to use a recording system to monitor that medication is being taken regularly.

'Ian, the principal says that David will just have to remember to take his medication, but he can't. What do you suggest?'

I would suggest that this shows a lack of understanding of ADD. More than likely David is taking medication because he doesn't concentrate on tasks or remember things. It is very unlikely that when David's first dose of medication is wearing off he will remember to take it again. If he could remember he might not have ADD.

If a school monitoring system is not possible I then suggest several strategies. The most important is to remember that David is forgetful and unless we distract him in a very obvious way he will not remember. If you simply slip the tablet into his lunch-box, expect a handful to be in the bottom of his bag by the end of term. If you slip it into his top pocket the washing machine will be very non-hyperactive.

One method is to purchase a weekly medication dispenser from the chemist. While these provide a good routine they are not usually distracting enough. If you are going to use a medication dispenser, tape it across his lunch-box each day with bright tape in such a way that he can't get to his lunch without handling it first.

If you wish to be a little more discreet sticky tape the tablet on the entry hole on the top of a small fruit-juice (popper style). Now the only way he can get the straw into the juice is by removing the tablet. This allows an instant drink to swallow it. I have also recommended alarms set on wrist watches. For those ADD kids who don't like taking it with water try placing it in a favourite lolly piece on the top of a recess or lunch bag, such as in an Apricot Treat, or small chocolate drop.

Keeping ADD kids on medication

Keeping ADD kids on medication can be very difficult and involves different problems. Here are some simple remedies. For ADD kids who will take tablets at school but not in the afternoon, tie the afternoon tablet into a treat. For example, 'If you take the tablet you can have a milkshake on the way home to take it — but no tablet, no milkshake.'

For those who have been going well but begin to regress off medication keep a record of detentions for a week off medication. When they see they are missing out on more play they may agree.

Sometimes formal testing will convince ADD kids of the benefits. By showing them improved test scores you can explain this means they will be smarter at school. Often teachers can help here by supporting that they are doing better in class. Similarly showing examples of work on and off medication can be helpful.

▶ ATTENDING OTHER THERAPIES

It is likely you will be seeing many professionals with your ADD child. Always prepare him or her briefly as to where and why you are going, but avoid long explanations that will cause anxiety or fear. If you have an anxious kid reassure them that there are not going to be any needles or anything else they may be phobic about. Try to keep explanations positive, such as 'This man is going to play some games and find what you are good at' rather than 'He is going to test you to find out about why you can't read.'

Try to keep longer-term therapy positively focused, such as 'We are going so you can be a very clear speaker, you'll be a great talker and everyone will understand' rather than 'We are going because you talk badly.' Any long-term therapy should be full of small, recognisable goals, at least several rewards every session. It will be hard labour for your kid, but this doesn't mean it can't be fun. Lots of stickers, showing you how your child has improved, charts showing improvement and genuine praise keep up motivation and willingness to attend.

A *word of warning*: ADD kids get bored with the same rewards. You or the therapist may need to change them regularly to maintain interest and novelty.

A *second word of warning*: ADD kids become very fatigued each school term. Avoid working them too hard. Generally it is a good idea to have at least a part of holidays off therapy, otherwise ADD kids become burnt out. However, long blocks of months away from therapy may see a loss of skills.

ADD is a confusing disorder for us all. The more we know, the more we have explained and come to understand, the more success we are likely to achieve.

Lastly, a caring and understanding professional can sometimes achieve what Mum and Dad can't. Such a professional needs to have a good understanding of ADD, be in tune with the kid and have a bank of success stories to draw on to help acceptance.

In summary:

▶ ADD kids of different ages need different explanations.

▶ Explain the strengths as well as the weaknesses of ADD.

▶ Don't use ADD as an excuse, rather own the problems and work on solutions to overcome them.

▶ Don't just try to change your ADD kid. We all need to change how we deal with problems.

▶ Good communication between home, school and the professional leads to success.

▶ Try to learn as much as you can about ADD.

PRACTICAL MANAGEMENT

chapter 3

Parents rightly complain that practical management of ADD has not been adequately addressed. It is what they struggle with most often. Before discussing symptoms or diagnosis of ADD we need to look at behaviour problems.

Most ADD children:

▶ have extremely poorly sustained attention

▶ have poor impulse control

▶ are very distractible

▶ are insatiable and constant

▶ are often very active.

These unique features most likely contribute to the lesser success of many treatment programs. ADD kids need very immediate, frequent and concise behaviour management. As was argued in the Introduction, many traditional treatments are not very successful, although some areas are very useful if adapted to suit ADD. Other specific therapies, while effective in different cases, can be totally unsuitable for ADD management. For example, many abused children have responded excellently through play therapy. Similarly, I have seen quite anxious little girls respond brilliantly to a traditional behaviour modification program. But ADD children are so unusual that these treatment programs are unlikely to prove successful. Further, parents of ADD kids need basic parenting support and guidance.

▶ THEY COME WITHOUT INSTRUCTIONS

When my first child, a son, was born, I recall at the end of his cot a small blue card that told us his sex, his length, his head size and basically that everything was okay. We received little about managing a child. Incidentally, at the same time as my son arrived, we bought a video recorder. An eighty-page instruction booklet accompanied it, providing great details on how to run the video. It even had trouble-shooting ideas, and a phone-in help line.

When I thought of ADD in particular, an analogy came to mind. It struck me that not only does the parent of an ADD kid not receive an instruction booklet, but in fact the ADD kid they receive does not function in the normal way. It would be like receiving a video for which the instruction booklet was written in a foreign language. There is no obvious way to see how to make things work successfully. Further, all the normal things the parent tries makes the machine backfire or work in reverse.

Those ADD children who are unfortunate enough to also have more severe problems, such as oppositional, conduct, anxiety or other disorders, need more specific treatment. The make-up of these disorders makes their management even more difficult. In later chapters I will also deal with these co-existing disorders.

▶ THE BASICS

Training not blaming

The most basic step in ADD management is to begin training parents, not blaming them. It would be more useful to accept the fact that ADD children are very difficult. In past decades parents have been held responsible as the cause of poor behaviour in ADD children. Often 'old faithful' statements from grandparents such as 'all the boy needs is a good hiding, send him to me for a week and I will sort him out...' have led to parents feeling very defeated and dejected about their own parenting ability. Despite the fact that smacking only hypes up most ADD kids, it remains as one of the cures most often suggested.

Jake and the grandparents

Parents might delight to know that only once have I really given in to grandparents' demands to 'sort out' an ADD kid. These grandparents constantly rang me to express their displeasure at their grandchild, Jake, being on pills. Further, they berated Jake's mum, until I felt she needed respite care. So we finally agreed to let Jake go to his grandparents in Surfers Paradise for a break. The grandfather rang delighted to say that they had experienced no problems after two days, although we presumed that keeping an ADD child happy on the busy, lively Gold Coast was within reason. Several days later Grandma was put through to my clinic in desperation. Jake had locked himself on the unit balcony on the eighth floor and was threatening to kill himself because Grandpa had got cranky at him and no-one loved him. Sound familiar?

We did get Jake inside and Grandma and Grandpa are now great ADD supporters.

Parents need family support

A general message to all families. ADD may be a controversial subject and take time to adjust to. But the first basic strategy of managing ADD is understanding that no parent has become a better parent as a result of loved ones, relatives or friends constantly criticising them or undermining their confidence. Parents need to trust their own judgement and build their skills through training, not blaming.

The dad's role

Dads have often told me that they are much better than mums at managing their ADD child. They even criticise their wives for not handling the situation. I think it is important to recognise several factors.

▶ Firstly it is easier for dads as they are not nearly as involved with ADD children.

▶ Secondly we might learn a little from some of the things that Dad does that might explain why his performance is sometimes better.

▶ Lastly criticising wives rarely makes better mums, but tends to lead to less motivation.

As a busy dad myself (who works too-long hours every day trying to solve ADD problems) I am fortunate in that I don't have to get through 'Grizzle' hour. Rarely have I had to have one hand in the frying pan preparing dinner, with my little one tugging at my shorts for attention while my ADD child screams as I try to get him through homework — all this before the battle to get them bathed or fed. Dad doesn't have to deal for as long with that same ADD child who demands sole attention and knows which buttons to push when it gets boring and he needs a little stimulation. It is important to realise that by the time Dad gets home it is easier because by then the children are often bathed, fed and ready. Similarly Dad only has a short time with the children. He can come in and be wonderful and playful, not having to get through the difficult chores. ADD children are often perceptive enough to know, too, that if they don't behave for Dad, time quickly runs out and they don't have a good time.

This is not considering the dads who have ADD themselves. They seem able to arrive home just as Mum finally manages to settle the kids down. Dad is full of energy, ready to wrestle and play, but then wonders why the children won't settle to go to bed. Hyped-up ADD kids don't switch off miraculously when bed-time comes around.

▶ DON'T FEED THE ADD PROBLEM

Many strategies that have been helpful in managing more typical children in fact feed the ADD problem. Parents are often told to reason with their ADD children. While reasoning is a very good strategy for many typical children, the more we reason with an ADD kid the more we feed their high demand for attention and stimulation. Often reasoning can go on endlessly and at irrelevant tangents, only making the problem worse. Similarly, parents are often told to be far more positive with their ADD children and to ignore any bad behaviour. The more parents ignore the behaviour, however, the more they increase the level until it is impossible to ignore. The child acts up more and more to the point where the situation is beyond resolution, because the child is so hyped up. Ignoring the ADD child actually feeds the problem.

The power of the voice

At the risk of generalising, I believe dads tend to use a firmer and more consistent voice than mums. This supports the point that I made earlier regarding dads' special management qualities. We know that a firm, steady voice is more effective with ADD children. We also know that dads tend to act more quickly, applying immediate consequences, rather than spending a long time reasoning. While Mum's gentle reasoning is much more effective with an anxious or nervous girl, generally dads are a bit more naturally successful with ADD children. While Mum is gently and patiently reasoning, her ADD child ties her in knots with irrelevant arguments.

As most parents know, ADD children are hypersensitive. Not only do they react to some specific foods, colours, salicylates and other food ingredients, they often get more hyped up when it is a windy day, react more when things go wrong, are more emotional and react more dramatically. This has led us to find that ADD children also react to our voices. When an ADD parent is reduced to screaming, with the higher pitch voice comes a more hyped-up ADD child. While it is very difficult to achieve, a more steady, monotonous voice will have greater success. The aim is also to slow down the rate of speech. Try to speak in a fairly boring, carefully punctuated and firm tone when your child is behaving badly. Again try not to feed the problem. We are trying to bore your child, not feed his attention-seeking.

Aim not to race words together but to speak in a very slow, determined and firm manner. Most ADD kids are very intuitive. Your child will perceive a rapid, shrill voice as one out of control, but a punctuated voice of lower pitch as being a sign of control and calm authority.

Be brief, don't reason

A strength of ADD is that kids have good lateral brains and divergent thinking skills, which may be helpful eventually in a problem-solving or creative career. For now, however, it is important to understand that most of them are experts in turning a reasoned discussion into an irrational and irrelevant argument, that ends up quite removed from the original problem. They are brilliant at destroying parents' best arguments, turning parents inside out. This is an example of an attempt at reasoning:

> 'I want a biscuit.'
> 'No, it will spoil your dinner.'
> 'No it won't, I promise.'
> 'You promised yesterday and you didn't eat your dinner
> 'You never believe me, everyone thinks I lie.'
> 'I never said you lied.'

> 'You did, you always pick on me and let Tim have what he wants. This sucks.'
> 'Don't swear at me or you'll lose your bike for a week.'
> 'You can't take it, you're not the boss of my life, you can't make me . . .'
> And so on.

With a more difficult ADD child, reasoning will usually lead to your child demonstrating how little he cares for you and how talented he is at debating and arguing. Any reason you give will provide an escape door from admitting blame. This will finally only lead to further distress and frustration.

Similarly, how often have you pleaded and begged your ADD child to get ready for school, only to arrive at the school gate arguing about whose fault it is that homework and lunch were forgotten again.

As a parent of an ADD child, if you hear yourself saying too much, try to remember to be brief, be direct and to the point. In fact, the less you say the more likely you are to achieve success. Again this explains why dads are sometimes better, as they are less likely to reason and spend a long time talking. They are more likely to quickly state what is to happen.

Again remember to avoid yelling or screaming demands, as this will not solve the problem either. Rather try to use a calm, firm but brief statement indicating what is expected. For example, a statement about the biscuits (above) might be 'No, I'm sorry, the rules are no biscuits before dinner.' It is equally important, however, that we are not too quick. An ADD child also needs a chance or two. Dads who fire off like a machine gun, never giving a chance, will also fail.

Communicate simply and clearly

ADD kids often have language and auditory processing problems. If you talk too much your child will switch off and begin gazing around the room. Using abstract or complex language will surely make your ADD child turn off. Long lectures are destined to failure. Try not to hype up your ADD child by lecturing for a long time, which can only lead to you becoming frustrated when your child is unable to tune in at length.

Act quickly, don't ignore

If I see a family with a more typical child, who has no ADD but seeks attention, I might tell the parents to ignore the attention-seeking behaviour. Most ADD children, however, respond very differently. They are insatiable and constantly demand stimulation and attention. Therefore they will not give up when you ignore them, but will keep trying.

As I saw my wife heading off to the shops one day with a brief list of things that she wanted, it came to me that ADD kids have similar mental lists of behaviour to call on when being ignored. For example:

▶ if whingeing a little does not get the demanded attention, perhaps stamping the feet will

▶ if stamping a foot doesn't succeed then perhaps beginning a yell will

▶ if yelling doesn't work, then perhaps lying on the floor will

▶ if screaming doesn't work then perhaps threatening to throw something will.

The difficulty is that eventually the situation becomes so out of control and unmanageable that you are never going to be able to rescue it. By the time ignoring becomes impossible your ADD child is so hyped up, emotionally intense and extremely upset that it is impossible for you to successfully discipline him or settle him. Furthermore, five minutes later your ADD child will have forgotten all about it, happily playing with the toy that distracted him and not disturbed at all, while half an hour later Mum and Dad are still destroyed.

By ignoring you have fed the ADD problem.

When your ADD child is attention seeking act quickly and do not ignore it. This does not mean that you jump on your child negatively or critically. I would suggest you begin the Four Step procedure that is detailed in Chapter 4. The first step, the Awareness Step, is to let your ADD child know that the behaviour is not acceptable when it first appears. Again, by ignoring you will tend to feed the ADD problem. Instead, aim to act before your child gets too hyped up and difficult to manage.

Identify what is not acceptable and begin working on a solution.

No yells, no stops

We must understand that ADD kids' behaviour is governed by impulsiveness, or more correctly poor impulse control. Their behaviour is not governed by deliberate intent. They are not intentionally and deliberately bad. This rule does not always apply to the more severe

Oppositional or Conduct Disordered ADD children, who can be malicious or manipulative. In simpler terms, the typical ADD child often acts without thinking or being aware of consequences, rather than maliciously planning their behaviour.

How often I have met mums of ADD kids who wish that their ADD child would just 'stop and think'. Again yelling 'Stop' will likely feed the problem and is not even fair. It hypes them up and it is unfair as they often don't mean it.

If you are not sure that impulsivity is a problem try this exercise. When your ADD child is bouncing up and down on the lounge, yell 'Stop'. He will briefly stop because you shocked him by yelling, but he will then look from side to side to see what he has actually done wrong: the consequential connection has failed. Rather than seeing his own wrongdoing, he will over-react to you having yelled, and an argument will begin. Further, when you check five minutes later, he will be bouncing again, having forgotten all about what has just happened. He failed to stop and think again.

In the Four Step procedure, I often refer to the Awareness Step. Rather than screaming 'Stop' try to make your child aware of what you expect, in a calm, brief statement. 'John, what are the rules about sitting on the lounge?' or 'John, is it okay to jump on the lounge?' Obviously this needs further work but it is a beginning. If we return to the example of the ADD child who demands a biscuit at 6 p.m. you might begin with 'Sorry John, the rules are no biscuits after 5 p.m.' No reasoning, no yells of 'I've told you a hundred times', no screams of 'Stop!'; instead a firm, brief monotonous statement.

No why's

Asking an ADD child *why* they are behaving in a particular way is another strategy that feeds the ADD problem. I have seen some very impassioned dads pleading with their ADD child in my waiting room as to *why* they tipped Lego all over the floor. I am sure that if little Jason realised that his father was going to make him pick up all the Lego, piece by piece, Jason would never have tipped it out in the beginning. Jason never thought about what he was doing and therefore has no reason to give. He did it because he had an impulse to do it and never thought otherwise about the consequences.

To answer *why*, you must have had a reason for behaving.

I have come to believe that the more we ask an ADD kid *why* they did a particular thing or *why* they behaved in a certain way, the more we encourage lying. Because they are impulsive and their recollection is so poor, they can't recall why. Thus an ADD kid will often come up with a very good excuse. Rarely is this either the truth or the real reason for bad behaviour: it is whatever pops into his brain. Asking why leads to lying or avoiding as a means of covering what is actually impulsiveness, and this only leads to an escalation of problems.

ADD children have very lateral, inventive and creative minds: they often come up with very plausible excuses, which bear no relation to the truth.

Why, Simon?

I learnt this lesson well in my early days with ADD children, in the waiting room of my first small office. I came out from talking with parents to the waiting room where I clearly saw Simon punching his brother, Alex. Foolishly, I asked 'Why are you hitting Alex?' Naturally he had a very plausible reason or excuse. Not only that, he convinced me that I didn't trust him because I didn't believe him. He was so convincing that by the time five minutes had passed he had me believing I was at fault for not believing him.

How did I get myself into this dilemma? By asking why. The lesson therefore is not to ask why but instead to move forward to an awareness of what is appropriate behaviour and what will happen should this behaviour not be followed.

Did you hit your brother?

On a different occasion I heard a loud series of whacks, followed by a younger brother's cries of pain. I again foolishly asked, 'Did you hit your brother?' The answer I got was an impassioned 'No! No, of course not, he's just acting to get me into trouble.' This particular ADD child then began an Academy Award performance. He wouldn't possibly hit his brother. Why would I think that he would dare do something so mean? I had let him down because I accused him unfairly, etc. etc. After several minutes of this discussion I had to look towards my secretary to confirm that I had heard what she had seen. Again he was so convincing that I had begun to doubt my own ears. I am sure many parents have been in a similar situation. This is why you should try to avoid questions of 'why?' or 'did you do this?' Rather move towards a clear statement identifying the behaviour, making them aware of what is unacceptable, leaving no room for their impassioned pleas or creative lies. 'You hit your brother. You keep hitting and you are choosing to sit in isolation.'

► *FIRM BOUNDARIES AND STRUCTURE*

When looking at an ADD kid, I am often reminded of a very bouncy 'super ball' that I played with as a child. It would bounce fast in all different directions when I least expected it to. If I ever tried to contain it in a large room it ran wild and would end up lost. However, if I kept it in a small space with limited boundaries I could control it to some degree. I am sure this holds true for ADD kids. By setting up a fairly firm and consistent environment and a structured routine greater success is likely.

Often parents of ADD kids are distraught when they hear mention of developing firm boundaries and consistency. However, most ADD parents know that their kids will try to push the boundaries one or two steps beyond the set point. It is important to establish firm boundaries well before situations arise. These boundaries need to be the same every day, wherever possible. If we imagine that an ADD child is like a wild bull running rampant, it is no good chasing the bull and madly trying to throw fences in front of it. We need to have prepared firm, tight fences, with a little room to expand, before we begin trying to deal with the bull's behaviour.

Every ADD child I know tries to gain a metre if we give a millimetre. Later on when he is in business, this negotiating skill will prove very successful in winning great deals. At the moment, however, it is sure to drive parents crazy, as the ADD child constantly pushes past what is accepted or expected. Therefore you need to firmly rein in the boundaries and support this with fair but mildly strict rules. The aim is for you as parents, as well as your ADD child, to know where you are coming from each day.

The rules should be the same today and tomorrow as they were yesterday and the day before.

Rely on the rules

In the basic program for ADD that I have given to hundreds of ADD families we rely on tight boundaries and structured routines. We rely on tight boundaries because it allows for a set of rules that can be referred to at all times. When your ADD child tries to divert you to irrational arguments you can rely on going back to the rules to avoid losing control. Without a strong, strict, reliable set of rules, it is inevitable that you will be drawn back into arguments. If you can build and keep rules established, then less often will you find yourself trapped in the reasoned arguments that you are losing against your eight-year-old. When a child begins distracting reasoning or laterally diverting, you remain determined to rely and return to the rules.

> 'Can I have a biscuit?'
> 'What are the rules about biscuits after 5 p.m.?'
> 'But it won't spoil my dinner.'
> 'Sorry, rules are no biscuits after 5 p.m.'
> 'But I'm really hungry.'
> 'Sorry, rules are no biscuits after 5 p.m.'
> 'This sucks, you're really unfair.'
> 'Maybe, but rules are no biscuits after 5 p.m.'

Your aim is that each time your child tries to divert you, then you respond with the same boring line. This does not feed the problem or open the door for an excuse.

▶ DEVELOPING CONSISTENCY IN AN ADD FAMILY

Developing consistency is one of the most difficult tasks for parents, as often one of the parents of the ADD child will also have ADD symptoms. We know that ADD is predominantly a genetic disorder; that is, ADD is inherited. Unfortunately parents with ADD symptoms will often favour inconsistency, irregularity and creativity. They rarely run organised and ordered lifestyles, governed by routine and good memory for responsibilities. If an ADD adult runs their life in such a chaotic manner, this will only lead to further difficulties, problems and confusion. Similarly, the greater the level of regular routines and structure existing in a classroom, the greater chance an ADD child will have of success in school.

Build consistency slowly

Given that consistency is very hard to achieve, it is very important to work at it slowly. Don't expect to immediately become a consistent, structured and highly organised parent. In the busy life and rat-race we now live in there is no such thing as a household run absolutely on routine.

Develop weekly not daily routines

The theory books might tell us to keep a daily routine. I believe this is impossible in ADD households. Rather I suggest you work toward a consistent week-long pattern.

For example, each Monday you might expect 4 p.m. — homework, 5 p.m. — bath time, 5.30 p.m. — free TV time if homework is complete. However, on Tuesday Peter goes to soccer at 5 p.m. Therefore he needs to hop in the bath at 6 p.m., as soon as he comes home. Again, rely on the rules: 'Peter, it's Tuesday, rules are bath straight after soccer training before TV.' If Peter argues that he just wants to watch this show, go back to the rules: 'No, Peter, rules on Tuesday are soccer, bath, then TV. If you choose to argue then no TV.' Again, don't venture into reasoning or divergent arguing. (I will explain the ensuing steps in the Four Step procedure.)

When you hear yourself reasoning about irrelevant matters, try to return to relying on the rules: 'That is okay, but the rules are still the same: soccer, bath, then TV.'

▶ REMOVING 'I' STATEMENTS

I am fortunate that my eldest son is a fairly compliant child. As such, the tried and true strategy of expressing my parental disappointment is a reasonably effective strategy. This method is sometimes referred to as 'I' statements, for example 'I am distressed by your behaviour' or 'Can you see how you caused trouble for the family? I am disappointed that you'd behave in that way.' My son fortunately has no ADD, and if I use an 'I' statement he becomes concerned, aware of the consequences of his behaviour, and will generally try to amend his behaviour.

Most ADD children are very impulsive and generally only concerned at a time of conflict with themselves and their own well being. They can be very self-centred. ADD children often wrongly interpret 'I' statements as rejection from their parents, to which they over-react, for example an ADD child will react by claiming 'See, you hate me.' An 'I' statement will possibly lead to further arguments.

Other 'I' statements can lead to their total ignoring of your feelings. It can be very frustrating when you receive a reply such as 'Who cares what you think?' The 'I' statement, which can be a good strategy normally, only feeds the ADD problem. I strongly suggest to parents with an ADD child: try hard not to make 'I' statements, such as 'You're upsetting me' or 'I am upset with how you are behaving.' Replace 'I' statements with those that show behaviour is their choice.

Do not own their problem

ADD children rarely, if ever, accept the blame for their own bad behaviour. It is always someone else's fault. If as a parent you use an 'I' statement, you own the problem. An ADD child may interpret that the problem is not with her own inappropriate behaviour, but your problem because you are the person who is upset. If you state 'I am annoyed . . .' your ADD child might respond 'Don't get angry at me, you're always yelling at me for something'. Thus your ADD child managed to blame you for getting angry, rather than accepting that her initial bad behaviour was the problem.

Your choice, not my problem

Several years ago I put a McDonald's voucher for a free family meal in my top desk drawer. It was put there in waiting for the first ADD child who came in and within the first few sessions admitted that a problem was his or her own fault. Needless to say, after many years the voucher is still in my drawer. I have heard countless numbers of excuses, such as 'It was my sister's fault'; 'He made me do it'; 'Well, Mrs Smith is a bitch, she deserved it', etc. But never have I heard 'I chose to muck up' or 'It was my fault' in initial sessions. Many ADD kids I have worked with end up seeing it is their choice of behaviour that causes problems, but not until some extensive counselling has been completed.

Rather than accepting excuses, generally I suggest that we replace 'I' statements with making your child increasingly aware that it is their choice of behaviour that causes problems. As a simple brief example, excuses such as 'You made me cranky' are answered with 'No, you chose to yell and hit out, you chose to go to Time Out.'

▶ *Do not say 'maybe'*

After much berating and whingeing do you finally say in desperation 'Maybe we can think about it, John'? Two hours later John says 'This isn't fair, you promised.'

The mistake here was saying 'maybe'. When dealing with an ADD child try to be definite and firm in what you are doing. ADD kids generally respond to definite and consistent boundaries. Parents, because they are fearful their child will throw a tantrum or because they are simply worn down, will often revert to statements such as 'Maybe we can do that later' or 'I'll think about it'. To an ADD child this means we *can* do it. Alternatively they become very distrustful, thinking we are just putting them off. Particularly Oppositional or Conduct Disordered ADD children know that we may not keep up the commitment. If you are going to promise something or make a stance be definite about it and try to avoid being wishy-washy or unsure. It is better to finish an argument firmly if your child is wearing you down: 'We have talked enough, any more whingeing will mean Time Out.'

▶ *Limit choices*

Don't give your ADD child too many choices; giving too many choices can feed the problem. ADD kids have difficulty in making choices and often become bewildered and overwhelmed. Try to keep to one or two only. For example, at breakfast ask 'Would you like cereal or toast?' Do not put out five options and then offer more choices.

▶ *Balance positive and negative*

Most ADD kids attract a mass of negative attention, but little positive recognition. One sure way to feed the ADD problem is to concentrate on negative behaviour only and not try to find even little positives.

> It is very difficult to manage an ADD child as so many normally successful strategies fail. As parents you need to be aware when you are falling into the trap of using strategies that feed the ADD problem. However, as we all grew up with these strategies and see them in use every day it is very easy to fall back into using them. Give yourself time to adjust and gradually replace them with more successful strategies.

In summary:

► We should aim to train, not blame, parents or teachers.

► Try to avoid strategies that feed the ADD problem.

► Try to avoid long-winded reasoning or emotional reactions. Act, don't reason.

► Use a firm monotonous voice and speak simply and briefly; don't reason.

► Act quickly before problems escalate.

► Don't ignore bad behaviour, but only act on what is important.

► Avoid yelling, asking why this has happened or saying 'maybe'.

► Try to keep firm boundaries and a very consistent structure.

► Rely on consistent rules to avoid irrational arguments or diversions.

► Don't use an 'I' statement, make it your child's choice of behaviour.

► Limit the number of choices you allow your child.

THE BASIC FOUR STEP PROCEDURE

— chapter 4 —

The basic Four Step procedure was developed and refined to deal with very impulsive children with little or no idea of the consequences of their actions. It also aims to gradually teach responsibility for one's own behaviour, rather than blaming others. The Four Step procedure tries to deal with difficulties quickly, firmly and consistently.

► *LACK OF IMPULSE CONTROL*

You spent hours preparing dinner and tell her it is nearly ready. So did she forget when she devoured three biscuits? No, she acted on a hunger impulse without thinking. You have told him twenty-five times, so did he really forget again not to run out onto the road? Yes, he did forget the twenty-five reminders, because he is very impulsive. He saw the ball across the road and his impulses said 'Run and grab it'. No other governing messages, such as 'You might get run over' or 'Mum has warned me about this', entered the decision-making centres in his brain.

ADD kids are now referred to as lacking impulse control, rather than just being impulsive. The reason for this change in thinking is that all children are impulsive. However, more typical or non-ADD kids govern or control impulsive thoughts, through alternative messages being transmitted in the brain. Whatever the message, it governs the response. It is very important that as parents you understand that a good deal of ADD kids' behaviour is not deliberate, but governed by impulsiveness or, more precisely, extremely poor impulse control. Similarly teachers need to see that a good deal of disruptive school behaviour is the result of poor impulse control behaviour.

Impulsive but remorseful

There are several characteristics to generally describe ADD kids:

1   They are often impulsive and thus don't realise what they are doing.

2   They can be so impulsive that they are unaware of expected behaviour or rules that apply to a situation.

3   Rather the ADD child has forgotten the rules or is simply acting on exactly how they feel at that moment.

4   Their behaviour is not deliberate misbehaviour or based on malicious intent.

5   Rarely have they thought past what is immediately in front of their face.

6   Once caught, when they realise they've been misbehaving they are remorseful.

Therefore the first step is to *build awareness* and *overcome impulsiveness*.

▶ STEP 1 — AWARENESS

'Stop doing that. I've told you a hundred times. I'm sick of you not listening.'

But they are unaware of this, thus they think you are on their backs all the time. Because ADD kids are so impulsive Step 1 was developed to help make them aware of their behaviour. In effect, I am trying to overcome the first problem of ADD, namely that the ADD child is unaware of their own behaviour.

In a monotonous, non-emotional voice you make your child more aware of what he is doing, more alert to expected behaviour, or you remind him of the rules. If your child is jumping on the lounge you would make him aware that jumping on the lounge is not acceptable: 'Is jumping on the lounge okay, Jason?' or 'What are the rules about jumping on the lounge?' If Sally comes out of school demanding that she have a treat we would go back to the rules, saying 'Treats are only given on Fridays, not Tuesdays.'

Again, at this stage you need to remember our earlier points of not saying too much, not getting into reasoning and keeping a firm, consistent and monotonous voice. You should avoid reasoning, such as 'You'll ruin the lounge springs' or 'Why do you ask all the time when you know I haven't got the money?'

Relying on the rules in the Awareness step

In the Awareness step it is very important that you begin by relying on rules. This allows you to fall back on them when your ADD child begins to argue or sidetrack you. In later steps it becomes apparent how important the rules are in managing an ADD child. It also helps consistency, as the rules remain the same from day to day, whereas our emotions as parents change. As you become more consistent with the basic Four Step procedure, after several days you can add statements such as 'No biscuits before dinner; same rules every day Sally, no biscuits before dinner.' ADD children tend to interpret this consistency as my mum knows what she is doing and therefore I'm less likely to get away with tantrums, yelling, arguing and so on. This is not to say that ADD kids may not try to argue or divert the conversation.

Generally you should only make your child aware of the rule or expected behaviour once or twice at most. At that stage you have overcome the first problem of ADD, which is impulsiveness. Your child should now be aware of both their behaviour and expectations or rules. After this point you will be dealing with inappropriate behaviour. In order to gain control you must move rapidly. In moving to Step 2, it is important to move quickly and not get into a long-winded battle.

Repeat the Awareness step for auditory processing difficulties

There is one exception to the rule of giving the Awareness step only once. I have occasionally suggested to parents of ADD children with severe auditory-verbal processing difficulties that they calmly and firmly repeat the Awareness step to make sure the child has tuned in, processed and understood the rule. This is because many of these kids listen, but do not absorb and process what they first hear. With these kids it also important to attract their complete attention through either a visual or a tactile cue, for example touching their chin or waving your hand to indicate 'stop'. It is even more true when dealing with ADD kids who have auditory processing difficulties that yelling from the kitchen will rarely work. Talking to an ADD child while not in their immediate sight and attention-span area will not be successful, as they will be too distracted.

▶ STEP 2 — CHOICES

Step 2 involves several complex parts, although I refer to it as one step.

Parents will note that in discussing Step 2 I will often refer to 'choices'. This term refers to the emphasis on the relationship between what happens to an ADD child and the 'choice' he has made. It is the result of his 'choice' and not due to any other factor. At this stage parents should avoid involving themselves in the argument through using words that suggest they own the problem, at least in their ADD child's eyes. If you state 'I will send you to Time Out' your ADD child will turn this to 'You are being mean to me' or 'You hate me, you don't love me, because you're sending me away.' Their perception is that of *you* doing something to *them*. This is because they have short attention spans and forget their own behaviour, only now paying attention to the fact that *you* are sending them away. ADD kids don't accept that their behaviour caused them to be sent to Time Out. I suggest parents remove themselves from taking blame or being the person making decisions. Rather concentrate on your child's choice of behaviour.

Behaviour is their choice

In the many years I have been working with ADD kids I am overwhelmed by ADD kids' creative and impulsive excuses for their behaviour. It is always the dog's fault; my brother made me do it; I can't help it, I've got ADD; everyone else does. It is always someone else's fault but never theirs, even the Man in the Moon's.

On a more serious note, is very important that we begin at the earliest possible age to teach ADD children that they must be much more responsible for their own behaviour. The aim is to almost brainwash them into seeing that *their* choices lead to their own consequences. I use the term 'brainwash' because an occasional message about responsibility will not sink in. ADD children learn only from highly repetitive, consistent messages. If you begin using 'choices' it will not have an immediate effect, but over time I have seen ADD kids finally accept that their problem has resulted from the choice of behaviour they made. By using 'choices' you are also more able to avoid being distracted by an ADD child's diverting arguments, in that you can come back to the rules and the child's choices.

Never a neutral outcome

Your ADD child needs to hear and know that there is a positive outcome if he complies, but that a negative consequence is likely if he chooses not to comply. It is very important that an ADD child is never allowed a neutral response. This refers to a certain amount of argument or reasoning with no outcome. You should try to offer the child a choice of two outcomes linked to a choice of two behaviours: one choice of behaviour will provide an immediate positive reward for the child; the other choice will involve an immediate, brief form of discipline. The outcome is based on your child's choice of behaviour.

Similarly you should not ignore bad behaviour: this is a form of neutral response. If you ignore behaviour, your ADD child does not see that there are consistent consequences for all their behaviour. This can convince an ADD child that he can get away with misbehaviour. Alternatively, if an ADD child is determined to get your attention, he or she will engage in increasingly bad behaviour until your attention is attained.

Obvious, simple and immediate rewards

Normally rewards for a choice of good behaviour would lead to a very simple and straightforward reward, which must be made obvious to the child. Similarly, refusal to comply leads to immediate, brief discipline. If we return to the example of the chocolate biscuit before dinner, at Step 2 you might state 'If you wait, you can choose to have this chocolate frog here on your dessert. If, however, you keep arguing, you are choosing to go to Time Out for five minutes. It is your choice.'

In our other example of getting Jason into the bath, you might state 'Jason, it's 5 p.m. The rules are if you get into the bath then you choose to watch the Simpsons right after the bath, but if you refuse you are choosing Time Out with no TV. It is your decision.'

Keep to the choices

As with Step 1, it is important that Step 2 is also brief and that you do not become distracted. If your ADD child is good at arguing you can repeat in a boring, monotonous voice the choice terminology. The following dialogue might demonstrate:

> 'Jason, it is 5 p.m. Remember that is bath time.'
>
> 'I just want to watch this.'
>
> 'Jason, the rules are 5 p.m. is bath time.'
>
> 'You never listen. Why can't I watch this? It's my favourite. Ben's allowed to, his mum's not mean.'
>
> 'Jason, the rules are 5 p.m., bath time, if you get in then you choose to watch the Simpsons. You choose not to get in, you decide on Time Out. It is your choice.'
>
> 'This sucks.' (Don't get distracted by taunts.)
>
> 'Jason, rules are bath and you choose Simpsons, but no bath means Time Out. This is two. Three is out.' (I will discuss Step Three (Three is Out) on page 42.)

You will note though that each time Jason tried to distract, I came back to the rules, rather than answering his arguments. If I rely on the rules I can be boring and repetitive. ADD kids hate being bored. Therefore it does not feed the ADD problem. They gain no stimulation from my boring responses and I am staying on track.

A change of terms

At a later time other terms can be used to replace the term 'choice'. This becomes necessary as ADD children become bored with the same words. Initially it is important to keep just to the terms 'choice' or 'decision'.

A quick solution with a definite end

In the above example you can see we got to 'three is out' quickly. We are trying to avoid drawn-out arguments and long lectures. Try to produce a quick and definite end to the interchange. You will remember we have discussed firm boundaries. If you allow your ADD child to draw out the debate, you are again chasing the wild bull, trying to throw fences in front of it. The idea is to have a definite fence or boundary set before we begin, the same boundary that exists day-to-day. If I begin this strategy with younger ADD kids I will recommend that parents hold up fingers as they work through the steps. The aim is to more clearly demonstrate that there are firm boundaries and a definite end to this interchange. Once I have held up three fingers that is it. An ADD child must know that the issue will be dealt with briefly and be finished before they become too hyped up. Similarly, with teenagers we set a three rule as the limit.

More complex problems

Parents with an ADD child who also has Oppositional and Conduct Disorders will realise that their children are more difficult. As they present with different and more severe problems we would need to slightly amend the above Step 2 of the basic Four Step procedure (see Chapters 8 and 9).

▶ STEP 3 — THREE IS OUT

You should aim to move quickly from Step 2 to Step 3, so that your child understands that there is a rapid setting of a definite boundary to their choice of behaviour. It also helps to convince your child that arguing at tangents or reasoning is no longer as effective in distracting you. Lastly, they do not become too hyped up.

In the early stages of trying this strategy your ADD child may not respond quickly. He may even try to tantrum more, because he is used to being in control through prolonging the event and wearing you down. Now we have turned the game upside down and set new rules that don't appeal to your ADD child as much. However, with repeated practice at getting through Steps 1 and 2 quickly and applying Step 3 firmly, gradual gains are made.

Step 3 means the quick choice

If your ADD child does not comply then Step 3 involves simple application of the choices made in Step 2. If your child continues to behave badly or refuses to comply then they choose that the negative option is applied. As with Step 2, the child must keep ownership of the problem. You should remain withdrawn from the central conflict. Punishment is applied based on your child's choice of behaviour. Again, you are not *sending* him to Time Out; he *chose* to go to Time Out by getting to Step 3. Similarly, we didn't take away his beloved CD; he chose to have it taken away through his choice of behaviour. He could have chosen the other option that was offered, but he chose not to.

Examples of Step 3

We can return to Jason who was reluctant to get in the bath. As a parent you moved through Step 2, offering him two choices of outcome. However, Jason still refuses or argues. You would then move through to Step 3, by stating 'Jason, you decided not to get into the bath. This is three. You chose to go to Time Out for five minutes and to have the TV turned off.' There is a very heavy emphasis on your ADD child's choices or decisions.

Similarly, we can demonstrate this step with Sally, who wanted chocolate biscuits before dinner. After letting Sally know this is two, you would then move quickly to Step 3, for example while holding up three fingers you would state 'Sally, this is three. Three is out. You chose to go to Time Out by still choosing to argue.'

Stay calm and on-track

When making the statements in Step 3, remember to use a very low, monotonous voice, avoiding reacting to your child's taunts. When you first begin this procedure, your ADD child will become desperate and use every bit of available lateral judgement and argumentative skill to try and take you off-track. Try to keep to the original problem and their choice of behaviour. Do not be distracted by other arguments.

I often envisage driving along the highway with a passenger who keeps trying to turn the wheel from left to right. The most important thing at this stage is trying to remember what we started on. If the child attempts to take us off-task and says 'You're a cow, this is unfair' our answer becomes 'No, Tim, you chose to not stop arguing, therefore you chose no Simpsons for ten minutes.' Similarly, if Jason argues that we didn't listen to him, we stay on-track, for example, 'No, Jason, you decided not to move to the bath. You chose Time Out.'

Don't give in

ADD kids are so good at diverting and arguing that parents are tempted to give in at Step 3. Once a child has got to Step 2, they must understand that each and every time they push it past Step 2 they will automatically have Step 3 applied. There is no option to return because it was their decision to continue to behave in this way. Again because we have removed ourselves from the argument, it is the child's responsibility. If the child emphasises that you are being mean, remove yourself and state 'No, you chose the behaviour Sally. Your problem. You decided on Time Out.'

He refuses to go to Time Out

As I write this, I can hear parents screaming 'But what if he refuses to go?'; 'What if he argues further?'; 'What if . . . ?' (I will attempt to answer some of the 'what if' questions below in Step 4.) Many of the children who refuse to go, or violently fight back, in fact have Oppositional Defiance or Conduct Disorders. The different strategies for these groups are covered in Chapters 8 and 9.

▶ STEP 4 — BE REPETITIVE

Most ADD kids, as parents are only too aware, are brilliant at creating diversions by introducing new arguments and thus taking parents off-track. Therefore it is very important that at Step 4 you try to be very repetitive, boring and non-emotional. This counters their diversionary strengths. Do not fall into the trap of feeding the ADD problem by beginning a long-winded lecture, getting into threatening behaviour, beginning to scream or demand. At this time, the most effective strategy is to deliver the same boring message, no matter what your ADD child says. We repeat the same statement over and over again, in the most boring, monotonous voice that we can possibly use. There is no limit to the number of times we will repeat Step 4 in a boring, monotonous voice.

If we were dealing with Sally; and the chocolate biscuits we would answer with 'That's fine, Sally you chose to keep arguing, you chose the Time Out corner.' No matter what taunts or diversions Sally comes up with, we give the same boring line repeated over and over.

Time Out taunts

Step 4 (repetition of the choice in Step 3) can also be used to deal with ADD children in Time Out. Parents often ask what happens when their ADD child begins yelling out for attention or screaming in Time Out. The most likely reason your child is yelling out is that he is bored and wants some attention. The answer to this is continue with Step 4, no matter what the child does, by keeping up a boring, monotonous line. As an example, if your child begins to build up a screaming charade such as 'How long do I have to stay here? When can I come out?' we answer each one of these with the same boring line. You could try statements such as 'You are there until the five minutes is up' or alternatively 'When you start being quiet the five minutes starts, then you can come out.'

Again, the most important tactic is not to fall into the trap of arguing or answering your child's debates or irrational arguments. Try to keep to a boring, repetitive statement, such as 'You chose to muck up, you chose Time Out, you're out for five minutes.' Again, it is very difficult to demonstrate adequately in a book rather than in a seminar, but the following dialogue may prove helpful.

'Jason, it is 5 p.m. Remember that it is bath time.'
'I just want to watch this.'
'Jason, rules are 5 p.m. is bath time.'
'You never listen. Why can't I watch this? It's my favourite. Ben's allowed to.'
'Jason, the rules are 5 p.m. is bath time. If you get in, then you choose to watch the Simpsons. You choose not to get in, you decide on Time Out. It is your choice.'
'This sucks.'
'Jason, rules are bath and you choose Simpsons, but no bath means Time Out. This is two, three is out.'
'I'm not going, you're not the boss of my life.'
'Jason, this is three. You chose Time Out and TV off.'
(To Time Out and TV off)
'How long do I have to sit here?'
'Till the five minutes are up.'
'When can I come out? This is unfair.'
'When the five minutes are up.'
'I hate you! Why do I have to stay?'
'You can come out when the five minutes are up.'
'John never has to sit here.'
'Fine, but you can come out when five minutes are up.'
'No-one loves me. I want a cuddle.'
'Fine, when the five minutes are up.'

Why the Simpsons or similar programs?

To ADD kids rewards are only effective if they are worthwhile. Again I believe that what works with ADD might not fit the theory book but it is what works. While these alternative shows have their problems I believe it is better to use them as a reward to keep a sane household than ban television and leave parents nothing to negotiate with.

The Four Step procedure has its limitations, but it is the basic strategy for dealing with ADD kids' behaviour. The procedure detailed in this chapter is a basic program, whereas each ADD household is unique. Therefore parents are encouraged to alter it minimally to suit their household. Further, it is a difficult procedure to adjust to. If we were in my clinic now I would suggest I would be seeing you again in a month. I would suggest that I hoped you might be only ten to twenty per cent more effective with this strategy by the next time I saw you.

In summary:

▶ Step 1 is to make sure your child is aware of rules or expected behaviour.

▶ Step 2 is to make them responsible by emphasising their choice of behaviour.

▶ Step 3 is to quickly apply Time Out.

▶ Step 4 is to be repetitive, using statements that are boring and non-emotional.

▶ Don't get sidetracked. Stay calm and keep to the behaviour problem.

▶ Never allow a neutral outcome, always have a positive and a negative consequence.

▶ Use simple rewards or punishment that can be applied immediately.

▶ Don't give in. Keep to consistent discipline day to day and between parents.

REWARDS AND PUNISHMENT
chapter 5

*T*he rewards and punishments used to manage ADD kids are slightly different from those used with other children. We cannot use:

▶ delayed reward systems
▶ occasional praise and recognition
▶ meaningless rewards.

The most effective rewards for ADD kids are immediately given at highly frequent intervals and must be worthwhile to the child. Discipline and punishment rely on using ADD children's dislike of boring episodes. Discipline is quick and relevant. Most of all, rewards and discipline need to be suited to the uniqueness of ADD. Many traditional rewards and punishments fail with ADD kids because they rely on delayed responses.

An ADD child's attention span lasts only a few minutes. Their awareness of what is happening even two hours ahead, let alone in three days' time, is very poor. Therefore saying to an ADD child 'If you keep misbehaving then you will be missing out on the dance on Friday night' will have very little effect, as this is not in their current thinking. Similarly, telling an ADD child that if they behave at eight o'clock in the morning by getting ready for school then they can stay up later that night will prove ineffective, as the ADD child will not see the relevance of this suggestion.

Reward either immediately or very soon after good behaviour. Apply punishment immediately after misbehaviour, for example going to Time Out straight away, rather than threatening a punishment such as no ice skating in three days' time. The younger an ADD child, the more immediate rewards and punishments need to be. Punishment can be delayed to a degree occasionally with teenagers, but in general using either delayed or very complex punishments and rewards will prove ineffective.

▶ REWARDS

Problems with delayed rewards

'If you are good you can go to McDonald's on Friday.' There are two problems with this strategy. The behaviour required to get the reward is not specific enough; what exactly is 'good'? Further, an ADD child is not likely to think about going to McDonald's through all of Monday to Thursday. However, like most ADD children, the child will produce the amazing ability to remember details at rare times, and at 5.30 p.m. on Friday will suddenly remember that she was promised McDonald's, having forgotten totally that she had misbehaved all week, except for the last half hour. She will demand her right to go, and if Mum dares to refuse, justifiably, she will resort to tantrums and claims of gross unfairness, and war breaks out.

Delayed reward systems at school

I have visited ADD children in schools where a behaviour modification program has been recommended to manage the child. This usually involves the child receiving a 'smiley' stamp if he behaves from the beginning of school until recess and another 'smiley' stamp for between recess and lunch without losing concentration on the goal. The ADD child begins at 9 a.m. trying to stay in his seat and not call out, but by 9.20 a.m. he has been distracted from this task. However, at 10.15 a.m. he remembers. ADD kids somehow always know when a break is near. So he tries for the last fifteen minutes, thus expecting his stamp. He has little recall of his poor behaviour in between. He then yells at the teacher for not giving him his reward, as all he remembers is the last fifteen minutes. Again, we have fed the ADD problem.

The problem is not the behaviour modification; rather the long-term concentration required for delayed rewards does not work with ADD children. Putting an ADD child on this type of behaviour modification suggests a failure to understand ADD itself (see Chapter 14).

Immediate rewards

Examples

It is best to use rewards that you can give very quickly:

▶ five minutes of your time playing a game or watching them perform an activity

▶ ten minutes extra television time

▶ extra time with Dad reading to them in bed

▶ ten minutes of Dad playing with them

▶ extra treats with dessert.

Rewards will need to be based on each child's desires.

Frequent and small

It is likely you will be giving frequent small rewards, other than in exceptional circumstances. I suggest you keep rewards in balance with the time used for Time Out. As an example, if Time Out lasts for five minutes then for very good behaviour your child may be able to earn five-minute slots of extra TV time or five-minute slots of stay-up time at the end of the night. If you reward your child with too much or promise too much it will be too hard to follow through with it. If you don't fulfil your promises don't expect your child to forget. ADD kids' memory for this type of information is amazing.

When immediate rewards are impossible

If a reward cannot be given immediately it is important to make it visible and evident. For instance, if we were dealing with Sally who wanted a chocolate biscuit before dinner, obviously we cannot give her a chocolate replacement immediately, but I might place a Freddo Frog in a dessert bowl, ready to go with her ice-cream dessert. At least by having it made visible and evident Sally will accept it as an immediate reward. If you are trapped in a car use a token system. Perhaps try giving your child a five-minute card that means Dad owes him five minutes as soon as he arrives home, or a five-minute block to shoot basketballs in.

Worthwhile rewards

The rewards given to ADD children must be worthwhile and meaningful to them. For example, if an ADD child with severe language-based learning difficulties received a photocopied merit award for 'Meritorious Respect', not only would he perceive it as not being a real merit award, he would also have no idea at all what 'Meritorious Respect' meant.

Some parents have been unwilling to compromise. A mum I saw recently said 'Well I like minties, if he doesn't bad luck.' Is it a wonder her son didn't improve? Rewards must be motivating, or an ADD child will not strive for them. Further, as ADD children are easily bored and insatiable, what is new, novel and a good reward this week may have become boring and old in two weeks' time. You will need to keep changing.

Tight boundaries to rewards

Rewards must have definite limits. You can get yourself into trouble by having loose boundaries on rewards. If you promise a treat at the shops for good behaviour your ADD child will be thinking of a new Nintendo game when you are thinking of a small lolly. If you say you will play with him if he completes his homework without yelling or whining, set a definite amount of time for play.

Is this bribery?

Occasionally in seminars I have been criticised by professionals for bribing children. I clearly agree that some of these strategies are very close to bribing. However, the reality is that dealing with an ADD child is difficult and sometimes bribing is simply all that works, as it is a good immediate reward the ADD child really wants.

Despite this I would implore parents to try as much as possible to come up with natural consequences, such as providing children with a little extra reading time in bed, an extra five minutes with Dad when he gets home, the right to go outside and shoot an extra ten hoops of basketball, extra special cuddles, extra TV or computer time, etc. I would rather parents rely on these natural rewards than Mars Bars philosophy.

Star charts

The star chart system awards a star to a child who behaves all morning each day, and these add up to a reward in two weeks' time once twenty stars are achieved. Many ADD children begin enthusiastically, but the novelty soon wears off as the reward is not immediate. Parents become self-critical, believing they must not be good parents as it works for everyone else. It is not poor parenting, but the star chart itself. While it is a good strategy for many other kids, most ADD children do not have the concentration or attention span to wait for weeks to get a reward. They need to be replaced with far more immediate reward systems, such as a point for each job done in the morning, even cleaning teeth and brushing hair. A quick ten points gets ten minutes' TV time before school. These systems are really only useful for breaking bad patterns of behaviour. They rarely last long term.

▶ PUNISHMENT

I have seen some very determined and well-meaning parents try to ignore their child's difficult behaviour for hours on end to avoid becoming distraught. Finally at the point of exasperation and total exhaustion they break, resorting to an extreme and harsh punishment. It is better to deal with behaviour as it occurs rather than waiting until you have reached boiling point.

Is it important?

ADD kids will always do some minor things wrong, but picking on every little thing will lead to a very negative home, and diminish the effectiveness of your efforts to deal with more serious problems. Try to decide what is important. Pick on things that will affect your child's life but let a few little unimportant trivialities pass by.

To demonstrate, a typical mum launched into a tirade about her son, describing many difficult problems. However, she finished by complaining that her son didn't put his pyjamas under his pillow. I felt a little sheepish at this time as I often forget my pyjamas too. I agree it is annoying, but it is more important to avoid a disaster over little events. Otherwise I will change my business card to include 'and puts his pyjamas under his pillow'.

Don't punish yourself

Parents who delay until it is too late, as demonstrated above, can create other problems. They tend to use very long-term, severe or large punishments, which make life harder for themselves. For example, if you ban your child from his bike all weekend you are asking for a very difficult weekend. If the bike is the one thing that your ADD child enjoys, he will destroy the whole weekend by pleading and arguing every ten minutes to get his bike back. He will attack you for having dared to take his bike away. He is very unlikely to realise what he did wrong in the first place or why the bike was taken away. He might simply see the situation as 'Mum is unfair and a bitch because she took my bike away.' I suggest, unless you particularly like painful and long difficult weekends, that you revert to very simple, short punishments.

James

I recently worked with James, a child who had a very bad habit, like many ADD kids, of jumping on his bike and riding impulsively onto the street. The rules were rather simple. If he rode his bike carefully his mum would reward him with an extra five minutes of riding time at 5 p.m. before homework started. However, if he rode recklessly without looking, his mum called him back and he was made to sit on the front patio for five minutes only. We certainly did not take his bike from him for the whole afternoon, which would have caused mayhem. Once the five minutes was up James was allowed to immediately return to riding, without any further criticism or punishment. Again large amounts of reasoning about the danger of this behaviour were avoided. As with most ADD kids James would switch off after the first five words.

If James refused to come back, he lost ten minutes TV time after homework was completed. This strategy had a definite structure. If James refused to come back, Mum placed a red card on the fridge, which James was reminded of at 5 p.m. On the card was briefly written the inappropriate behaviour: 'refused to come'. Thus, even though we had slightly delayed punishment, it was made immediate and definite through the use of the card. As the punishment was short we were never forced to give in.

▶ MAKING AND MONITORING PROGRESS

Progress with your ADD child will be slow and gradual. Don't expect too much. You will face some failures, but hopefully have more good days than bad. It is interesting to note that as I work with parents they often lose sight of the gains made. It is like having a new puppy. Everyone else notices how it grows but you don't because you're with it all the time. The same is true with ADD. The small ongoing problems often cover the real progress that has been made. Sometimes I deliberately go back in a file and read a parent the problems their ADD child was initially referred with. When they compare them to the current problems they realise the struggle is not really so bad after all.

Reassuring kids and parents

Sometimes when a crisis arises ADD kids or parents become very discouraged and fail to remember the overall progress. All effort and concern is concentrated on the current problem. We need to look at all gains.

Only a flat tyre

I recently saw a teenager and his parents. I had explained ADD to them many months before as being like a prestige car that was not cared for and had no brakes, so it often crashed. I took them back to this image. We looked at how we had polished the car up and had worked out how to apply the brakes. We had made great progress. Even though we now had the equivalent of a flat tyre, we weren't going to forget what had improved. We simply needed to look at how to solve this problem. Given the great changes we had made, fixing this minor problem should not be too hard.

ADD kids often need to be shown the progress they have made to encourage them to keep moving. Parents can look to see how they have improved. Weigh this up on the positive side when a negative problem occurs.

Never give up

This is a good time to mention never giving up on your ADD child. There is no more positive message than this for a troubled child or teenager. Perhaps one of the most pleasing aspects of my job is having ADD kids come back and tell me how well they are doing many years later. I am certain a part of this success is due to the fact they perceived we would not give up on them easily.

ADD children require very immediate and definite rewards and punishment. Many strategies and programs have been unsuccessful because they failed to recognise the characteristics of ADD itself. Success can be gained with ADD children if we look to use rewards that cater to their short attention span, limited concentration and distractibility. If you find punishments or rewards are not working first check they are immediate, have definite boundaries and are meaningful to your ADD child.

Look for the balance of good and bad.

In summary:

► Use only immediate rewards or punishments.

► Use small rewards that can be given frequently.

► Don't use big rewards that are given after a time delay.

► Rewards must be worthwhile and meaningful to your ADD child.

► Use natural rewards where possible rather than artificial bribery.

► Don't delay punishment or punish yourself by using too-harsh discipline.

► Keep punishment brief, simple and related to bad behaviour.

► Keep track of improvements to reduce the effect of a crisis.

► Let your child know that you will never give up easily.

TIME OUT

Time Out has long been used as a strategy for dealing with attention-seeking, difficult and defiant behaviour. However, as with other ADD strategies, special consideration needs to be given to the unique personality of any ADD child. Generally the Time Out area for ADD children has a number of important features.

► SPECIAL FEATURES

Boring Time Out

The first important feature is that you choose a Time Out spot within the house that is not stimulating or full of distractions, otherwise we will feed the ADD problem. It needs to be a boring spot. The aim is that the ADD child is not gaining any reward, attention or means of stimulation. Rather the aim is that they will be bored.

Use a boring corner in the dining room, that is well away from everything else, a spot under the staircase or even the third step leading upstairs. Look for a place where there is very little stimulation and interest. Try to avoid heavy activity or traffic areas or places from which your child can lash out. For example, one well-meaning mum sat her ADD child at the end of the kitchen bench, near the fridge, where mayhem could be created. With younger ADD children, particularly in their restless defiant years, we often make the Time Out a place down on the ground to give you some further power.

A name for Time Out

It is very important that the Time Out area have a set name. This is especially true with young children. If the name changes from day to day, it gives ADD kids just another thing to argue about. They can then feign lack of understanding. If we can have a consistent name what we are talking about becomes immediately obvious to the ADD child and reduces the chances that they can distract you or take you off-task. Try to keep the name as simple as possible and avoid the use of very negative terms such as 'naughty boy's chair' or 'horrible place'. Often we have used terms such as 'the corner' or 'the chair'. With some sporting kids we have found the term 'sin bin' very effective. In the basic Four Step procedure you would refer to choosing a reward or choosing to go to 'the corner'.

A definite name for Time Out makes it more transportable, overcoming the problem parents have in disciplining their children when they are out. If you have established a name for the Time Out area you can just as quickly establish it in almost any environment. This also allows you to cut down on reasoning or arguments. For example, at Grandma's, when your child begins mucking up we would state 'Jason, this corner here is "the corner" at Grandma's. Play nicely and share and you can put on a video at 3 p.m., but keep fighting and you are choosing "that corner" for five minutes. It's your choice.' I have even used a corner at McDonald's with a class of behaviour-disordered kids. We can find a corner there too, even if it is, for example, against the light-pole outside.

Definite boundaries for Time Out

ADD kids are very creative and clever. If you do not set boundaries they will gradually edge back towards TV, slide towards their little brother, and so on. Therefore an important feature is that Time Out has a definite boundary. It is not necessary to permanently mark your floor or carpet. Sometimes it is simply adequate to set the boundary as the corner itself. I have even recommended using a small chair. For the very defiant kids we have used a small felt or carpet square, and they must keep their bottoms on this. Don't use a plastic lid or they'll be skidding all over the floor on it.

▶ BEDROOMS AND TIME OUT

Sending a child to a bedroom is effective with typical kids, but not with ADD kids. Generally Time Out in bedrooms is not recommended for ADD kids. Can you recall sending your ADD child to his room, and going in two minutes later to check on him to find him sitting intently playing with his Lego on the floor? He is seemingly unaware that he has been in trouble and is wondering why you were stupid enough to ask what he is doing.

Similarly, parents send ADD kids to their bedroom to think about their behaviour, only to find they didn't make it because they were distracted by something else. They have forgotten all about their bad behaviour. Sending an ADD kid to his room is often feeding the ADD problem and unlikely to prove successful.

Teenage ADD kids and severe ADD children seem to perceive their room as their own fortress, to attack parents from. I have lost count of the severe ADD kids who have trashed their room to get even with parents. Similarly, many teenagers delight in storming to their room, swearing as they go, slamming the door and intermittently letting go with verbal abuse from the safety of their doorway.

Many Conduct-Disordered ADD kids believe their room is sacred territory and no-one will enter it without penalty. This is where they store their knives, draw their dark, bloody and death-obsessed pictures and write hate notes. I believe it is unhealthy to allow them to retreat to this fortress easily, get depressed, hate the world and plot against it to get even. I would rather they have to briefly face and accept their choice of behaviour.

The anxious and bedrooms for Time Out

ADD children who have anxieties and depressive cycles will retreat to their room to internalise negative feelings. They stew about how unfair and depressing the world is, talking themselves deeper into anxieties and depression. Again, I would rather they learn bad behaviour is dealt with quickly but then forgotten, and effort put toward positives.

▶ THE WALL-KICKER'S TIME OUT

For most ADD kids the corner or chair works effectively. However, a few of the more Oppositional or Conduct Disordered ADD children see this as an opportunity to improve the air conditioning in your place by kicking a hole in the wall. For this small group alone I have recommended using the felt square in a different manner. We have set the boundary for Time Out as keeping bottoms on the 'spot' (felt square), which is placed one metre out of the corner. If your child gets off the square Time Out starts again. You can allow them to swing round a little and fidget, but not move off the square. I have used felt for several reasons. Felt slips less on carpet and vinyl than other materials. Further, for very difficult ADD children, it is the ultimate in transportable Time Out. We have had several mums carry one felt square in their handbag to take to Grandma's, had a similar felt square at kindergarten, and so on.

The other alternative for wall-kickers is to choose a room that is less easily destroyed. For a very few, very severe ADD children we have used a room, such as the laundry, where less damage can be done. Washing machines, baths and tiled walls in a laundry or bathroom can better withstand little kicking feet. It is critical though that you install locks on cupboards or remove all detergents, laundry cleaners, washing powder, etc. It is also very important with very difficult, severe ADD children to allow them a small amount of control in this situation. This is discussed in 'Boss of the Clock' on page 102.

▶ HOW LONG IN TIME OUT?

Sending an ADD kid to Time Out is difficult. For the ADD child five minutes is an eternity. For Mum and Dad three hours wouldn't be long enough. While I understand their frustration, I also wonder if they enjoy punishing themselves. Trying to keep an ADD child in a small confined space like a bedroom for an hour of Time Out is like putting a new-born puppy on a mat and expecting it to stay. While short Time Out would prove useless with a more typical child, long periods of Time Out with ADD children can amount to parental abuse or self-torture.

Time Out based on attention span

An ADD child has only a short attention span and therefore it is inappropriate and meaningless for them to be punished at length. The rough rule I have applied is to limit Time Out to approximately one minute for each year of the child's age, with a maximum of ten minutes. Therefore a five-year-old typically would be in Time Out for five minutes, a ten-year-old for ten. This is not a hard and fast rule and can be adapted as parents find it effective. The important thing to realise is that five minutes is an eternity for a young ADD child. It is unwise and unworkable to expect an ADD child will sit in the corner for half an hour. Their level of stimulation, and reluctance to be bored, would make it unworkable and would almost certainly lead to a disaster.

I have also found that the more difficult, severe ADD children will accept a short period of Time Out. At the early stages of trying to gain control of your child it is more important to initially get him to acknowledge that he has behaved badly and accept a punishment. Up to this stage many ADD kids have not begun to accept they are in the wrong. Severe ADD, Oppositional and Conduct Disordered children will never accept an hour's Time Out.

Time and sequence— definite times

Most ADD children have very poor understanding of time and sequence. Many well-meaning ADD parents might say 'You stay there for a good while' or 'You stay there until I decide you can come out' or 'You're in Time Out until you're good.' Most ADD children will believe 'a while' is forever, and thus will fight against accepting it. ADD children do not understand loose time concepts, such as 'a while' or 'until later'.

Try instead to continue with the practice of set boundaries, in this case a set time boundary. Not only does an ADD child need to know the length of Time Out, but the Time Out period also needs a definite end point, such as a bell ringing or timer finishing. This again removes arguments, such as whether the five minutes are up.

Measuring time

There are a number of options available for measuring time. In simpler cases we have been able to deal with the mild ADD kids by simply putting on the oven timer. Any challenges such as 'When can I come out?' are answered with 'When five minutes are up, when the oven timer rings.'

Moderate, more classical ADD kids need even more obvious time mechanisms. They need to see the time. As an answer to this problem, I have found that many of the disposal or two dollar shops around Australia stock simple cake-timers. They are very effective for ADD children to measure five minutes' Time Out. However, it is generally important that your ADD child can actually see the clock. If she were placed in the dining-room corner then you would place the clock on the kitchen bench, within her sight. By being able to see the clock count down she has a good idea of when Time Out is over. As the bell rings, there is a definite finish. Your child cannot complain that five minutes is up before it really is and argue about how long they have been there.

The timer can give you some extra strength. If your child continually argues, there is the possible further step of stating 'If you keep screaming you are choosing to start the five minutes over again.' (Never let the child hang on to the clock though as most ADD children are good at pulling things apart and will have the clock in pieces or will have worked out a way of winding it down more quickly than the five minutes.)

If a cake-timer clock is not available, other options are an egg-timer or a standard clock on a wall nearby. If using a clock, your ADD child must still be able to know definitely when time is up. Possible ways of managing this are to put a small sticker, star or chalk mark on the clock. When the hand reaches this mark they are able to come out. Overall, it is important that the ADD child has a very clear indication of when the Time Out period is over.

A word of warning: Beware of using some older-style microwaves; if the microwave has to run when the timer is used you run the risk of burning it out.

▶ GOING IN AND STAYING IN
Don't buy into grumbles

If your ADD child heads off to Time Out but mumbles under her breath, don't buy into a worse argument over a new problem. Unless it is very abusive and foul swearing let it go. Otherwise you will have been diverted from the real issue. If the swearing becomes too abusive keep your response simple, such as one quick warning: 'Swearing is not okay. It is up to you. Keep swearing and it is ten minutes. Be clever and go quietly and you keep it down to five minutes for yourself.'

Staying in Time Out

Experience has shown that when the strategy is first developed ADD children refuse to stay in Time Out. The more difficult, oppositional and severe ADD children are already well practised in non-compliance, so refusing to go into Time Out is only the next step. In fact they will fight tooth and nail to stay out of Time Out, so we need to separate out the severe, Oppositional and Conduct ADD kids. I refer parents with this type of severe or difficult child to Chapters 8 and 9. For more classic ADD children, however, we can work on a number of simple strategies.

Breaking down defiance

Obviously with very difficult ADD children the Time Out strategy is not going to work the first time you try. With some ADD kids we have had to complete the in and out routine twenty to fifty times over, before they have begun to realise that we meant business. I often suggest that if you have a supportive partner, that you begin the strategy on a weekend. It is often more effective if both parents can be involved and the child sees a combined force. Take turns in returning the child to Time Out or repeating the boring, repetitive step. It is important that one parent does not take over totally from the other. Many ADD kids will perceive that one parent is stronger than the other and begin to divide and conquer.

Try to use terms such as 'we', rather than 'I'. Try to avoid saying 'I told you to go to the corner.' Rather try a line similar to 'Your behaviour meant that you chose the corner, and we have decided that you are still misbehaving, therefore *we* can see you still have to stay in the corner.' The following example shows parents alternating in the role.

> Tim: 'I don't want to stay here any more.'
> Mum: 'You are there until the five minutes are up.'

Tim: 'I'm not staying. You're not the boss of my life.'
Dad: 'You came out. We said that if you come out you choose the five minutes to start again.'
Tim: 'Mummy, Daddy is being mean.'
Mum: 'You chose to come out. We still see you choosing to behave badly. We see you've chosen to start five minutes again.'

In this way you are less likely to get worn down by an insatiable ADD child. Try to appear off-hand and prepared to return him to the corner dozens of times over without any concerns. This can be followed with 'If you stay you can be back watching television in five minutes.' As with other strategies, try not to be drawn into diverting reasoning or to get distracted. Each time your ADD child begins a new argument return to the same boring statement.

Keeping the very young in Time Out

With very young ADD children, who come out of Time Out constantly, there are several possibilities. One is to state repeatedly 'If you keep coming out of the corner, then you choose for the clock to be turned back to five minutes again.' For some ADD kids, actually seeing the clock moving back to the five-minute starting point, thus realising that they will be there for much longer, is enough to motivate them to stay in Time Out.

For other very young children, it is necessary to physically force them back into Time Out. This does not mean that you can exert physical violence. Be quite strong and determined without exerting physical violence. Don't attempt to grab them from the front and battle with them. The stimulation they receive from your angry face, as well as kicking you in the shins and lashing out, will be enough to reward them. The effectiveness of the punishment will be lost. Generally in a teaching seminar I demonstrate a tactic of grabbing a child by one arm, quickly spinning them around, placing their elbows in at the side and marching them into a corner with their back to you. In this way they do not even get the attention and feedback of your upset face or frustration. It also makes it difficult for them to kick out and hurt you.

Keeping older kids and teenagers in Time Out

With slightly older children it becomes somewhat more difficult to physically deal with them. Certainly with a teenage ADD kid it becomes totally inappropriate. At this stage we try to use the alternative strategy of showing them that by complying with the five minutes it will be quickly over and they can go back to what they want. Continuing to battle, however, will mean missing far more privileges. Generally, given an ADD teenager's insatiability and need for quick fixes, they will at times comply with this invitation. Often we might state 'It's up to you, a quick five minutes' Time Out and then you can finish your Nintendo game, but keep refusing and you choose for Nintendo to go off altogether.' Try to make it appear worthwhile for your child to do a quick punishment and get it over with rather than losing a great deal of what they want.

▶ ALTERNATIVES — TIME AWAY

We have discussed at length using Time Out because it is the most effective strategy. The next most effective strategy is Time Away; that is, time away from favourite pastimes or pleasures. For example, we might take small parts of time away from watching a favourite TV show. I usually recommend taking away segments between ads. For example, being abusive means choosing not to be able to watch and listen to a favourite show until after the first ad break. If you have definite boundaries, such as an hour's TV time after dinner, you can reduce this in ten-minute lots. If you read stories you can cut reading with Mum from ten minutes to five minutes. With teenagers we often remove parents' support. You might remove agreeing to drive your teenager to sport training, you might take away paying for karate lessons for one night, you might reduce agreed phone time to talk to a boyfriend from thirty minutes to twenty minutes. These punishments still need to be immediate.

A simple tip to find what is important:

▶ Look for what your child goes to first in the afternoon or weekend.

▶ Consider what shows they talk to mates about most.

▶ Listen to what they say was cool when discussing the weekend.

In summary, Time Out is a useful strategy for ADD children. Its success largely depends on suiting the age and personality of the child to the period to be spent in Time Out, the method of measuring this, and the nature of the area chosen.

▶ SIBLING RIVALRY

Family play in most ADD houses is like a war zone, where fights are regular events, and Time Out is often required to restore peace. ADD households seem to have more than their fair share of sibling rivalry problems. Often ADD kids are blamed for the trouble, because they are louder and more visible, although it is not always the ADD child's fault. Many kids become very adept at figuring out how to stir up their ADD brother or sister, knowing that they will react. There is often a double reward for the quiet stirrer: they get to enjoy their brother or sister reacting and getting into trouble while they are praised for being the good one. It is very important therefore in sibling rivalry battles that we deal with both kids.

The 'white-haired boy'

Many years ago I had the resources to videotape a child in his own home. His parents were very determined that their ADD kid was causing all the mayhem in the house. We watched the video at length to discover an encounter between the ADD kid and his brother. Both children were lying happily on the polished wooden floor of the lounge room. Suddenly a marble rolled from the 'white-haired boy' of the family and hit the ADD kid. This happened several times. Each time the ADD kid reacted more until finally he got up and walked over and hit his brother. The mother then raced into the range of the video, disciplining the ADD kid for his physical aggression. Needless to say, the 'white-haired boy' sat back in delight as his mother gave him a pat on the head and praised him for being such a good boy.

Both — or all — out

'Both out' is a strategy we use for dealing with most sibling rivalry fights. The idea is that you avoid trying to decide who began or finished the argument. Instead, you should use a broad term to describe what both children are doing, and give one warning only. For example, you would state that both children are causing problems and therefore both will be out. He started it, he hit me, she's biting. Try to ignore distractions. If both children are fighting over a computer then you would enter and say 'You are both squabbling. If you keep fighting then the computer is off for both of you for five minutes. If you share then you can keep playing.' Try to avoid distractions such as 'He started it' or 'He hit me harder.'

Any back answers such as 'It is all his fault' or 'He started it' are met with a bland response: 'No, you are both fighting, therefore you both lose the computer if you keep squabbling.' Try to avoid refereeing or attributing blame.

If you return again a few minutes later and they are still squabbling then stick to the broad term of squabbling. Do not make the mistake of identifying each behaviour such as 'You're yelling and you are hitting' because then we would have to decide which is worse. Simply state blandly 'You both did it, therefore you are both out.'

If you have more than two children involved, then substitute 'all out' for 'both out'.

Separate Time Out

Don't send both children to the same Time Out spot or the war will continue. They will need well-separated places for Time Out. It is best, in fact, if they are out of sight of each other, in their own well-defined areas.

Re-starting after Time Out

After turning off the computer for ten minutes you must decide who should have first turn again. Your ADD child will be insatiable and demand his turn first. Your daughter might feel that she always misses out. The most successful strategy is to rely on on a rule, such as on every odd day of the month your ADD child gets first turn and for every even day of the month your daughter gets first turn after Time Out.

Similarly, my wife adapted this rule to overcome fights about who sat in the front of the car. On the way to anywhere my son sits in the front and on the way home my daughter sits in the front. There is no argument to this. Whenever the argument arises such as he had more turns my wife says 'No, the rule is we are going somewhere, he is in the front, when we come home she is in the front.

When sibling battles occur try to invent a rule, and consistently stick to it. For example, don't try to have one child wash and one dry up the dishes as fights will start. Rather, on even days James washes and wipes, and on odd days Peter washes and wipes. Have a rule about who sits where for dinner to avoid races for the best seat.

Try to avoid getting into arguments about unfairness. Rely on the rule, repeating it no matter how they argue. Remember to reward agreement with the rules or pleasant sibling interaction, for example. 'You all get to stay up a little longer tonight because you all agreed without fighting over TV. Great work, kids.'

Protect siblings

When I first began helping ADD kids, I was so concerned with how little acceptance ADD got, and how often ADD kids were disadvantaged, that I forgot the other children in the family. I concentrated heavily on making sure the ADD child's needs were well looked after, perhaps to the detriment of the other kids in the family.

Even though I helped ADD kids to develop positive lives and overcome problems, several years later I was asked to see their brother or sister. The brother or sister had no ADD symptoms, but was often depressed, withdrawn, non-assertive, subject to abusive relationships or very angry about their childhood.

Many of these siblings develop a co-dependent personality, similar to co-dependency that affects the children of alcoholics. A child with an alcoholic father will learn coping strategies, such not asserting themselves, keeping quiet when Dad is angry, learning not to speak out, keeping quiet even though you have been unfairly treated. They can develop weak and ineffectual personalities.

Many siblings suffer similar problems because ADD kids dominate families' time, resources and emotions, through their demands and aggression. Their siblings learn to cope by staying out of the way, being non-assertive and giving in rather than fighting.

Siblings can develop a type of co-dependent personality. Their ability to deal with difficult relationships, aggressive bosses, abusive people and other similar problems is poorly developed. Another problem can be that an older sibling is expected to be the guiding, sensible one.

Encourage assertiveness and self-esteem

Encourage the other children in your family to stand up for their rights and not be dominated. Encourage them to be calmly assertive, for example firmly stating 'Your screaming is not going to work today, it is my turn to bat.' Try to avoid telling them to just give in to tantrums to keep the peace. If we encourage giving in we are rewarding ADD tantrums and teaching siblings to be non-assertive and weak. Try stating 'It is one turn each to bat, if you keep screaming you are in Time Out for five minutes, or you can wait your turn and get a bat in five minutes, then we can have a treat for sharing.'

Equal rules

Try to develop consistent routines that lead to equal sharing of time so that your ADD kid won't try to bend and manipulate you for more time and involvement. For example, with homework, have turns to ask Mum for help. In more difficult situations use a 'magic cup' to define turns clearly. Each child takes turns with the magic cup to tell about his day. Only the child with the magic cup can talk. Remember that we are trying to reward good behaviour; for example, sharing turns might mean Dad will play cricket for an extra ten minutes or waiting to talk at dinner earns a treat with dessert.

Don't dismiss siblings' feelings

Many tired and frustrated parents of ADD kids are worn out by the end of the night. They are more likely to dismiss the other children's troubles with remarks such as 'You'll be all right dear, don't worry about it.' I understand the fatigue and frustration parents experience; try to be aware that the other children need listening to. As they are more resourceful we can help them develop strategies to deal with their difficult brother or sister, focusing on solutions to the problem. Listen to their feelings, discuss their emotions at length, accept their pain and help them to build stronger lives.

Avoid the 'good girl' role

Many ADD kids fill the role of the black sheep in the family very comfortably. However, this often means that a brother or sister feels undue pressure to be the good child in the family. Try to avoid statements like 'Thank God, you're my good girl, you never do anything wrong.' All kids need to be occasionally naughty and learn from their mistakes. Often siblings grow up to complain that they were always made to be the good one, now finding that is a role they fill in life, always serving other people's needs but neglecting their own.

A word of warning: If your ADD child suddenly improves and the behaviour of the good child deteriorates at the same time, it may be a result of the 'good girl' role. When an ADD kid improves and gets all the praise, rewards and recognition, the 'good girl' is now confused as to what her role is now. Often, at this time, the 'good girl' will adopt some of the behaviours of the bad ADD kid.

Often siblings will also need counselling or self-esteem work to develop more assertive, effective personalities to deal with their ADD siblings and others. If a sibling shows signs of depression, anxiety, withdrawal or gross timidity, seek professional help for them to develop the necessary skills to deal with their ADD brother or sister.

In summary:

▶ Time Out should be boring, dull and brief.
▶ Don't use stimulating places full of distractions, like bedrooms.
▶ Only expect to keep your child in Time Out for a brief period.
▶ Make sure your child can see how long they are in Time Out.
▶ Don't debate taunts. Keep to a boring, repetitive reply.
▶ Don't use Time Out for teenagers.
▶ Use withdrawal of priviledges or time away from activities for teenagers.
▶ Use 'both out' to Time Out for sibling rivalry and separate all kids.
▶ Help siblings to be more assertive and avoid high expectations about being good.

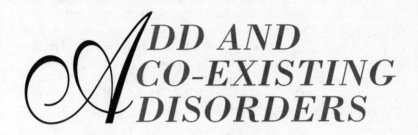

ADD AND CO-EXISTING DISORDERS

chapter 7

A n argument used against ADD is that children with very different behaviours are all labelled ADD. A teacher might complain that a hyperactive, aggressive, defiant and rude boy is diagnosed as ADD, while a quiet, anxious, dreamy and mildly obsessive girl has the same label. It is likely they each have ADD, but they also have conditions or disorders that exist at the same time as ADD. The aggressive boy might well have an Oppositional Defiant Disorder, as well as ADD (see Chapter 8). The quiet, anxious girl will also have ADD, but might also have an Anxiety Disorder (see Chapter 10).

► *CO-EXISTING CONDITIONS OR CO-MORBIDITY*

Many ADD kids have one or more co-existing conditions. Where this occurs we refer to the ADD child as having Co-morbid Disorders. Co-morbidity is used as a general term to describe any group of disorders presenting at one time. The fact that ADD kids can have Co-morbid Disorders explains why all ADD kids are not the same.

If a child presents with Co-morbid Disorders it is important to treat all the disorders, not just ADD problems. The reasoning behind this is simple. If a teenage boy without ADD were referred to my clinic with very defiant, aggressive behaviour I would treat that behaviour. Similarly, if a young girl with no ADD had intense separation anxiety and school refusal problems I would treat the anxiety and school refusal as a problem on its own. It therefore makes sense that if an ADD child also has these problems, we should treat them in the same way, as well as treating the ADD. Thus an anxious ADD girl will receive ADD treatment, but her anxieties will also be addressed.

Co-morbid behaviour increases with age

Co-morbidity problems tend to increase as children move into adolescence and adulthood. For example, it is common for a classic ADD child to develop oppositional defiance in adolescence. This may develop to Conduct Disorder or anti-social delinquency, and finally to Anti-social Personality Disorder by early adulthood. Many ADD adults have co-existing problems, such as alcoholism, depression, and substance abuse. The increase in co-morbid behaviour makes a very good argument for early intervention rather than waiting for an ADD child to grow out of problems. A parent's fears that if I don't deal with his problems then I won't control him as an aggressive sixteen-year-old are warranted. If untreated, the risks of greater problems in later life are increased in ADD kids.

▶ SECONDARY EMOTIONAL BEHAVIOUR

There are many behaviours that ADD kids display that are not technically Co-morbid Disorders. They are secondary behaviours that result from having ADD, for example:

▶   poor motivation
▶   low self-esteem
▶   frustration
▶   rejection
▶   emotional upset
▶   lack of drive.

In simple terms, they are not psychiatric or emotional disturbances.

Secondary emotional behaviour stems from problems associated with ADD. For example, an ADD child with learning difficulties is likely to have higher than normal levels of frustration, show less motivation and have low self-esteem. That child might be more irritable and tend to withdraw or explode unduly. As another example, an anxious ADD child might be more suddenly reactive, irritable, withdrawn and non-communicative. An ADD child who is in constant trouble at school might develop a distaste for teachers and eventually lose respect for many authority figures.

Secondary emotional factors need treatment or equal attention, just as much as other disorders, even though they are not technically Co-morbid Disorders. A problem for professionals, teachers and parents is that it is often difficult to distinguish secondary emotional factors from Co-morbid Disorders.

► LEARNING DIFFICULTIES

Is a learning difficulty a Co-morbid Disorder?

There has been great controversy and confusion as to whether a learning difficulty is separate from ADD. Some professionals argue that they are one and the same, even that ADD is really just a sub-type of learning difficulties. Another group, with the support of the majority of specialists in the field, argues that ADD and learning difficulties are separate and distinct conditions, although there is a high number of ADD sufferers who also have a learning difficulty.

It is my opinion that the second group is correct. My simple reasoning is that there are a very small number of all ADD children who do not have any learning difficulties. Similarly, there are some children with learning difficulties who do not have ADD. Therefore I believe they cannot be the same thing.

At a technical level, learning difficulties are accepted as a Co-morbid Disorder, but most professionals don't include learning difficulties when referring to Co-morbid Disorders or when discussing behaviour, social and emotional problems, such as oppositional defiance, anxiety, social deficits, and so on.

Learning difficulties and ADD

There are many descriptions and definitions for learning difficulties. I commonly use a simple, more recent definition: 'A learning difficulty exists where there is a significant discrepancy between the child's assessed intellectual potential and their performance level in specific areas.' An important development is that progressive professionals no longer suggest that only children working far below their chronological age, have a learning difficulty. We now accept that very bright children who are under-achieving, perhaps struggling to be average, can also have a learning difficulty.

Analysis of ADD studies has revealed that up to 92% of all ADD kids have a co-existing learning difficulty. If the definition limits learning difficulties to a difference between performance and chronological age, lower figures are recorded. Where a definition of discrepancy between intellectual potential and performance is applied, higher figures are recorded. In summary, the greater majority of ADD kids have a learning difficulty, which should be dealt with along with ADD symptoms.

Do all learning difficulty children have ADD?

As it is true that not all ADD kids have a learning difficulty, it is also true that not all learning difficulty children have ADD. A good percentage of all children who experience learning difficulties do not suffer with ADD. The most important related factor is that there is little evidence to support the use of stimulant medication, such as Ritalin or Dexamphetamine, with what are sometimes referred to as pure learning difficulty children (that is, those who have no ADD symptoms).

▶ OTHER CO-MORBID DISORDERS

It is highly probable that many ADD kids will present with more than one disorder at the same time. Some may present with as many as three or four. The following are some other co-existing conditions (the figures in brackets are approximate percentages taken from research studies that indicated how many ADD kids are likely to be affected with this condition as well as having ADD):

► Oppositional and Defiant Disorder (60%)

► Anxiety Disorder (20–30%)

► Conduct Disorder (35%)

► Socialisation Disorder (40–60%)

► psychosomatic illness (20%)

► bright ADD children (5–10%)

► Thought Disorder (4–10%)

► hypo-active children (2–5%)

► anti-social delinquency (5–20%)

► suicide (2–5%).

I will look at different strategies to manage these children. As I have stated, ADD kids need unique treatments and each of these groups needs its own slightly different management strategies.

► *ADD* AND *ADHD*

In order to help parents' understanding, many of the major and minor symptoms of ADD are described in the following pages. It is important to note these are symptoms of both ADD and ADHD (Attention Deficit Hyperactivity Disorder), in more classic forms, rather than symptoms of Co-morbid Disorders.

Late diagnosis hinders, early intervention helps

Perhaps the saddest feature of this problem is that in clinics across Australia reports are still made of later adolescent children who have obviously had symptoms of ADD all their lives but have never been accepted as having ADD. Late diagnosis often occurs despite the ADD child's parents' cries for help or their own awareness of possible problems. These children are chronic under-achievers, are very inattentive, often show low self-esteem and are much more difficult to deal with because of late diagnosis. It is well accepted that early intervention leads to better long-term outcomes. Perhaps if parents had been listened to earlier when describing ADD symptoms in their children diagnosis might have been earlier and far more accurate. Further, parents and teachers have taught professionals about other symptoms of particular ADD children and given us a greater clinical understanding of ADD.

Definition of the term ADD

ADD is the most commonly used and accepted term, so I have chosen to use it throughout this book. Technically, we should refer to Attention Deficit Hyperactivity Disorder, or ADHD. Within the major diagnostic criteria of ADHD are four sub-groups:

▶ The most easily recognised is the ADHD group, who are both inattentive and very impulsive and hyperactive.

▶ A second group is predominantly inattentive, but less hyperactive or impulsive; this group is often referred to as the ADD group.

▶ A third group is highly hyperactive and impulsive, but not so inattentive.

▶ A final group has inattention and hyperactivity problems but technically does not meet the Diagnostic and Statistic Manual (DSM-IV) criteria for ADHD.

In simple terms, there are several types of ADHD, in which some slightly different behaviour is noted. We are all very good at spotting the very hyperactive, difficult children, the kids current affairs TV shows love to portray. It is the more inattentive or finely hyperactive children, with less obvious behaviour, that slip through the education and diagnostic systems. I will continue to refer to Attention Deficit Disorder or ADD to cover all these groups.

A neurological and neurochemical disorder

ADD is a neurological disorder, most likely caused by neurochemical imbalance in the brain. While debate exists as to the cause of this imbalance, it is a fact that ADD is not caused by poor parenting, environmental factors, poor diet, laziness, family stress, etc. It is rather caused by poor neural transmission within specific receptive centres of the brain. In simple terms, there are some minute differences in the wiring of the brain.

If we accept that ADD is subtle faulty wiring in the brain, we must also accept that we cannot simply fix this faulty wiring. However, we can own ADD, not use it as an excuse. We can learn to modify behaviour, control environments around ADD children and use medication (where necessary) so that ADD children can reach their potential and operate on a more level playing field. ADD children in the past often had to operate at a disadvantage.

A genetic link

Often when assessing an ADD child, professionals have become aware that a parent or close relative had similar behaviour. For example, when I explain ADD to many dads they comment that I have just described their life. Recent research has indicated that genetic links have a great deal to do with ADD, more than any other cause. Unfortunately this means that if one child in the family has ADD, there is a much greater chance, in fact a 30–40 per cent chance, that brothers or sisters will have ADD.

Is ADD abnormal behaviour?

ADD is a disorder, but it is not a set of abnormal or bizarre behaviours. We all have minimal signs of ADD. The difference is in the frequency or intensity of those symptoms. ADD kids present with the symptoms on such a highly frequent and extremely intense basis that they interfere with the kids' daily functioning. For example, we all occasionally become bored in class, but we do not lose concentration every ten or fifteen minutes. We all occasionally act impulsively, but not to the extent that we are reckless or constantly and repeatedly in trouble. There is no perfect cut-off level for ADD symptoms. Rather, we consider at what point the severity or intensity of symptoms causes significant dysfunction in a child's life.

Core symptoms — inattention, impulsivity and hyperactivity

It is generally believed that there are three core symptoms of ADD. However, not all ADD children will have the same levels of these core symptoms, nor is there one clinical picture of ADD. In fact there are many different types of ADD children. Perhaps to explain this we can think of the brain not as a huge lump of jelly, but as a bunch of grapes with different interconnecting features. Each grape has a particular job.

Each ADD child is affected in different ways, with particular grapes being sour rather than the whole bunch being sour. Which particular grapes are sour grossly affects how each child is affected by ADD and other co-existing conditions. There are also many 'soft' symptoms or softer signs of ADD. When examining these soft symptoms of ADD we will find that there are even greater and more significant differences between individual ADD children.

CORE SYMPTOM 1 — *Poorly sustained attention*

ADD children have difficulty paying attention and remaining on-task. Not all ADD children have the same attention problems; in fact under certain conditions they may be able to pay attention. However, typically ADD children:

▶ lose interest faster

▶ have a higher level of distractibility

▶ receive fewer impulses to stay ont-rack

▶ actively search for stimulation in boring environments.

As a result they:

▶ often fail to complete tasks

▶ fail to pay close attention to detail

▶ appear not to listen or tune in

▶ fail to follow through with instructions

▶ can be forgetful and disorganised

▶ too often lose their possessions.

An important fact is that ADD is not simply a filtering disorder, an inability to block out distractions. ADD children also actively seek stimulation and interest. For these reasons simple programs such as keeping distractibility to a minimum have failed because ADD children, and particularly adolescents, will constantly need stimulation. For instance, an ADD adolescent or adult who is doing well might deliberately sabotage a program simply because it has become boring and is no longer a challenge.

CORE SYMPTON 2 — *Lack of impulse control*

In the past we have looked at ADD children being impulsive. We looked at behaviours such as acting without thinking, blurting out answers, not waiting turns. interrupting talk and playing recklessly. There have been recent moves away from the concept of impulsivity toward describing ADD kids as having poor impulse control. This better clinically describes neurological evidence of what occurs in ADD kids' brains. The reality is that we are all impulsive; however, non-ADD people have much better inhibition and impulse-governing methods

As a simple analogy, if you entered a room and found a chocolate on your chair you would have the same impulse as everyone else, to pick the chocolate up. But very quickly, perhaps in milliseconds, a governing response in the brain says 'Don't pick it up.' Whether it is your mother's voice from childhood, a moral message, concern that it is a trick, or whatever, this governing message controls the impulse. In ADD kids it is likely that the failure of the governing message to be received causes impulsive behaviour. In more real terms, it is this failure to inhibit behaviour or govern impulses that leads ADD kids to be, for example, impulsive enough to jump recklessly from a high balcony with no sense of what may happen next. Similarly, it is this lack of governing of impulses that leads ADD kids to:

▶   blurt out answers

▶   break social rules

▶   repeat recently corrected behaviour

▶   talk incessantly

▶   display many other similar behaviours.

The reality is that ADD kids have great difficulty in inhibiting both motor and cognitive activity. They lack a feedback system to govern or block inappropriate responses. A critical feature is that the classic ADD kid's behaviour is not malicious or planned, but often constant, with poor awareness of consequences and responsibility. Many parents describe their children as failing to ever *stop and think*. This expression of parent frustration in fact describes ADD kids' impulsiveness. ADD kids rarely get the governing *think* message to control their impulses.

Tied into this problem is that most ADD kids have very poor sequencing skills. They fail to see the sequence of events, either where their behaviour is leading or what the sequential consequences for their impulsive behaviour will be. If ADD kids knew this they probably wouldn't do it over and over. They just forget.

CORE SYMPTOM 3 — *Hyperactivity*

Not all ADD kids suffer with hyperactivity. There are also very widely varying forms of hyperactivity. The most easily recognised is gross hyperactivity, such as:

▶ being on the go
▶ being overly active
▶ fidgeting
▶ wriggling
▶ rarely being still
▶ wandering about
▶ wanting to climb, run or crawl excessively in situations where settled behaviour is expected.

The very hyperactive ADD kids appear to be overly active in play and have difficulty staying within boundaries. There are, however, other forms of hyperactivity. There is a group that shows only very fine motor movements, such as:

▶ picking
▶ flicking their fingers
▶ wriggling their toes
▶ constantly touching and preening, etc.

This group is not as easily diagnosed but certainly still has symptoms of fine motor hyperactivity.

The absence of hyperactive behaviour does not mean that a child cannot have ADD. The broad community image of ADD, often shown in the media, generally includes very hyperactive and naughty behaviour. This distorts people's understanding of what ADD really is. There are a sizeable number of ADD kids who are not hyperactive.

This group is:

▶ very inattentive
▶ disorganised
▶ dreamy
▶ distractible
▶ forgetful

► less badly behaved
► less on the go.

~~This group is less frequently recognised.~~

Increasingly hyperactivity is no longer seen as the main feature of ADD; rather inattention, poor impulse control and poor inhibition are seen more as principal features.

Hypo-activity

There is a very small group of ADD children at the other extreme of the activity spectrum. Rather than being severely overactive, the hypo-active are chronically underactive. They are not so impulsive; rather they suffer with lack of movement. They often have problems with speed of processing; that is, they are very slow-moving individuals. Their brains are capable but work at a slower speed. They are often the dreamy, bewildered and ineffectual kids who are difficult to motivate. They can suffer with obesity, depression and social withdrawal.

Other major symptoms

Not all ADD children present with all these symptoms. They represent a mix of problems any one ADD child may be affected by.

Hyper-reactivity

For a long time only hyperactivity was discussed as the main symptom of ADD. There is increasing evidence that ADD kids are also hyper-reactive. Hyper-reactivity is a symptom that parents have long complained about and is now being accepted by professionals. Hyper-reactivity refers to over-reacting or responding too dramatically to stimulation. Hyper-reactive ADD children don't seem to handle situations as other children do. For example:

► They are often more reactive to tones in parents' voices, criticism, or rejection.

► They often react more to foods, allergies and irritants.

► They over-react to peer teasing, bullying or rejection.

► They are more disturbed by environmental changes, such as changes in routines, windy days or temperature change.

► They are much more reactive to parents' moods and emotions.

Not only are they more reactive, their emotional responses appear very rapid and intense. Perhaps the most difficult feature of hyper-reactivity for parents is that while their ADD kid may react very intensely, five minutes later they have forgotten all about it, while the parents are still extremely disturbed.

Insatiability

Well-recognised paediatrician Dr Chris Green, ADD expert, colleague and friend, has suggested that insatiability should be included in the core symptoms of ADD. Chris refers to insatiability as 'an ADD child getting an idea into their mind, going on and on about it long past the point where other children would have let it drop'. I agree with Chris that this insatiable behaviour is extreme in many ADD kids. Their desire for stimulation, need for affection and demand to have their needs constantly and immediately met can drive parents crazy. They are not prepared to wait and will demand over and over again until their needs are satisfied. This is not only a childhood problem. Teenagers can be even more unreasonable and demanding. ADD teenagers want to be driven immediately to activities, don't want to wait for the phone and refuse to give up when told they can't do something. They will nag and nag until Mum finally gives in and lets them go to the disco that they were barred from before.

Constancy

Further to Dr Green's arguments regarding insatiability, I would add another very closely related symptom: constancy. It is in fact the constancy of ADD behaviour that I believe also drives most ADD parents crazy. Long ago I began to believe that some of the more difficult disorders of life were easier to handle than ADD. While there are some severe behavioural disorders, many of these children react only every week to month or so. ADD kids are constantly at their parents. Parents often experience a never-ending, constant barrage of attacks.

Other symptoms and soft signs of ADD

ADD and IQ

There is no definite link between ADD and intelligence. Despite ADD children often claiming they are dumb, their intelligence is not significantly different from the normal population. Occasional research reports have found very slightly lower IQ scores in ADD children. This is more likely due to specific weaknesses that pull down the overall average of scores that makes up an IQ score. A child can be very clever, average or slow-learning and still have ADD.

Learning difficulties

Meta-analysis of many ADD studies has revealed that up to 90 per cent of all ADD children suffer with learning difficulties. Technically, learning difficulties are not a part of ADD but a secondary feature. Despite this, they need to be paid great attention. Learning difficulty is a very complex topic, because there are literally hundreds of different learning disorders. In general a learning difficulty refers to a child not reaching potential. Thus a parent might describe her son as seemingly bright, having good oral skills, but being poor at reading and spelling and forgetting previously learnt material.

Discrepant learning difficulties

One of the most poorly diagnosed groups of ADD kids with learning difficulties are the very bright ADD children where there is a discrepancy between the child's bright ability and their actual functional levels. As a simple example, a seven-year-old child who has an assessed mental age of eleven years might be expected to be performing academically near this level. If the child fails to do this, rather struggling to be average, the child is under-achieving and likely to be frustrated. It would be like owning a Ferrari that performs like an old family car. We should apply the same principle to bright ADD children. I sometimes also refer to this group as having 'bright masked' ADD; that is, the child's ability masks or covers the symptoms of ADD.

Distractibility

ADD kids are much more susceptible to distractions. For example, small noises, changes in light or changes in environment can distract them from a task. Once they are distracted, they usually lose concentration and forget what they were doing. Similarly they find it extremely difficult to remember where they were up to in a learning task. They might even need to start all over again.

ADD kids' distractibility problems particularly interfere with their language skills. ADD kids often interrupt because they are fearful that if distracted from what they want to say they will not remember the message. Therefore they speak quickly, trying to get the message out before they forget. Regardless of this they need to learn to wait, perhaps with the help of a prompt or a reward.

Better in a one-to-one situation

Most ADD kids will be better in a one-to-one situation. They have trouble waiting turns, sharing, waiting for attention and not having constant supervision. Occasionally I have had parents comment that they wish they had had only one child, believing their ADD child would cope better as an only child. In fact this is not always true. Some only children who have ADD have had great trouble adjusting to the real world as they reach adulthood, seemingly having failed to learn to share, wait and cooperate. I would also wish many parents the opportunity of having a more typical child, so they realise they can be normal parents, and not always struggling.

Inconsequential

ADD kids may not foresee the consequences of their behaviour. Whereas other people can see particularly where their behaviour is leading to, ADD kids are very rarely aware that they are engaging in risky, socially inappropriate or dangerous behaviour. ADD kids may not see all the steps that lead to failure in many environments, but rather tend to concentrate only on the last immediate action that took place.

Sequencing disorders

ADD kids can have extreme difficulty with sequencing (that is, working in a logical or sequential order). They cannot see easily how to approach a task, so they may attack it randomly. They often don't see the process of first ... next ... next ... last. This can lead to difficulties such as inability to remember maths tables in order or to repeat directions, trouble writing sequences or difficulty in recalling phone numbers.

Disorganisation

As a result of sequencing problems many ADD kids can be very disorganised. Their rooms look messy, their desks are untidy, their bookwork has no flow or sequence to it and they constantly misplace items. They struggle to organise their work and keep their day in order. They struggle to remember and meet all necessary responsibilities.

Forgetfulness

ADD children may be very forgetful. Even though they have been reminded a dozen times they will simply forget what they were doing. Once an item distracts them they tend to concentrate on this new item, thus losing focus on the first and forgetting it. For example, if they are at lunch and they are distracted by play, their lunch-box remains where it is. If they are working on a maths sum, but are distracted by a noise outside, they completely forget that they were working on maths or where they were up to. You may give an ADD kid a message, but if they are distracted, they may fail to remember it. ADD kids can promise to do jobs but forget. They may leave behind or lose personal items. They can have trouble remembering directions. They often forget chores or miss appointments.

Time

Many ADD kids have a very poor concept of time or little understanding of it. They don't understand chronological time and are confused by terms such as hours, minutes and days. They have difficulty paying attention and keeping within time boundaries.

Recall deficit

A great number of ADD kids will suffer with recall difficulties, of two main types. One group has extreme difficulty in concentrating at the time a task is taught, so that they do not absorb an adequate amount of information when it is first taught, nor do they absorb what is important information.

The second group has significant delayed recall deficits: they actually learn work but then forget it later. You can teach your child his six times tables on Thursday night, until he has got them all, but by Friday morning he forgets half of them. Similarly ADD kids can be taught a word when reading, learn it, but forget the same word several lines later. Thus past mastered learning is lost.

Organised or sequential memory

ADD kids have very poor organised or sequential memory, for instance being unable to remember the steps to complete a task, being unable to remember their alphabet in order or recall the months of the year. They struggle to recall their tables in order, or to remember sequentially what happened in their day. Thus ADD kids cannot easily answer Mum's question about school, 'What did you do today?'

Good sporadic long-term memory

Despite their very poor short-term memory, ADD kids often have good sporadic long-term memory. For example, many parents of ADD kids are mystified as to how their child cannot remember even what they did that day, but then on the way to Aunty Sarah's, where they haven't been for three years, they can suddenly describe what is around the next corner. They can recall one-off incidents with a small prompt, but their overall sequential memory is poorly developed.

As we discussed early in this chapter, the brain is not one large lump of jelly. We have many memory systems attached to different functions in the brain. It is also possible for an ADD kid to have good recall from one area but not from another. A child may have good practical memory, for example being able to take apart or put together a machine, but have very poor auditory memory of what he was told.

Distractible memory

Most ADD kids have very distractible memories. This means that they can begin to work on a task, but once distracted, forget what they were doing. The most common example of this is that a parent will send an ADD kid to her bedroom to follow two instructions. The child will begin but, on seeing a doll half-way to the bedroom, will forget what she was going to do because she is distracted by the bright doll.

Over-perceptiveness

Many ADD kids are overly sensitive, emotional and too perceptive. For example, ADD kids may very quickly perceive that a person dislikes them. Unfortunately they don't have the social skill to manage this stronger perception. Therefore, rather than backing off and waiting to see what will happen if they perceive a dislike from others, ADD kids can charge in head-first without thinking, attacking the person. If they can learn to manage this impulsive behaviour ADD kids' keen perception can be turned into a great strength.

Escapists

ADD kids rarely like being confined or kept within tight bounds. They escape confinement in one of two ways. Often the very active, on-the-go group of ADD kids would simply prefer to be outside running around, building things, climbing recklessly or digging in the dirt. In fact, when they are very stimulated, even letting them run around for a little while may help to calm them and avoid explosions.

The more inactive, withdrawn and anxious ADD group escape through fantasy worlds. For example, they may withdraw from difficult social situations by immersing themselves in computers, Nintendos or similar electronic games. They need very tight limits on how much fantasy playtime is allowed each day.

Poor social skills

Very few ADD kids have good social skills. The very wide variety of social problems that ADD children present with can include smothering friendships, being over-dependent on friends, being too demanding, having difficulty sharing or not playing within rules. As examples they might have a friend for a week but quickly destroy the friendship by being overdemanding, or they miss the social clues when a new friend tells them to back off a bit. ADD teenagers can develop more withdrawn, defensive and occasionally aggressive behaviour. When they don't succeed with friends, they can become highly defiant and demanding of their parents. They might also engage in risk-taking or delinquency to gain peer approval. They are more likely to engage in substance abuse, and are at risk of suicide due to social failure.

Older and younger friends

Most ADD kids prefer to play with either older or younger children, even in teenage years. I believe this is due to the more clearly defined social rules involved. If playing with younger children, they are clearly the boss and know how to react in this world. If playing with older children or associating with adults, they clearly take a more submissive role and again fit into the set boundaries. Most ADD kids have the greatest difficulty in associating with peers their own age. If managed well, however, in later life ADD sufferers have great ability to adapt and relate to others, for example coming down to young children's level or being mature with adults.

Low self-esteem

I believe that low self-esteem is common to almost all ADD kids. There are two sub-types of self-esteem:

▶ very obvious low self-esteem, distrust of themselves, often appear sad, lack academic, social and personal confidence

▶ more brash, seemingly outgoing nature, but in fact very scared kids underneath, having low confidence but covering up with false bravado.

Perhaps amongst the most common statements ADD kids make are 'I'm dumb' or 'I'm stupid'.

Jekyll-and-Hyde characters

ADD kids can be rightly described as Jekyll-and-Hyde characters, with more variable and extreme moods than other children. They have extremely good times, when they are very affectionate, caring, loving and giving, more so than peers. Then there are the other times when they are very obstinate, defiant, overactive and restless. Unexpectedly an ADD kid is often the first to help when Mum is really sick, or the teenager who comes to the fore in a crisis.

Coordination

Many ADD kids have poor coordination, fine motor and gross motor skills. This more often applies to the inattentive, disorganised and learning disabled group. They can be clumsy, can have poor lateral dominance and poor spatial perception, can have difficulty with coordination and often have poor handwriting, poor drawing skills and generally present messy work.

In contrast, a number of the more hyperactive ADD group are very well coordinated, being very good at sport and motor activities. Their high activity levels and stamina become a strength in this area. For this reason they are often able to continue longer in some sporting tasks than others. They have good sporting perception, for example being able to read a football game or anticipate an opponent's moves.

Immaturity

Many ADD kids are appropriately described as immature. A common parental complaint is that 'Joseph is ten going on seven'. Generally it is believed, because of neurological deficits of the brain, they in fact do act in a less mature way. As a result, ADD kids do not build on social successes to gradually show more maturity.

Paranoia

Many older ADD kids and adolescents suffer with mild paranoia. They often believe that people are talking about them, trying to get at them or deliberately upsetting them. Their hyper-reactivity seems to lead them to make very impulsive decisions, rather than taking in all factors. This can result in paranoid thinking. ADD kids' aggressiveness can lead to others becoming defensive towards them, which increases their perceptions of attack to the point of mild paranoia.

Sleep difficulties

ADD kids can be affected by sleep difficulties, of varying kinds:

▶ difficulty getting to sleep

▶ significant problems remaining asleep, often waking feeling very insecure, unsettled or restless

▶ nightmares, night terrors, sleepwalking and similar sleep problems

▶ disturbed sleep but early waking

▶ awake with the dawn although last asleep in the house

▶ late in getting to sleep, but chronically difficult to wake in the morning, often being over-tired, irritable and fatigued.

Noisy children

Many of the ADD kids I have seen are very noisy, loud and overly talkative. We have often described them as having a 'Foghorn Leghorn' voice. ADD kids appear not to be able to talk in a quiet voice, but believe that everyone is at least one football paddock away. They can also talk incessantly about irrelevant topics, going off at tangents.

Diet and medication

Hyper-reactivity to foods

While diet is not the total answer to fixing ADD, a number of ADD children are hyper-reactive to foods such as flavours, colours, salicylates (naturally occurring sugars) and similar substances. More recent research has shown that a small group demonstrates a high level of hyper-reactivity and do need very restrictive, well-managed diets. The large majority are only minimally affected. This group can be controlled with sensible eating, without driving the family crazy with exhaustive shopping and special food preparation.

Medication dulls creativity?

It has been theorised that brilliant achievers such as Winston Churchill, Yeats, Einstein, Edison and Mozart had symptoms consistent with ADD. The non-believers and cynics use this as an argument against medication, claiming it would have dulled their creative brilliance. However, my experience with talented ADD adults on medication is that they achieve more. They are more able to remain on-task to complete brilliant ideas, to organise their work and make fewer forgetful or silly errors. Further, I believe multi-modal ADD treatment allows brilliant ADD sufferers a better chance of taking higher studies to realise their potential. Many women have reported that their ADD husbands change from having a dozen unfinished projects on the go, without any being completed, to only two or three projects, which are finished, with attention to detail and greater precision. One woman summed it up when she said her creative teenage son went from being a 'gunna do' to a 'good finisher'.

Looking at the good side

Lateral thinking talents

ADD kids may have difficulty staying on-task but they can also have very well-developed lateral thinking skills. Thus they can be very good at lateral problem-solving, creative solutions and brainstorming. They will see and deduce tangents that others may not see. They can make quick, determined decisions.

Energy and drive

ADD kids may be more hyperactive, but a positive sign is that they have more energy and drive. If their energy can be harnessed and focused in a positive direction they can be very determined and singular in their purpose. They have the ability to over-focus on stimulating and interesting material. Unfortunately this means they can occasionally block out the world around them.

Creativity

A great many ADD kids are more creative and inspirational than their peers. They are often more perceptive and talented in diverse or unusual areas, where they often achieve during later life. Many ADD kids have a natural talent for computers, electronics, welfare work, creative design and engineering, advertising, mechanics, art, cartooning, drama, construction and many similar areas.

Sympathetic, empathic and protective

In even the most difficult ADD kids I have seen a genuine empathy, and a warm and protective nature. They are the kids who will bring home a lost bird, help a disabled kid in the playground or take a defeated kid under their wing and protect them from others.

However, their perception can still be a little distorted. While they may think it is their given right to abuse and attack their little brother or sister, they are also extremely protective should anyone else dare attack that same brother or sister in public. Although it is acceptable for them it is certainly not acceptable for others. At least we know they have this other side, a great character trait in later life.

Teenage years and adolescence

Many of the symptoms described certainly apply to teenagers. However, by the time many ADD children reach adolescence, they are displaying more significant symptoms. They are often more oppositional and defiant, thus less willing to accept authority. By this time they are also more often obsessed with trendy clothes or alternative group cultures, making sure they fit in socially. Unfortunately they are very much more prone to substance abuse, because of their impulsiveness and low self-esteem. This is not caused by medication, but rather by their impulsive desire to fit in and do what is cool, without thinking about the consequences. They are also more prone to behaviour that leads to motor vehicle accidents and similar risk-taking adventures. At this time they are more likely to have had broken arms, stitches and injuries. They are more likely to now be involved in truancy, because of their dislike of school. They are often more chronically under-achieving and more prone to depression and aggression. A very small group is more subject at this time to suicide, particularly adolescent males. Some anxious, hypersensitive girls are very prone to bulimia.

More recent research has theorised that many ADD teenagers and adults are not as hyperactive or severely impulsive. As they pass through puberty they seem to start maturing past some of the more obvious symptoms while inattentiveness, disorganisation and forgetfulness tend to persist longer.

ADD in adulthood

ADD does continue into adulthood. Obviously these adults had ADD through their whole early life span but it was not a known condition in their time. However, ADD adults are rarely just grown-up ADD kids. They have different problems and needs but there are strategies, practical help and coaching techniques which I have successfully undertaken with adults. This book does not have the space to discuss the strategies used to treat ADD in adulthood, as it is an equally complex and demanding disorder. There are a number of adult ADD texts. The late Dr Gordon Serfontein's book *ADD in Adults* is an excellent Australian text. Dr Lynn Weiss, an American writer with much personal experience with adults with ADD, has several good texts on ADD in adulthood. A more practical guide is *Driven to Distraction* by American writers Edward Hallowell and John Ratey. (This text is written by an ADD sufferer and while this aids understanding, many readers complain that the text is a little disorganised and difficult to comprehend.)

Will they grow out of it?

Recent developments have led us to believe that hyperactive symptoms appear to reduce as adults mature and mellow. Thus many ADD kids will not continue to be affected all their lives. Rather it is the inattentive, disorganised, forgetful, fidgety, learning-disabled ADD group (often girls) that appear to be more likely to continue to present with symptoms in adulthood. This may account for recent research that indicates that the male to female ratio of ADD in adults is closer to 1:1 instead of the 6:1 ratio in childhood. There are other neurological indications that might explain the differences in ADD adults.

There are dads who say they coped and grew out of it. This may be in fact true. However, I believe the world is far more complex now; there is a greater need for education and a far higher rate of youth unemployment. Many dads have also admitted they struggled excessively to cope. Maybe they too could have had the opportunity to complete school without being at a disadvantage. For example, an under-achieving ADD student may miss a university place based on not reaching his full potential. Lastly, many ADD children are late maturers. Even if they do grow out of problems, by the time this occurs damage may have been done.

When do symptoms present?

The question of timing largely relies on the type of ADD affecting a child. The most obvious group are the more hyperactive, aggressive, and unmanageable children. More often these are boys in a ratio of approximately 6:1. These children will often present almost from birth. I have mothers (whom I believe) who felt their children were more active even in the womb. From day one these children will always be on the go, constantly touching and into everything. They often suffer colic, are poor feeders, scream constantly and demand attention. Even in pre-school they tend to reject social boundaries and are very often referred early for behavioural problems, leading to early diagnosis.

A second group is slightly less hyperactive. Although still mildly hyperactive, they may in fact be quite good, placid babies. It is not, however, until they get up onto their feet that they begin to be noticed. These children are often described as going straight from sitting to running, never crawling or walking in between. Again this group is highly referred and easily diagnosed, leading to good early treatment.

A third group of more classical ADD children are not severely hyperactive and often are not noticed until they begin school. It is only when they have to sit in a structured classroom, fit into social and academic structures and complete formal learning tasks that their ADD is more easily noticed. Again though, because they are not fitting into the normal behaviour patterns, this group is fairly easily recognised.

A fourth group is often not noted until they reach the abstract learning stage, when everything is not straightforward. If we study report cards of this group we might find comments such as 'A delight to teach, but slightly dreamy' or 'Could do better if she concentrated, but is a most polite student.' This group often in fact are not diagnosed until they are some eight to ten years old. As an aside this group often has another interesting label, simply 'girls'.

A fifth group is perhaps the most disturbing group of all, with symptoms from a very young age, often being recognised by parents and alert teachers as being different. They are constantly referred to as 'immature' and 'not reaching their potential'. Despite their parents' screams for support, they are told 'Not to worry, he will soon mature out of it.' This group no doubt has ADD, but educators or parents had failed to recognise them. When finally diagnosed, they are the very difficult, rebellious or depressed teenagers who are seen as very difficult to work with. As a result of their late diagnosis they are less likely to respond to treatment. Unfortunately, well-ingrained patterns must be overcome before treatment can begin to be effective.

As a precaution against over-diagnosis, it is worth nothing that ADD does not suddenly appear. Symptoms should present consistently over an extended time span, often through most of the life span. They certainly do not suddenly appear in later adolescence or adulthood.

In summary:

ADD is a very complex and confusing disorder. There is no one picture of ADD but many styles of the same overall disorder. while you may recognise features in the above description, careful diagnosis is necessary to confirm that your child may have ADD. Once diagnosed, try to look not just at their weaknesses, but at their strengths. Similarly, try to teach to their strengths as well as their weaknesses to increase the likelihood of positive outcomes.

OPPOSITIONAL DEFIANT DISORDER—ODD

chapter 8

Approximately 60 per cent of all kids with ADD may develop an Oppositional Defiant Disorder (ODD), particularly if they are not managed well. Fortunately, as we are seeing ADD kids at a younger age, fewer are developing ODD problems later. However, some ADD kids present with ODD symptoms from infancy. For example, I saw an infant who had pulled out his breathing tube over thirty times while in a humidicrib. The neonatal nurse had marked his card 'Very stubborn'. He is now one of the most oppositional kids I see.

Unfortunately, because most kids with an Oppositional Defiant Disorder are very difficult to manage, they are among the most trying kids that parents are faced with. It is less likely that ADD kids with ODD will have a positive future than will classic ADD kids. However, many people have been too hasty in writing off oppositional ADD kids. They are difficult but success can be realised. A critical step towards success is to adjust the basic strategies for classic ADD kids to suit the unique problems of ODD.

▶ A BRIEF DESCRIPTION

In general an oppositional and defiant child is one who performs very much as the label suggests. They are consistently very hostile, negativistic and defiant. They can often lose their temper, argue excessively, refuse to accept authority, annoy people deliberately and be very angry and spiteful.

They will often deny the consequences of their behaviour and are liable to resist any discipline programs. Unfortunately an oppositional child may go beyond either seeing reason or accepting that it is time to give in. While you may feel you have an ADD child who also has ODD, it is necessary to consult a professional, such as a paediatrician, psychologist or psychiatrist, for a formal diagnosis. A child with a Conduct Disorder, Mood Disorder or Psychotic Disorder can be similar in some ways. However, there are risks to inaccurate diagnosis. A technical description of ODD is listed in the Diagnostic and Statistic Manual (DSM-IV).

Simple examples

A simple example of a young ADD child with ODD would be a three-year-old girl who, when smacked, will state aggressively 'It didn't hurt.' Even when she knows she is in real trouble she still will not accept that it hurt. At a later age these kids are obviously very much at risk. A simple example in adolescence might be a thirteen-year-old saying 'Try and stop me' when you try to tell him that he cannot leave the house. Similarly a fourteen-year-old girl with ODD may seek approval from her girlfriends, feeling it is more important than accepting your discipline. She will display all sorts of defiant and aggressive behaviour in order to see her friends. For simplicity's sake I often refer to ADD kids with ODD as Oppositional ADD kids, whereas normal ADD kids are often referred to as classic ADD kids.

Oppositional ADD kids absolutely refuse to own any problem and will be resentful and aggressive if you push the point. Even more than classic ADD kids, Oppositional ADD kids will constantly deny responsibility. They may do everything possible to avoid blame themselves. They are very apt to create excuses for their behaviour and embark on threats and swearing as a way of covering their problems.

Some parents have been wrongly told by professionals that oppositional defiant behaviour is just normal ADD behaviour and to expect and tolerate it. A classic ADD child or teenager will not elevate their behaviour to such extremes and is often more remorseful. Oppositional ADD kids rarely show remorse.

Anxiety and Oppositional ADD kids

A smaller number of Oppositional ADD kids have underlying anxieties, which are often not realised because they are masked by aggressive behaviour. For example, some Anxious ADD children may turn into Oppositional ADD teenagers. Success will not be achieved unless underlying anxieties are resolved. It is hard to see the anxiety under the defiance, but it needs attention.

Any attempts to overcome nervousness must be taken in tiny steps. Never attempt to throw your Oppositional ADD child in at the deep end. Instead, gently encourage forward progress. It is important that your child is not overwhelmed by the task at hand. Realistic examples of when he or she has coped with similar situations in the past will help build confidence. Again giving some responsibility should also help overcome these problems.

► MANAGEMENT STRATEGIES
Change and improvement are slow

I have generally found that we need to embark on a more complicated, individual management plan with Oppositional ADD kids.

It is important to remember that change with Oppositional ADD kids comes very slowly. Most Oppositional ADD kids practise from a very young age, even maybe as two- or three-year-olds, to defy authority. Unfortunately, too often parents have finally had the problem recognised and diagnosed when their child, typically, is in the teenage years, by which time it is unlikely that they are going to give up easily and immediately change. The tactics that I am about to describe, however, are generally found to be more successful over time, but no strategy will always succeed with this group.

An example of managing ODD — Tom

Tom was one of the most Oppositional ADD kids I had seen. Like many similar kids he had never shown me this behaviour, determined to prove his mum was really a liar who made all these problems up. That was until Tom stormed into my office, furious that his mother had refused to buy him McDonald's, which is downstairs from my office. Although I had trusted his parent's descriptions I now saw Tom in his full fury. He slammed the chair against my desk, leaned over close to my face and began a verbal assault. He was trying his hardest to lock me into a head-on battle. I could have yelled back and attacked him for swearing, but then Tom would have had me. I quite deliberately stood slowly and sat on the side of the desk, at an angle to Tom. Then in a non-emotional voice I said, in my best detached manner, 'Gee Tom, I just spoke to Mr Flannery (Tom's principal). I wanted to tell you what he said about you improving, but I guess I can't if you keep yelling, can't really talk to you then. Tell you what, I need a coffee. You see what you want to do, it is up to you.' I then left Tom for a few seconds to turn the kettle on, not that I really needed a coffee. I simply wanted to momentarily avoid the immediate battle.

When I returned I was again determined to be off-hand. Tom was still visibly upset, but not quite so loud. I again moved off to an angle and said, in a detached manner, 'Still loud Tom, guess I can't talk to you then, but then again you could calm a bit and I can tell you what Mr Flannery said about you. It's up to you, not me, Tom.' Because Tom did not calm immediately I still wanted to avoid the battle so I said 'You decide Tom, kettle's boiled, I'll just make the coffee. You're in control, Tom, of what happens next.'

When I returned Tom had calmed slightly. At this point I tried to distract him from the battle. (If ADD kids are going to be so distractible, we might as well use it to our benefit sometimes.) I said enthusiastically and involved now, no longer detached, 'Hey Tom, everyone said you couldn't calm down and you've just proved you can. I'm just going to write this down as being great. Hey, hang on Tom, I'm going to tell Mum how well you started to calm down.' I was determined and enthusiastic to 'jump on the good' rather than concentrating on the bad. While we needed to go back and do some counselling about Tom's initial anger, I could only do this when he was calmer and felt I was on his side, not against him.

I do not imagine this strategy would work every time at home with your Oppositional ADD child, but it provides a guide to strategies to deal with this difficult group. Some parents have felt they could never master this type of strategy, rather preferring I come and live with them. The answer is that you too can learn strategies to deal with Oppositional ADD kids with time and practice.

Avoiding head-on battles

Most oppositional kids enjoy head-on battles or confrontations. When Oppositional ADD kids walk head-first into an argument, rarely will they be in compassionate or conciliatory mode. More likely their whole aim is to have a head-banging session with you as parents. Therefore it is important initially that you do everything you can to avoid a full head-on confrontation. You will remember that when Tom pushed the chair into my desk to confront me I moved to the side at an angle. I have similarly trained parents to simply try to take a step back or a step away and to the side when the initial confrontation begins.

Watch the tone of your voice, your facial expressions and open aggression. Many Oppositional ADD kids almost delight in watching their parents get angry. One of the more Oppositional ADD kids I saw described vividly how red her father's face became, how the veins bulged in his neck and how white his eyes became. By the time he finally threw her into her room the battle had already been lost.

In dealing with Tom, I kept the tone of my voice very deliberately cool and detached. This is very difficult to achieve, as Oppositional ADD kids deliberately annoy and frustrate. It is important that you do not fall into their traps.

Try to use an offhand or detached voice, almost as though you don't care. I sympathise with how hard it is to stay calm but the more you can appear to be in control, although internally you are very frustrated, the better your chance of success. The more detached or off-hand the tone of your voice the better, even though your normal automatic response is to yell.

I try to train parents in also using a non-confrontational, off-hand stance. The aim is to use non-verbal language, tone and physical position to suggest that you are not overly concerned by these events. If you fall into the trap of criticising, backing the child into a corner or being aggressive in either voice or stance then the oppositional child perceives that you are losing. The original issue can be lost in their desire just to win. Therefore we quite deliberately use detached terms. You will remember in working with Tom I said 'Guess I can't talk to you' rather than 'Don't dare talk to me in that voice.' Try to use terms like 'Well, it doesn't really matter to me' or 'Okay, but it is not really my problem.'

Try to avoid using statements such as 'you do it or else', unless you are sure of what 'or else' is and that you can carry it out. Most Oppositional ADD kids will test 'or else' because they feel they are being backed into a corner.

Slow the procedure or walk away

Oppositional ADD kids can become very heated and aggressive very quickly. Because of their impulsive nature they will take only a few seconds to refuse to comply. The explosion is often only short-lived. Therefore, it is very important to change the basic Four Step ADD procedure (see Chapter 4). In the basic procedure we aim to get the 1 . . . 2 . . . 3 Steps over quickly. With Oppositional ADD kids it is helpful to slow down the procedure.

Aim to give the oppositional child time to cool off for a second and calm down, rather than get on the heated oppositional treadmill. Sometimes their explosiveness will have dwindled. You will note that in working with Tom I walked away twice for coffee, quite deliberately, to allow a little cooling off and avoid a head-on battle.

If Oppositional ADD kids are hastily confronted and pushed to give quick responses, they will explode and become more oppositional and defiant. Those kids who have language problems will act aggressively if they can't think of a quick answer. Give them the choice of taking their time or try walking away briefly.

Let us return to the example early in this chapter of a teenager who is about to walk out the door. Rather than aggressively threatening him, you might say 'Well, you could prove you can go, but probably I couldn't drive you to baseball tomorrow. Or you could choose to stay in, it is up to you. You think about it while I check Sam's homework for two minutes. You tell me what will go on next.' (I will expand on this response later in this chapter.)

Walk away for a definite time to a definite place

When you walk away, it is important that your Oppositional ADD kid knows where you are going and for how long. Because they have time and sequencing problems they may not understand coming back 'in a while'. Further, if you don't walk away for a definite period or to a definite place they may become exasperated that you are just deserting them or running away. This could lead to another conflict. Be definite about your times by saying, for example, 'I am just going to put the kettle on. I will be back in one minute and you can tell me what you want to do next' or 'I'll be back as soon as I put my briefcase away.'

When you return from walking away, try to let your Oppositional ADD kid know straight away that he is in control. Therefore in an off-hand manner say 'Oh, by the way, what have you decided?' Try to use an off-hand tone and a detached manner. Often I would not even look directly at the child.

If your Oppositional ADD kid does not make an appropriate response at this time, it is quite acceptable to try walking away one more time. Don't escalate the situation by judging him: 'I can see you're still being silly.' If your ADD kid still appears to be oppositional, you might say 'No problem, I can see that you still haven't made up your mind. I have another little job to do and then we can decide the next time I come back.' Another example might be 'No big deal; you still can control what happens next. You think while I just get the telephone messages, mate, then you can let me know what you want to do.' Try to walk away and give your child a little more time to calm down and space to think about it further. Limit your walking away to two or three times, otherwise your ADD child will string it along and become too hyped up, and this will lead to greater problems.

Limit debates

Some Oppositional ADD kids are quite confident both orally and verbally, and long-winded debates will often lead to failures. Give a certain amount of time to rationalise thoughts, but then quietly apply a reasonable set of rules.

For the Oppositional ADD kids who have language-processing difficulties, if the debate goes on for too long they will feel they cannot keep up with verbal responses. Once they become too frustrated they will 'blow up' rather than facing more verbal embarrassment.

Avoid stand-offs

Your child will go to extraordinary lengths to prove you are being ineffective. Remember the three-year-old who, when you smacked, says it does not hurt. She taunts us to smack her again, but she will refuse to admit it hurts, even if she has a tear running down her cheek.

If you try to get on top of your teenager, who feels she is being backed into a corner, she may even dare you to come up with more extraordinary demands, such as 'Go on, ground me for a day; go on, make it a week then, I dare you.' This behaviour is just to prove you are not in control, and screams out for a parent to react more aggressively. We must try, however, to remain calm, detached and off-hand. Try to slow the process down, walk away if necessary and let your child or teenager have some control in the situation, within reasonable boundaries.

If faced with a real confrontation, you can offer an altogether different outcome. For example, at the point of screaming you might say 'Do we really want to do this? What about I make a coffee and go out on the back verandah. You put your music on and let's try again out on the back step in fifteen minutes. What do you think?'

Jumping on the good

When Tom was in my clinic, I immediately concentrated on the first sign of improvement. This is what I mean by 'jumping on the good'. Many oppositional kids believe that everyone is absolutely against them. Therefore it is very important to ease the confrontation by shifting the focus from what your child is doing wrong. Rather if your child makes any tiny step towards appropriate behaviour then try to jump on the good thing that he is doing. If he shows that he is calming down a bit, immediately praise him, even if it is not total calm. If your child even considers making a good decision then praise him and show him how that system is going to work out for him. For example, with our teenager who wants to leave the house, but then shows some intent to stay we say 'Hey, great! You are starting to do really well and I am very proud about how you are thinking about things. We could think about a video now.'

Involve yourself when they improve

As soon as your ADD child starts to improve, stop being detached and become very involved. We might say 'I am very proud of you' or 'Gee, you did some great things there, we are doing well together now' or 'That was smart thinking, we can work this out well.' These statements also help ADD kids to not feel the whole world is always against them.

The Four Step procedure for Oppositional ADD

The Awareness step (Step 1) of the Four Step procedure (see Chapter 4) for classic ADD kids remains much the same with Oppositional ADD kids, with minimal changes only. It is still important to recognise that Oppositional ADD kids will often be unaware of their behaviour because of their impulsiveness. The only change we make is using a more off-hand tone and less direct confrontation. Examples might be: 'Hey Timmy, watch jumping on the lounge, mate' or 'Biscuits before dinner? Not really in the rules, Sally.'

Step Two of the basic Four Step procedure involves two options of outcomes based on your child's choice of behaviour. When dealing with an Oppositional ADD kid, we should remain with the basic strategy of giving the child two choices. However, we do this in a more off-hand way. For instance, if the child is standing at the door saying that he is

▲▲▲▲▲▲▲▲▲▲▲▲▲▲▲▲▲▲▲▲▲▲▲▲▲▲▲▲▲▲▲▲▲▲

going out and you cannot stop him you might well initially agree to some extent, but then move to choices. 'Well, I probably can't stop you, that's true, but then if you go out you know that the front door is locked at ten and driving you to baseball tomorrow probably is not going to happen. Then again you could choose to stay in and that is probably a smarter choice because I can drive you to baseball and you can have take-away pizza with us and a video.'

The aim is to keep the choice a little softer so that your Oppositional ADD kid hears it almost as though he is in control. Again, try to do everything possible to avoid ultimatums. You will note that I gave Tom the choice of finding the good things Mr Flannery said or not talking at all and missing praise and recognition he usually receives from me.

Use 'in-control' terminology

I use the phrase 'in-control' terminology to help the parents understand that it is important for their Oppositional ADD kid to figure that he or she is in some form of control. Thus we change the terminology or words we use. Many Oppositional ADD kids merely want to ensure that no-one else is telling them what to do. Once they have been given no choice they are likely to become more defiant and more irrational in their behaviour, refusing to back down. A determined, very zealous teacher is giving no choices with 'Stand there and don't you dare move!' It is certain that the Oppositional ADD student will fight back just to avoid being totally controlled. An alternative might be 'Wait there, Tom, while we see if we can't both work this out better.'

You need to change the terminology we use in the basic Four Step procedure. We aim to use phrases that give the impression that your kid is making the decisions. For example, with a teenager who refuses to stay at home, we might say 'Well, the choice is up to you and you could go out and I probably can't stop you, but then again you could . . .' Similar terms we use are 'Okay, it is a decision for you to make' or 'Well, it's not really up to me, you let me know what's next.' You may have noted that I said to Tom in my office 'It's up to you what happens next. You control what happens next.'

Still encourage that behaviour is their choice

We are still trying to help even Oppositional ADD kids to see that it is their choice of behaviour that leads to consequences. As an example, you might say 'Well, you could choose to keep arguing and miss your favourite TV show. It might be a better choice to do the five-minute Time Out. You figure out what is best. You decide.'

Time Out and Oppositional ADD kids

It is extremely difficult to get an Oppositional ADD kid to go to Time Out and stay there. They believe they are being ordered about, which is against their nature to accept. I do not often recommend Time Out for Oppositional ADD teenagers; rather we use withdrawal of privileges. With younger Oppositional ADD kids we will use Time Out, but avoid backing them into it. Try to help your kid to see that complying has benefits. For instance, if your child says 'No, I am not going to Time Out' you might say 'Well, it is up to you. Choose not to go to Time Out and that probably means you would miss all of your favourite show. Or you could think about going for just five minutes, doing your Time Out and getting back to the TV. You decide what's best.' Again, you could use the walk-away strategy: 'You decide. I just need to turn the dishwasher on. You decide, just five minutes or missing all of your show. You let me know when I come back.'

Boss of the clock

'Ian, I don't want to wait outside for ages in the waiting room while you talk to Mum and Dad. How long have I got to wait? I bet it's ages.'

'Tell you what Tim, you can be boss of the clock. As soon as the clock reaches 9.20 you can say it is your turn and kick Mum and Dad out. Got it? When it is 9.20 on this digital clock you knock on my door and kick Mum and Dad out. You're the boss.'

I have often used this technique to keep kids patiently in my waiting room. Equally we have used it as another alternative to keep Oppositional ADD kids in Time Out. For example, you might put the clock on the kitchen bench near the 'corner', then say 'Zoe, you are the boss of the clock. As soon as it reaches five minutes you can tell me you have to be allowed out.' This feeds their desire to be in control.

Removing privileges

'I don't care'

One of the most common complaints that I hear from parents with an Oppositional ADD kid is that their child or teenager appears to destroy discipline by saying that they don't really care. For instance, if Mum dares to take his skateboard from him, he will scream back 'I don't care anyway, I didn't want it.' However, in almost 100 per cent of the times when I have brought up the same issue with the child, they have been extremely resentful that Mum would have dared to take this item from them.

Scott

The most glaring example of this was Scott, a very difficult child I saw many years ago. I had long suggested to Scott's mum that we remove his three most treasured items for very oppositional behaviour. After two months of this she came back saying that it wasn't working because Scott never cared. I got his mum to describe the items that she took away. Quite regularly, almost daily, she took Scott's skateboard from him. Of course he never ever would let it be known that he missed his skateboard, instead claiming he didn't care. After chatting with Mum, I asked Scott into my office, leaving a tape recorder on. I casually asked Scott how his skateboard was going, to which he responded abusively that the world 'sucks', how his mother was a bitch and had no right to take his skateboard from him. Scott kept this abuse up for some time despite the fact that he had his mum totally convinced that he did not care. Scott's mum was stunned to listen to the tape. My feeling now is that often when Oppositional ADD kids say that they do not care, they really do care. It is just a tactic that they use to defeat their parents.

When your Oppositional ADD kid says 'I don't care', play along with it. A good response might be 'Okay, no problem, I'll just put it up here anyway till the time is up.' Don't buy into worse arguments: 'Right, now it is two hours.' They will drive you to a final punishment you can't carry out.

Similarly, don't react to muttering under the breath. They are looking for a victory or to divert the argument. By buying into the argument you provide the opportunity to escape the real conflict.

What privileges to remove

I suggest that you keep up with strategies of quickly removing important possessions or privileges for very oppositional behaviour. It is, however, hard to decide what to remove. A general hint is to watch what are the things they first grab for when they come into the house. These are more than likely what they will miss most, even if they do not admit to it. Secondly, look at what is cool in society. Removing his bike if everyone is riding skateboards will not work. Thirdly, look for what they refuse to share with brothers or sisters; these are more important to them. Fourthly, listen to what they talk to their mates about most often. Lastly, note which TV programs they can't wait to see.

Short total entertainment loss

With some young, very Oppositional ADD kids it is necessary to remove everything for a very short time. These kids often say 'I don't care, I can play the computer anyway.' As they perceive they have won, discipline is ineffective. Removing the Nintendo will not be effective if they can play Game Boy, watch TV or play videos. With some very tough kids we have made a rule of no entertainment at all for ten minutes; that is, no Nintendo, TV, CD or video. For example, you might say 'You kept going, that means no entertainers for ten minutes.' This must be established as a procedure beforehand, clearly stating what is included in the 'no entertainers' category.

Give a few minutes' warning of expectations

Older Oppositional ADD kids and teenagers may cooperate more if they have a few minutes' warning rather than springing expectations on them. For example, they resist being told to hop in the bath or do homework. Instead a few minutes before you might say 'Troy, it is nearly five o'clock, finish watching this show but remember we are doing homework at five.'

Removing teenagers' privileges

It is difficult to find what to remove from teenagers. A basic rule is that five minutes' Time Out will no longer prove effective. The second rule is that unless you have invested in your kid's life in childhood removing privileges will be harder as a teenager. Suddenly removing your approval and acceptance is ineffective if you have been critical and dismissive through most of their childhood.

There are no classic withdrawal methods with teenagers. As for younger children, I suggest you watch what is important to them. It is through this method that we have found more effective withdrawal measures. For example, if your Oppositional ADD girl immediately races to the phone when she gets in at 5 p.m., talking to Telstra about a phone lock might be worthwhile. If your Oppositional ADD youth hates walking to baseball training, try removing the privilege of his being driven for abuse in the afternoon. Similarly, one tough ADD youth loved a large hot country-style breakfast in the morning. We had simple rules. If he came home in time on Friday night Mum was happy to cook him this big hot breakfast. If he didn't he had to get cereal for himself.

One teenager stumped us as to what we could remove. Then I noted he always wore a 'cool' surf shirt under his white school shirt. In this case we began by not washing the T-shirts if he didn't help out. However, he just wore them dirty. So now Mum puts the T-shirts in a soaking bucket. If he cooperates then Mum moves one or two from the soaking bucket to the washing machine. Even though this means some late-night washing it has given Mum more control.

► *A MATTER OF TRUST*

Overcome their distrust of the world

Oppositional ADD kids often distrust the world. Perhaps because they tend to rip the world off they believe the reverse applies. Further, they bring many negatives on themselves, but don't accept the blame for this. At times we have found it necessary to make written notes to prove that we will carry through. For example, you might say 'You agree to cooperate now and I'll give you this ticket. That means as soon as we get home I owe you free computer time and you get to choose what to watch on TV after the news.'

The one-on-one-off strategy with older teenagers

'Why can't I go? You don't trust me, you are expecting me to do bad. No-one trusts me.'

Many Oppositional ADD teenagers manipulate parents by claiming they are never trusted, but the reality is they have denied themselves the trust. However, telling them this usually leads to an argument. The 'one-on-one-off' strategy is a method to gradually give control and trust. It also helps keep faith with your teenagers.

For example, if she wants to go the Blue Light Disco you might say 'It is up to you. If you go, stay inside and be home by eleven. You choose to keep my trust, but if you don't do the right thing, then you take the trust away for the next time. You decide I can't trust you next time. After that I am prepared to try again.'

If your teenager mucks up at the disco you would write on the calendar to remind yourself and avoid arguments that next Friday night disco is out. When Friday arrives and the argument begins, go back to the calendar. You might then say 'You came home an hour late last week, therefore no disco this week. You chose for it to be off for one week. Next week I trust you to try again. It is only one off.'

You will note that we are trying to display faith in teenagers as few adults have faith in Oppositional ADD teenagers. For example, you might say 'You chose one time off for being late home, but I trust you to do it next week. This week off but I trust you to have a go again next week. I have faith you can do it next week.'

Obviously, very severe behaviour would change this strategy. For example, getting caught smoking drugs or vandalising would be dealt with more decisively.

Avoid face-to-face discussions of problems

ADD teenagers are very sensitive and easily embarrassed under the tough exterior. If trouble arises or you need to discuss a sensitive issue avoid a heavy face-to-face discussion. Many teenagers find it easier to talk at an aside. Some examples are:

► while driving in the car where they can look out the window
► on the back step looking into the back yard
► sitting on their bedroom floor while they are in bed at night
► walking the dog together.

Often it is wise to go to an area your teenager is comfortable in.

Beware of conning or misleading

Oppositional ADD kids are like all ADD kids, in that they are extremely perceptive. They very quickly sense moods, feelings and emotions in others. It is just a pity that they don't have the social skill to go with this. They are so perceptive that as a parent you have to be very careful of ever attempting to con or mislead an ADD kid.

▶ *A SCHOOL REMINDER*

Most of the strategies discussed here also apply to school. Unfortunately I have seen Oppositional ADD kids backed into a corner thus becoming more defiant and aggressive. I recently saw an Oppositional ADD child who was told 'Face the wall, keep still and don't dare talk until I'm ready for you.'

As an alternative, for example, with one very Oppositional ADD child in school we decided to let him have five minutes to calm down and wait for the principal, allowing him a small, well-defined courtyard area to wander in outside the principal's office. The aim was not to restrict him, and to allow a cool-down period to get over the impulsive defiance and opposition. When previously dragged to the principal this lad regularly ran off, but once he had his calm-down period, we were able to resolve conflicts successfuly.

Many of the off-hand statements described above also work in explosive classroom situations. A teacher can try indirectly talking to an Oppositional ADD child, rather than embarrassing them in front of the class. I have seen several very successful teachers who could almost talk through an imaginary third person, thus avoiding a head-on battle.

▶ *LEADERSHIP OPPORTUNITIES*

Oppositional ADD kids often respond well to independent or leadership opportunities. Many oppositional kids have responded excellently when they have been given the opportunity to show responsibility, leadership or independence. They also enjoy one-to-one time with Mum or Dad separately, where they get undivided attention and have a chance to show independence and responsibility. They delight in helping underprivileged or weaker kids in the playground. They often make good sporting captains, house sport leaders, scout leaders, peer support leaders, and so on.

In summary:

Like most ADD kids the oppositional group also works better in a very structured, firm and consistent environment. They need very clear rules and expectations. Being flexible often entices Oppositional ADD kids to see how far they can bend the rules. Some oppositional behaviour is intentional but some is also governed by impulsiveness.

It is very important that Oppositional ADD kids always have the opportunity for brief negotiation in conflicts. They must feel that there is an option or way out of the situation by which they can save face.

CONDUCT DISORDERS

chapter 9

Perhaps one of the most difficult groups to deal with in the ADD spectrum of Co-morbid Disorders are those children who have not only ADD, but also a Conduct Disorder. There are many different types of Conduct Disorder.

A classic ADD child is fairly impulsive and unaware of consequences, but often is remorseful after the event. A Conduct Disordered ADD child is impulsive, but can also be very deliberate and is rarely genuinely remorseful. To keep it simple we often refer to this group as Conduct ADD children, as compared to more normal or classic ADD children.

▶ *A BRIEF DESCRIPTION*

Generally a Conduct Disordered child is one who is aggressive, who destroys things, is quite deceitful, steals or seriously violates the rules. Often these children will engage in one or more of a range of behaviours such as:

▶ bullying

▶ fighting

▶ using weapons

► being cruel to peers
► lighting fires
► stealing
► running away
► truanting excessively
► being involved in substance abuse.

They do not need to display all of these behaviours. The child can display as few as three of these behaviours over a period of time. It is important though that they are repeatedly displayed over a significant time.

I believe that a Conduct Disordered child is most difficult to deal with because they are largely amoral. This means that the child is not very interested in our moral or social values; in fact the child may not care at all about others or their feelings, social rules and responsible values. A Conduct Disordered child often perceives the world as deliberately against them. Therefore they will do whatever they feel is reasonable to get even, regardless of whether this means hurting others. As long as they see themselves as doing well and coping the Conduct Disordered child will generally be unconcerned if he has damaged someone else's property or hurt another person or an animal.

An important point to note is that Conduct Disordered children's behaviour must be intentional or deliberate, and frequent. The child who accidentally or impulsively injures an animal or very occasionally steals on an impulse is not a Conduct Disordered child. Generally we look for malicious intent and very little remorse. A simple way of differentiating is that an ADD child might be quite remorseful and sorrowful once an act is over, even trying to change behaviour, whereas a Conduct Disordered ADD child will in fact feel that they have been wronged and therefore will totally reject punishment.

While you may think that from the above description your child has ADD and a Conduct Disorder, it is essential that you consult a trained professional for a formal diagnosis. Other psychiatric problems can appear to be similar. There are high risks associated with inaccurate diagnosis. A technical description of Conduct Disorder is listed in the Diagnostic and Statistic Manual (DSM-IV).

A simple example — Jamie-Lee

Jamie-Lee is a pretty, very bright twelve-year-old girl. She was faced with the possibility of being left at home when her parents were to travel overseas on business. She impulsively rationalised that this was unjust as soon as she was told she wasn't going. Jamie-Lee did not think or reason this through; she just decided it was not fair. She then embarked on a scheme to upset her parents' departure. She deliberately upset her baby sister just as her parents were to leave for the airport. Then she refused to come and say good-bye. She had already stolen from her mother's purse. Finally, after her parents left she began swearing at her aunt, who was to look after her. Jamie-Lee showed little remorse for this later, rationalising that if her parents had only taken her none of this would have happened. She refused to accept how impossibly inconvenient it was for them to take her for a rushed three-day business trip overseas.

Another simple example might help. A classic ADD kid might tantrum at not being allowed out, but a Conduct ADD kid will retreat to his room, cut the flyscreen, climb out and scratch Dad's car on the way out to prove who is in control. If his little brother 'dobs' him in, he might feel justified in waiting to finally hit his little brother with the plastic baseball bat when he gets a chance.

The media and public image of ADD are often Conduct kids

Often Conduct ADD children are portrayed in the media as typical ADD children. They are not classic ADD kids, despite the fact that they make great television for sensational shows. I cannot possibly count the number of times at seminars a mum has questioned whether her child really has ADD, because her daughter is not nearly as bad as that horrible boy she saw on television.

▶ HOPE FOR THE FUTURE?

The majority of Conduct ADD children do not begin with Conduct Disorders, although they are born with ADD. They are most often either the product of seriously dysfunctional families or very negative schooling, or they gradually develop behaviour from Oppositional Defiant Disorder. A small minority of ADD kids appear to have been born with Conduct Disorder.

Many parents ask 'What will happen to my Oppositional ADD child if I don't seek support and guidance?' The answer is that he may well develop Conduct Disorders. One problem does grow into the next. If the kids see substance abuse, physical and verbal abuse, depression, and anti-social behaviour at home they have a greater potential to develop Conduct Disorders. Similarly, parents are often told their child will mature out of their problems. The reality is that an already difficult ADD student placed in a non-supportive education system, where they can't realise success and are constantly treated negatively, will very likely develop Conduct Disorders. If they cannot get support and acceptance at school, they will get approval and gang recognition from mates for truanting, drug-taking, stealing or vandalising. Thus every effort should be addressed to intense early intervention.

Professionals have tended to be very dismissive or negative about the outcomes for Conduct Disordered ADD kids. Unfortunately they can come from violent, aggressive or very dysfunctional homes, can be the children of more aggressive or negative males, may have had very negative school experiences, may see large amounts of anti-social behaviour and are amoral at times, so their outcomes generally are less positive than the typical ADD kids. While we should not be too optimistic it is important to recognise that there have been some Conduct ADD kids who turned out to have normal futures. There are Conduct ADD kids that professionals, including myself, have worked with and realised success. The success rate is small but nevertheless parents should not feel totally defeated.

▶ SPECIFIC MANAGEMENT FOR CONDUCT ADD

Impulsive or intentional and deliberate

One of the first problems a parent of a Conduct ADD kid faces is to decide whether behaviour is merely impulsive or deliberate and intentional. Unfortunately these different behaviours require different management techniques. The impulsive behaviour is treated in a similar way to treating classic ADD kids. However, intentional or deliberate behaviour must be treated from the stance that the child or teenager is amoral and capable of harming others.

Treatment difficulty

Obviously a Conduct ADD child is very difficult to deal with, and they are also vigorously resistant to treatment. Therefore I cannot possibly hope to cover all of the management techniques that we use with a Conduct ADD kid. I will, however, demonstrate some that I have found partially successful. A general rule is that a Conduct ADD child will need very intensive psychological or psychiatric help. It is beyond the capacity of most parents to develop strategies to deal with such a child. I am aware that many country parents have little access to such services and therefore these strategies are largely developed for those people who cannot have regular access to a counsellor, psychologist or psychiatrist who is well experienced in dealing with such complex and difficult children.

These strategies are primarily for Conduct ADD kids, not those with a Conduct Disorder and *no* ADD. Further, I have already demonstrated that ADD kids need unique strategies different from those for more typical kids. This is even more true when dealing with a Conduct ADD child or teenager because they have a self-centred, amoral and vengeful outlook that makes even the Four Step procedure less effective.

One of my worst experiences with a Conduct ADD child came through an attempt by a creative and well-meaning principal who tried to use an Oppositional ADD strategy for a Conduct ADD student.

Oops, wrong strategy!

In the preceding chapter on Oppositional ADD children, I described a strategy used to let a student have some time and space to cool off before going into the principal's office. The aim was to give him time, control and space, to avoid a head-on battle.

I gave this same strategy to the principal of a well-known private school in Sydney in order to manage a difficult Oppositional ADD girl, Annabelle. The principal was very impressed with the strategy, finding it very successful in avoiding head-on battles. Most times Annabelle calmed enough in the five minutes to be able to be dealt with.

Unfortunately the same principal also had a very difficult Conduct ADD girl, Suzie, in the school. She decided that since this strategy had been so effective with Annabelle, she might try it with Suzie. Remembering that Conduct ADD kids are amoral and are quite likely to get even if given the chance, you might see where this problem was going to end up. My well-intentioned principal decided that she would send Suzie to wait outside in the courtyard, near the teachers' car park, to cool down for five minutes. Suzie was still very annoyed. Within the five minutes she had managed to let down the tyres on six different teachers' cars. The Motorists Association found it a very rewarding afternoon as they charged each teacher a substantial fee to re-inflate all their tyres. Needless to say we have since recommended a Conduct ADD child never be given five minutes to cool down in their own area.

Don't reason with amoral characters

If reasoning with an ADD child is ineffective, it is even more true of reasoning with a Conduct ADD child. It is ineffective because most Conduct ADD kids are amoral and are only interested in their own well-being. Conduct ADD kids are totally nonplussed about whether they are causing other people hurt; in fact they may even intend to hurt other people. They may even mention the hurt as confirmation that they got even. They are unlikely to be concerned if they violate someone else's rights or privileges. Moralising or reasoning with a Conduct ADD child that they are causing damage to someone else or that their behaviour is unacceptable is a waste of time. For example, a child who openly steals is well aware that stealing is unacceptable and wrong, but they simply choose to steal because it is what they want to do.

Reasoning may feed the problem

Many Conduct ADD kids are very deliberate or intentional in their actions. For example, your teenage son may plot to trap and hit his little sister for revenge. If he intensely dislikes his sister, feeling that she is being more favoured and loved than himself, any message that he has hurt his sister is in fact a recognition of his success. He may even remember that this is a strategy that really works because it caused lots of upset.

Imagine you refuse to give your ADD girl money she feels she deserves, without actually having earned it. She retaliates by shoplifting from the corner store. Your saying 'I have been extremely hurt by your behaviour' will likely feed the problem. When you tell her that she has hurt you greatly, she takes it as a victory. I have seen many Conduct ADD kids almost putting marks on their wall for the number of times they 'got' their parents. Therefore, with a Conduct ADD child it is even more important that you don't tell them that they are hurting someone, reason with them, use 'I' statements or plead social responsibility. If you recognise the hurt your child caused, you are telling her what really works and encouraging her to do more of it in the future.

Let them believe they are winning

Because Conduct ADD kids are so self-centred and amoral, it is important that in some way during a confrontation you let your kid feel that he or she is winning, even if this means that you have to compromise or give a little bit at certain times. A Conduct ADD kid will fight simply to be seen as not giving in or allowing someone else to have authority over them.

We need to change the terminology used in the basic Four Step procedure. You might avoid the basic simple choice of 'If you don't do this there is no TV' by using a statement like 'I wasn't prepared to let you have TV tonight, but you can win some TV from me by doing your homework on time.' We often support this with statements such as 'That worked out well for you. Now you get some extra TV, even though I decided before on no TV.' In fact you might have been prepared to give TV but he doesn't know that. To some extent this means that as a parent you might not be absolutely 100 per cent open and honest, but otherwise your Conduct ADD child will always have you at a disadvantage. I am not suggesting that you lie, but rather that you leave yourself some room for movement and negotiation.

Selfish therapy

Successfully dealing with a Conduct Disordered ADD child often involves what I loosely term 'selfish therapy'. The reason that I have used this term is that unless the Conduct Disordered child sees they are winning and it is serving their needs, they are not likely to go along with any program at all. They will not choose to do it because 'Dad said so' or because 'It is the right thing to do, nice kids do that.' They will conform only if it suits them, because they are selfish. Therefore we use therapy that caters to this selfishness.

Avoid moralising. Rather try to present your Conduct ADD kid with limited choices, but allow them to choose what is best for them. In fact, we are encouraging them to look at it selfishly rather than morally. For example, you might say 'You work out what is best for you' or 'You figure what is the most you can get out of this situation.' The latter type of self-centred statement allows your Conduct ADD child to think they are winning. For example, you might say 'No homework means no wrestling with Dad, but even though I wasn't prepared to let you have TV tonight, you can win some TV from me by doing your homework on time, but you decide what's best for you. No homework, no wrestles; homework now and get TV. You work out where you can get what you really want.'

Naturally, I would prefer not to allow Conduct ADD kids to be so selfish. However, the reality is that this is almost the only way I have found to deal initially with Conduct ADD children successfully. Whenever I have seen parents reverting to moralising, long lectures or efforts to impart social values, behaviour management often has failed. Eventually psychotherapy may help to correct their amoral and selfish outlook.

Avoiding fights they pick

Some Conduct ADD kids deliberately pick fights by speaking in absolute or extreme language. They believe their opinion is the only right one and is not open to discussion. For example, they are unlikely to describe a teacher they don't like as 'not very nice', but more likely as 'the biggest jerk alive, totally a *?#@*!' As Conduct ADD kids are so extremely absolute in their opinion, it is not a wise idea to fight this. Again, to let them think they are winning or controlling a situation, we avoid reasoning. Rather recognise their opinion but don't accept it, then move on to a solution. *Avoid the fight, go to a solution.*

As an example, if a Conduct ADD kid hated a teacher I would not debate that hating is unacceptable or that Mr James is not that bad. Rather, I would use a statement such as 'Well, you might think it's not cool to go along with Mr James. You may even think that Mr James has been really unfair, but what we have to figure out is what is the best thing for you to do now.'

Similarly, if a Conduct ADD child tells us we can't make them do something and not to boss them, we might reply 'Well, maybe people shouldn't boss you, but if you don't help I won't be driving you to hire your Nintendo game. Then again you could help out and I'd owe you a special dessert, but it is up to you if you want to make me get you a special dessert. You figure what is best for you.'

Solutions that serve needs, but have parameters

At this early stage try to avoid reasoning as to what is right or acceptable and good behaviour, but simply try to figure a tactic that will serve the Conduct ADD child's needs. Usually it is wise to still set some parameters to their behaviour. The parameters are still loosely related to the Choices step in the Four Step procedure (see Chapter 4). While they often still choose between two outcomes or consequences, the terminology is altered. For example, after several tries to get some help in the example above you would impose a final parameter for behaviour. You might say 'You didn't accept the last chance; that means no getting the game now.'

Letting them have their say, within limits

Conduct ADD kids have very definite opinions. Interrupting them to tell them how wrong they are will usually lead to tantrums or to teenagers exploding. Instead of correcting I have found it useful to give them some time to have their say. For example, when your teenager is very heated and threatening you might say 'Tell you what, I'm going to let you have the next five minutes uninterrupted. You can have your say, as long as you don't abuse me. I'm happy just to listen for a few minutes.'

Going along a bit

As part of the 'selfish therapy' mentioned above I have also found it useful at times to go along with a Conduct ADD child to a small extent. Conduct ADD kids perceive the world differently. Unfortunately many of them have a very insecure feeling about the world, often believing that everyone else is out to get them. If they are willing to rip off the world regularly it makes sense for them to believe in turn that most other people in the world are prepared to rip them off. It is unwise to take on every inaccurate perception of the Conduct ADD child.

Therefore, in counselling or therapy, I tend not to challenge their statements about particular people and situations. For instance, if a Conduct ADD child came in and told me that her teacher was a real bitch I wouldn't go so far as to call the teacher a bitch. However, I might say 'Well, maybe I will accept that Mrs Smith is a tough teacher, but let's figure out now how you can stay out of being on detentions.' After brief discussion I might add 'Okay, but I'm still sure what's best for you is to stay out of detentions, so let's figure how we can manage that.'

If the Conduct ADD child replied 'So you think Mrs Smith is a bitch too' I would be firm in saying 'No. I didn't say she was a bitch, though if what you are telling me is true then she may be a hard teacher. But the problem still is let's figure how you can try not to get on any more detentions, because I know you're hanging out to get with your mates at lunch-time.'

Try to stay with the main problem

In this strategy you can see we constantly try to return to the main problem, rather than getting sidetracked by other issues. Although the teenager began with distractions such as 'My teacher is a bitch' we have ended up discussing behaviour at least in some way. Further, I have looked at trying to address the child's problems. The next lines would run something like 'Well, even if Mrs Smith is hard, we have to accept that there must be something you're doing that is part of getting onto detentions at lunch-time. Let's just figure what we can do to stop that.'

In a less direct manner, I am still trying to get Conduct ADD kids to own their problem. If they can accept that they can get out of their problem by changing their own behaviour, we are at least getting them to accept some responsibility for their own behaviour. While not a perfect situation, it is a beginning point with a Conduct ADD child or teenager.

A final boundary

As with more classic ADD kids, we still need a firm, final boundary for what we will allow with a Conduct ADD kid. If you fail to set this they will abuse the situation because they will believe that it is far too weak a system. Therefore if we talked about some sort of consequence, it must finally be applied. For example, we might finish with 'You figured it's best for you not to help, therefore your decision was no being driven to baseball training.'

Drawn-out debates lead to pathological lies

Conduct ADD kids try to draw out debates. They may get a perverse power thrill from abusing you. Therefore you need to try to finish debates reasonably quickly. Try to keep the basic 'three is out' strategy in your mind (see page 42).

Conduct ADD kids are often pathological liars. If you ask a question they may give a bizarre lie as an answer. While they may know this is a lie when they first make it up, after repeating it several times they actually begin to believe it. You will end up in a 'no-win' situation: you know they are lying but they believe they are telling the truth.

Three times for lying

If you are sure that your Conduct ADD kid is lying deal with it quickly. The most effective strategy we have used is three times the punishment for lying. If your kid tells the truth at the first chance he gets only a small punishment for the first behaviour. If he lies he gets three times the punishment. For example: 'If you took it and you tell me the truth it is only ten minutes Time Out, but if you are lying, then it is ten minutes for taking it, but also no Simpsons and to bed half an hour early.'

Don't let him off if he tells the truth. Many liars figure out a good system where parents let them off for telling the truth. They think I'll try to get away with it by lying and if I do that's good. If I get caught I'll just tell the truth and then I'll still get away with it. Either way I don't have to be punished at all. The only punishment is Dad lectures me but I don't care about that anyway.

Play out bluffs

'Mrs Bull, my teacher, said I could have the five glue sticks.'
'My friend gave me his new baseball jacket for two weeks.'

Conduct ADD kids often lie and bluff their way out of things or throw threats at parents. It is important to check out bluffs. For instance, in the first example you would say 'That's okay, but you know the rules are I check if anything comes into the house, so you won't mind if I ask Mrs Bull tomorrow.'

'If you smack me I'll ring the police and tell them you abused me.'

Again I suggest you play out the bluff. In my experience police and community services will act on genuine abuse, but are not interested in one smack on the bottom. In this situation I would say 'Okay, that's fine, let's ring them, but let's tell them that you refused to come inside, you swore at me and broke the flyscreen. Then again, we can try to solve this a bit more calmly; you figure out what's best for you.' You must remain calm at this time. Don't make it a threat.

▶ MEASURES OF YOUR TRUST

Conduct ADD kids distrust other people even more than Oppositional ADD kids. They often believe parents will rip them off. I have sometimes overcome this by giving tokens of trust. For example, one kid distrusted that I would give him half the appointment time next visit. So we agreed to write a note and staple it to the front of the file. With younger kids we can do this at home. For example, you might give out an 'I owe you' card. If he behaves in the car on the way home then you give him a card that means you owe him best out of ten shots on the basketball ring.

▶ RUNAWAYS

Don't chase runaways

Conduct ADD kids get great power from running away and having everyone chase them. I believe it is better to let them go. Most ADD children will not run away far: they generally hide in the tree out the back or up the street. When they threaten to run away you might say 'If you need to you run away, I love you and don't want you to, but if you need to it's your call. Only there's no warm fire and dinner out there, but you decide.' I have found with younger children that if we take the impact out of running away they are less likely to use it as a strategy as teenagers.

Runaways have to do punishment

'If you don't let me watch it, if you make me go to Time Out, I'm going to run away.' It is important not to get into such threats. The basic rule is if you run away you still have to do your Time Out. For example, 'Well, I love you and don't want you to run away, but if you do you still have to do Time Out when you come back, but you could just do five minutes and get back to your show. If you run away there's no Simpsons up the street.'

Let them save face to come back

Conduct ADD kids will not come back cap in hand ready to say sorry. It is wiser to let them come back and save some face. For example, if he is up the tree, wander out calmly and say 'I wonder if John's around. If he comes in now he can have lasagne for dinner and watch his favourite show if he just does a quick five minutes' Time Out. I'd be willing to let him do that, it is up to John.' If John comes back then let things lie; don't escalate the problem by attacking him for running away.

► *DAY-BY-DAY BOUNDARIES FOR TOUGH TEENAGERS*

Try to avoid ultimatums with Conduct ADD kids, such as 'If you go you are never coming back' or 'You stay out past midnight and you're never welcome here.' Instead try to set day-by-day boundaries, with firm parameters. For example, with a teenager who refuses to keep to curfews we might say 'Rules are you come in by twelve. At twelve the doors are locked. Then you have to sleep on the verandah. If you bash the windows I will call the police. If you stay out there's no breakfast tomorrow either. But at lunch I'm happy to forget it and start again.'

'You punch holes in the walls and I will call the police, but you can come back tomorrow. The door is always open to try again tomorrow. But if you are that abusive today you can't be here today. Then again we could try talking out the back.'

There are times when you will need to use authority figures, such as police, welfare, mental health for suicide threats. Conduct ADD kids need to know that there is a final boundary. For example, threats with knives or even guns can be dealt with only by having them removed by police. At this level, you need professional help also.

The best protection

The best protection against all these dramatic situations is to build good times, respect and commitment with your kids before they reach the teenage years. There is less incidence of conduct behaviour in families that spend time together, have interested parents who are good role models and build mutual respect, free of criticism or abuse.

In summary:
■ ■ ■ ■ ■ ■ ■

Conduct Disordered ADD children are generally amoral and self-centred. Their behaviour, rather than being simply impulsive, is deliberate, and they show little or no remorse. Reasoning and debating will prove ineffective and counterproductive. You can use your discretion to give them some sense of being in control, in other words compromising to a certain degree where necessary and useful. Their own selfishness can be used as a strategy. Ultimately you must establish firm and final boundaries, but avoid 'no-win' situations.

ANXIETY AND ADD

chapter (10)

A small and often misunderstood group of ADD kids suffer with a Co-morbid Anxiety Disorder. In simple terms these kids become overly anxious and distressed about situations that other kids manage with far less stress. A Co-morbid ADD and Anxiety Disorder can be confusing as it may take two common forms. Each displays quite different final behaviour.

One group of ADD kids with an Anxiety Disorder:

▶ are purely over-anxious and over-concerned

▶ are possibly perfectionist by nature

▶ lead highly driven lives

▶ are often on edge, being far too emotional and active

▶ can be hypo-active rather than hyperactive (hypo-activity refers to the fact that they are under-active, withdrawn and quiet)

▶ can also be over-focused, not being able to get their mind off certain thoughts

▶ often escape detection in class, being described as 'delightfully compliant; a pleasure to teach but a little dreamy'

▶ are often very minutely fidgety and will pick at clothes or themselves (nails and so on), preen, twiddle fingers, flap legs, giggle around, etc.

This last type of activity is often described as fine motoric restlessness; that is, rapid, very fine motor movement, which replaces the gross motor movement of the classic ADD kids, such as walking about in class, running excessively and being hyperactive generally.

The second group of Co-morbid ADD and Anxiety Disorder kids is far more difficult to diagnose. The members of this second group are:

▶ extremely anxious and distressed, covering up with aggressive behaviour (in this way people never get to see their real emotions)

▶ appear to be quite brash, aggressive and threatening on the outside, but underneath are very scared little kids

▶ are often inaccurately diagnosed as purely Conduct Disordered or oppositional.

Parents, in fact, can be very good diagnostic sources as they are often aware of what their kids are really like underneath the tough outer shell. Further, many such kids will not display the anxiety outside the home for fear of failure, but will allow it to be seen at times of crisis at home. Parents' description of this type of behaviour must be accepted as genuine, even though it contradicts what the child does in public. A more appropriate diagnosis can be Co-morbid ADD and Anxiety Disorder, leading to Conduct Disorder. Each of these ADD and Anxiety Disorder groups needs dealing with slightly differently.

To make a diagnosis of ADD and Anxiety Disorder it is necessary to follow a very complex diagnostic procedure. Inaccurate diagnosis can lead to poor outcomes. In clinical practice ADD kids with an Anxiety Disorder are often referred to as Anxious ADD kids.

▶ *A SIMPLE EXPLANATION*

This is a broad description of ADD and Anxiety Disorder symptoms. Not all Anxious ADD kids suffer with all these symptoms — in fact some suffer with only a few.

Anxious ADD kids take what are normal events and become overly anxious or concerned about them, to the point that they cannot function normally. Children without this disorder might become a little anxious, but this does not interfere significantly with their daily functioning.

Anxious ADD kids are very tense and demanding. They often fear failure and will in fact fail themselves by refusing to take normal risks.

They can be described as having a 'fear of failure' complex. Anxious ADD kids can also be obsessive, compulsive or ritualistic in their behaviour. They can experience nightmares, night terrors or phobias. They generally are unsure of themselves, for example being unwilling to sleep in their own rooms.

Simple examples

Many kids, including classic ADD kids, become anxious on the first day of school but this is a fairly normal event. In contrast, an ADD kid who wakes up every morning feeling sick, experiencing somatic illnesses such as stomach cramps, diarrhoea and headaches, and who cannot get to school without severe distress may be suffering also with an Anxiety Disorder, and perhaps somatic illness.

While almost all ADD kids dislike projects for homework, an Anxious ADD kid might become overwhelmed by the enormousness of a school project, and become upset that they cannot complete all the work. They may go as far as refusing to do the work rather than making an attempt that they think the teacher will fail. I have even seen Anxious ADD kids do the work, but then not hand it in for fear of being criticised or failing.

An Anxious ADD kid with associated conduct problems may be the tough guy at school, but then will con his little brother to sleep in his room at night, because he is scared of the noises and imaginary ghosts or wolves outside. Or he may wake with night terrors, sneaking into Mum's bed and refusing all attempts to get him back to his own bed, breaking down to sob emotionally and scream. These kids often delight in horror movies but then their fear later on leads to nightmares or terrors.

Anxiety and impulsivity

Anxious children without any ADD seem to take a little time to build up to anxieties, whereas ADD kids can very quickly get into a panic situation. Often this can lead to sudden panic attacks, somatic illness, extreme distress or severe over-reaction. Anxious ADD kids react so impulsively that parents often have no warning and no chance to alleviate symptoms, but on the positive side they are also somewhat more easily distracted from their stress. As I have commented elsewhere, if ADD kids have distractibility problems, we may as well use them to our benefit, in this case to partially distract them from their anxiety thoughts.

▶ IRRATIONAL FEARS
Reasoning and Anxiety ADD

In the basic Four Step procedure (see Chapter 4) I recommend almost no reasoning. With Anxious ADD kids, however, we do suggest a small amount. Because these kids become so anxious or distressed about many issues, they need a little more calming or reassuring. Unless they are given a brief explanation or gain some understanding their anxiety or fear may stop them from acting at all. Often Anxious ADD kids' fears are based on irrational thoughts or incorrect perceptions of situations, and these need to be corrected. To simply give them choices does not allow you to explain away such a situation.

An Anxious ADD kid might be fearful of a creaking noise at night, and simply sending them back to bed will be unsuccessful. You might need to explain the noise was just the house contracting after a very hot day. Similarly, an Anxious ADD kid might be convinced that they are going to fail an exam. Briefly reassuring them that since they have passed all of the previous nine exams they will probably pass this tenth exam will also be helpful.

Limit the amount of reasoning

The amount of reasoning you allow, however, needs to be very limited. Anxious ADD kids tend to think and worry over and over their problem, to the point where they cannot function normally. The more you talk the more anxious they are likely to become.

The general rule is a few sentences of reasoning. Try to keep to very straightforward logic, well defined and easy to understand. Irrational arguments are best dealt with by using commonsense logic or reference to past successes. Often very bright Anxious ADD kids will divert you, going off at irrational tangents. There must be a point where you stop the diversions by stating, for example, 'No, we have done this now. We are not talking any more on this topic. Instead we are going to make cakes.' You still need to avoid getting into long-winded discussions. Alternatively allow several questions about their fear but then say 'We have talked about this now, so no more questions. We can talk about anything else, though.'

Is their fear real?

Many Anxious ADD kids are overwhelmed by their anxieties. Simply reassuring them or providing a positive incentive is not enough to motivate change. Anxious ADD kids see the threat and fear as so immense, despite parents' reassurance, that they can't or won't act. To help you understand their anxiety, imagine a tiger standing in my office doorway. If I were to explain that the tiger in the doorway is tame and it is safe for you to walk past it, I wonder if could you pass the tiger. Despite my reassurance and promising you a reward it is unlikely you would be able to overcome your fear. Your fear is so intense and real that you can't move. Many Anxious ADD kids experience the same level of fear over simple factors; for example, they may feel as anxious over getting to school as you may be about the tiger. To them the fear is very real; it is not imaginary.

The 'comfort zone'

If we consider that Anxious ADD kids can be overwhelmed by their anxieties, then simply providing a positive incentive is not enough to motivate change. Given that their fear is so real, so sudden and so intense, a simple reward to encourage them is unlikely to be successful. They would rather stay in a 'comfort zone', where they are not forced to confront their fear and overcome it. An Anxious ADD kid will prefer not to take on their anxiety, to avoid fully facing the fear and risking failure and greater anxiety.

For example, an Anxious ADD kid who is fearful of school will not agree to go to school simply because he is promised a treat in the afternoon. Similarly an Anxious ADD girl will prefer being hassled a little for sleeping in her little brother's room to actually confronting and overcoming her night fears. Let me refer to our tiger example. If I placed chocolates beyond the tiger, would you move past the animal to get them, or prefer to stay in the 'comfort zone' of my office, even though you'd rather be heading home?

The carrot-and-stick approach

Because Anxious ADD kids prefer to stay in the 'comfort zone', we need to alter the Choices strategy (that is, Step 2), of the basic Four Step procedure (see Chapter 4). The normal Choices strategy, where there is a simple positive outcome and a negative consequence, is not enough to motivate them. Therefore I often refer to the 'carrot-and-stick' approach, which relies on having both a positive reward for overcoming anxiety, and a significant negative outcome that makes it very difficult for the Anxious ADD kid to stay in a comfort zone.

Parents of ADD kids who live in the country will have seen a sick cow lie in a paddock. Although you can put down hay and water to entice the cow to get up and move, unless there is some force applied the cow's fear of feeling pain will stop it moving. It will stay in the semi-comfort zone of lying cold in the paddock, rather than move. In the end the farmer has to make it very uncomfortable for the cow to stay where it is, by poking it with a prod. This applies to treating anxiety-ridden ADD kids. On the one hand we have to encourage them to move by placing very clear, immediate and consistent rewards in their near reach. However, we also need to make it very uncomfortable for them to stay in their comfort zone. Otherwise their anxieties will overwhelm the need for positive reward.

A successful case — Moira

Anxious ADD kids are difficult to deal with and rapid success cannot always be guaranteed. However, the following case demonstrates some successful strategies. Moira was a girl I saw who had failed to attend school for some eighteen months, always presenting with somatic illness. At this time she was so anxious that she was unable to attend school at all. There were two basic steps to Moira's treatment. One was that any goals we aimed for were very small. Secondly, because Moira was very anxious we also tried extremely hard to make sure that she would not be comfortable if she chose not to go to school.

As Moira was easily overwhelmed, we set very minimal goals to achieve rewards. If she made the first steps toward getting to school, such as even beginning to get dressed, we immediately rewarded her with a token. Each goal or step Moira had to achieve was only marginally more difficult than the last. We certainly never aimed to get her back to school in one day: just a little improvement each day. More importantly, though, she was not allowed to stay in a comfort zone. If she stayed home we had to assume that she must be sick. Therefore she was made to go to her room with the curtains drawn and lights off until lunch-time, no TV, boring soup for lunch and early to bed that night as she needed rest if she was sick. The aim was that the less threatening option, staying home, would not be too comfortable.

Other therapy was also undertaken to actually deal with Moira's anxiety, build her self-esteem and confidence and develop her parents' skills to manage her effectively. With gradual progress Moira returned to school fully over several months, even though she had been out of school, refusing to attend through anxiety, for over eighteen months.

► *MISSING THE BIG PICTURE*

Anxious ADD kids do not see the big picture. As a result of learning difficulties they often cannot put all the separate pieces of a situation together, so they are unsure about what is expected of them. As they are so uncertain, they often fear they will do the wrong thing, or worse, will become stuck and embarrassed, not knowing what to do next. More able kids trust in their own ability to find their way out of problems. Anxious ADD kids don't trust themselves and therefore become anxious in unknown, foreign or difficult situations.

I believe that this may be related in part to many ADD kids having sequencing and memory difficulties. Often ADD kids fail to see naturally the necessary sequence of steps or fail to remember the steps they followed yesterday. They cannot easily see that if trouble occurs, they just do this first, this next and that last. Thus they distrust their ability and become anxious. Even though you may reassure them they have done it before, they can't remember all the steps they took before.

It is important to always explain each and every little step as it occurs. If you are planning change or beginning a new adventure make sure that each step is very clearly described and that no possible confusion is likely to happen. Anxious ADD kids need to be reassured about where they are heading, why, what will happen step by step and how you will support them if they get stuck.

Check behind 'anxious logic'

As anxious kids often confuse the sequence of events, confuse steps or forget past experiences they are more prone to misperceive what is actually happening. Further, they may simply distort or irrationally deduce what is occurring in a social situation. Many Anxiety ADD kids have developed more severe anxieties because they have incorrectly interpreted outcomes or perceived situations in the wrong way. It is very important that you check the particular logic they are using as a basis for their reasoning.

Timmy

Anxious ADD lad Timmy's parents owned a passenger commuting business, which meant that Timmy's father was involved in commuting passengers seven nights a week. After months of therapy Timmy was making great progress and everyone was coping very nicely.

It was then decided that Timmy's mum would also obtain her commuter's licence, so that Dad did not have to work seven nights a week. Suddenly Timmy became extremely distraught. For no apparent reason his behaviour had regressed greatly over the month since I last had seen him. When I talked to Timmy in the clinic he explained that he was really anxious because Mum was going to be out all night. He never understood that if Mum went out to work in the commuter business, then Dad would be staying home and looking after him. Timmy was anxious that no-one would help him with homework, cook him dinner, put him to bed, and so on. Timmy became so anxious he couldn't even settle at school. But because Mum and Dad were enthused with Mum obtaining her licence he was too anxious to tell them his fears. Much of his anxiety was alleviated immediately, and thus his behaviour rapidly improved, simply by recognising that the logic he was following in fact had a sequential and logical flow.

▶ STEPS TOWARDS SUCCESS

Keep rewards visible and immediate

The rewards offered to an Anxious ADD kid must be visible and be granted immediately. Even more so than with classic ADD kids this group needs to very clearly see the reward and get it before their anxiety overwhelms them again. Unless it is completely real (that is, well within their immediate reach), they will not be distracted from their anxiety.

Small steps to achieve success

Many anxious kids are overwhelmed by the pace of the expectations to improve. If we need to make change slowly with classic ADD kids, it is even more true for Anxious ADD kids. I recommend that you expect your kid to change only in the smallest steps possible. For instance, in the earlier example of Moira, who eventually returned to school, much success came because each step we planned was only minimally harder than the step before. In fact, Moira's father credits this as being the most important strategy in overcoming Moira's anxiety.

Although Moira had not been to school for eighteen months it was not suggested that she should suddenly return to school. We began working in tiny steps, such as just getting her to stick her nose around the corner to look at school. If she achieved this that day, that was all we expected. Moira clearly understood our aim. If she didn't accomplish this she was back to 'sick' treatment at home, in her room, no TV, etc. The next day we asked her to stick her nose around the corner and take only three steps towards the kerb, but not yet to cross the road. Again she was assured this was all that was necessary. This process continued step-by-step over several months until now Moira has been back at school for nearly two years.

The only technique that proved effective for Moira was a series of small steps, supported by other self-esteem work and general counselling. I believe if we had pushed for too rapid improvement, we would have failed.

Slow and steady

Anxious ADD kids are overwhelmed if they are pushed to change too quickly. It is important to realise that because an Anxious ADD kid reaches a certain level, it does not mean that they have become totally confident or comfortable with that level.

We often stalled Moira's steps until she was comfortable with a particular step. For example, once she made the move to actually cross over the street to school, we gave her two or three days just to repeat that step without expecting any more. We needed to alleviate her anxiety and teach her that she could confidently master this step repeatedly, before moving on.

There is a tendency with Anxious ADD kids to move too quickly once gains have been made. I understand parents' desire once a gain is made to keep quickly moving forward. However, Anxious ADD kids quickly become fearful that they are going to be forced to take on new fears too fast. They may even think if I do this they are only going to expect me to do more tomorrow. Therefore Anxious ADD kids may deliberately fail steps to stop or slow the program themselves. They need to move slowly and steadily, having time to reassure themselves they can do it again.

Recognisable achievements

Many Anxious ADD kids become so consumed with their immediate problems that they often forget what they have achieved already. Their impulsivity seems to make them only concerned with what is happening now. I have seen many Anxious ADD kids who have made quite exceptional gains, hit a stumbling block and become overwhelmed with this step. As a result they begin to consider themselves a total failure and completely useless. Although they might have improved 60 per cent, because they got stuck at a stage for a little while, they negate all the steps they have made.

Hannah

This problem of stalling affects many tutors working with Anxious ADD kids. Hannah is a good example. She had a great tutor, Joan, who had helped her overcome many of her maths problems, building her confidence. Suddenly Hannah was confronted with fractions, which she could not grasp. Suddenly she hated going to Joan's. She refused to do maths homework, claiming she was really dumb and never would be any good. She lost sight of how many other problems she had overcome. Luckily, Joan had kept all her old tutoring sheets, and we used these to get Hannah off the impulsive thought 'I can't do maths' and to focus on the fact that, as she had beaten many other difficult maths problems, she could beat this one too. Without a tangible record of improvement we might have been lost.

Keep a record of gains

When working with Anxious ADD kids I have found it very effective to keep some sort of record. In your record constantly note in very clear steps every small gain your child makes. When they falter, you can bring it out to encourage them to keep going rather than concentrating on today's failure.

Nathan

Nathan is a very successful ADD youth. He wanted to make the school walking team, even though he was very young at the time and was not sporting in nature. To qualify even to join the training squad, a lad had to beat a certain time on a walking machine. Nathan began training with great desire. Then, at his first attempt on the walking machine Nathan's time was well over ten minutes. Because Nathan knew that he had to get down to eight minutes thirty to qualify he immediately saw that he was failing.

However, we began a small-step procedure of recognising gains. Rather than getting overly anxious with this result, we began keeping a day-by-day record of times. After several weeks Nathan had a daily record chart that showed that each day he had improved his time by five or more seconds. Nathan still claimed he was failing, but as I mapped out his improvement he recognised for the first time that he was actually making progress.

Small steps into big leaps

Nathan and I plotted each of the twenty improvements he had made. I drew each small step as a small jump. When they joined together they looked like a caterpillar crawling along. I then drew a much larger leap to show how far he had come altogether. It relieved Nathan to see that if he had taken this big a step overall, then achieving the qualifying time was possible. However, we still planned to achieve each little step one at a time, rather than looking for a total goal. Each time Nathan made another step we recorded it so that he constantly had feedback on what good progress he was making. It is well worthwhile to keep records of your Anxious ADD kid's progress in any field in which they are improving.

▶ *FOCUSING ON OTHER IMAGES*

Parents and therapists have long thought that Anxious ADD kids are extremely sensitive and reactive, possibly because they feel things more intensely or process information at a higher level. Interpretation of very complex brain scans appears to indicate that the centres where information is processed in ADD adults is in fact overactive. This would seem to confirm what we believed. More recently this has been referred to as hyper-reactivity. The result is that they appear to worry more over problems than other kids. Coupled with their impulsivity, this can make them almost unmanageable.

In other sections I have described how we might use an ADD child's distractibility to our benefit. This is never more true than with an anxious kid. When they first start to become anxious I teach many ADD kids to focus on an alternative. For instance, if a kid is anxious about going to school, in the morning when the first anxiety messages begin we teach them to focus on something very good, such as receiving presents at Christmas time.

To make this strategy effective, however, it is very important that the kid focus on the Christmas image intently, actually describing to you what it looks like, what presents they receive, how they feel, what people are saying, and so on. The more involved we make this step the more likelihood there is of success. Again, we would need to record in some form the success in managing this strategy. These are later built up to show an ADD kid with anxieties that he is capable of overcoming fears. If he can have a record of how he has managed this ten times it gives him confidence that he will be able to manage it again.

Security items

Another form of alternative focusing is to allow Anxious ADD kids to carry the equivalent of security blankets in their pocket, small security items such as worry beads, small furry stuffed toys, favourite miniature dolls or Mum's earring.

▶ DON'T USE TIME OUT

In the basic Four Step procedure Time Out is used as an effective strategy. However, with many Anxious ADD kids I have found Time Out to be ineffective. Anxious ADD kids can be mildly depressed and quite happy to withdraw. As such, sitting in the corner rather than having to complete a difficult task is probably preferable. Therefore I suggest that you be very wary as parents of using Time Out with Anxious ADD kids. There are a number of alternatives.

Remove their escapes

One alternative to Time Out is to withdraw those supports that the ADD kid uses to escape the world. That is why I use the demonstration of withdrawing John's computer in the sample conversation on page 139. Because many Anxious Disordered kids see the computer as providing a fantasy world that they can escape to, its removal disturbs them and so this is more likely to have a positive effect.

Give them onerous tasks

Another strategy to replace Time Out is to give Anxious ADD kids an onerous task. An example might be having to sweep up the leaves in the back yard or complete a chore that they particularly dislike. Again this fits into the theory of making it uncomfortable for them to stay where they are. If you simply say 'If you don't do your homework you will be in Time Out' your Anxious ADD kid might be quite happy to sit, drift into a dreamland and in fact spend too much time worrying.

Rather we would set up a strategy such as 'Well, if you don't do your homework, then you have to do the job sweeping up the back porch leaves. However, if you are happy to do the homework then I am happy to do your job. I'll sweep up the leaves for you.' Try to find tasks they dislike, which will not allow them to drift into a withdrawn, fantasy world.

▶ PERFECTIONISM AND HIGH ACHIEVERS

It is important that parents of Anxious ADD kids look at their own lifestyles and needs, to ensure that they are not contributing significantly to their ADD child's behaviour. A good majority of Anxious ADD kids I have seen have either a perfectionist or a high-achieving parent. This type of family obviously needs some family therapy or counselling to overcome problems. In particular it is important with Anxious ADD kids that you do not place too great demands on them, have too high expectations or rush them through life. They need to slow down. Go gently and be reassuring all the way rather than setting them unattainable goals.

Anxiety can be inborn

While perfectionism in parents contributes to anxiety, I have in fact seen many anxiety-ridden ADD kids for whom I believe the anxiety is inborn. From day one they were insecure, needed constantly to be picked up and held, cried at being left alone and always showed phobias. I have often found a long family history of anxieties that appear to have been there since birth. These kids are somewhat more difficult to deal with because the anxieties are so ingrained and are almost a family trait. Changing this type of severely Anxiety Disordered ADD kid is possible but needs more time and more gradual steps towards success.

▶ DON'T DISMISS FEELINGS

Sometimes well-meaning adults give inappropriate messages to Anxious ADD kids or dismiss the child's feelings. I have heard many parents or teachers say 'Don't worry about it; there is no need to worry.' Anxious ADD kids experience very real fears, and to them their feelings or emotions are being denied or ridiculed by such statements.

Instead of dismissing their anxiety, which in a way tells them that we think there is no problem, it is more effective to give them messages such as 'We can cooperate on this and get over the problem.' Generally it is important for an Anxious ADD kid to know that they have someone supporting them, but who, at the same time, does not own the problem. Try to work on solving the problem as a team, but your child must take the lead.

Don't own their problems

An equally common fault is well-meaning parents actually owning their kids' anxiety problems. They overprotect their anxious kids from the world and attack anyone who creates fear in them. This gives the kids greater permission to be anxious and the parents become responsible for the problem. It is more important that we give them support and guidance in overcoming the anxiety, but they must finally achieve the success.

▶ 'HOME DUMPING'

'But Mrs Smith says Tanya is very quiet and compliant at school. She's no problem there. She's horrible as soon as she comes home. My husband even doubts Tanya has ADD.'

Our first assumption might be that Tanya can't have ADD. There are reasonable doubts that need investigating. It could be that Tanya does not have ADD; it could be that the teacher does not accept ADD; it could be that Tanya is 'home dumping', a term I use to describe the rather unusual occurrence of an overly anxious ADD kid curbing or controlling behaviour at school. They manage this because they are so worried and concerned about getting into trouble. They will actually go to extreme lengths to avoid doing anything naughty in the daytime. However, the minute this Anxious ADD kid gets out of the school all that stored anxiety, frustration and aggression is suddenly dumped on the parent at home, most likely Mum.

There are two notes of interest regarding home dumping:

▶   Anxious ADD kids often are seen as being compliant at school. The reality might be that they will still fail to pay attention, will in fact fidget incessantly in the classroom, but will not outwardly muck up. Their fidgeting is likely to be fine motor activity such as picking at nails, preening, touching items on the desk, etc. They are still very active, but not grossly hyperactive.

▶ The second important note to consider is why they dump on Mum. Obviously she is there as soon as they are outside school. I believe, however, that they sense that Mum is the only person who will tolerate this abuse and still love them in the morning and care for them unconditionally. Unfortunately, they attack the person they love most.

Stored-up anxiety

The worst case I have seen of home dumping was a mother who twice within three years had to replace the headrest in her Volvo sedan. Each afternoon her little boy would come out quite happily from school, but immediately on getting into the car would begin thumping the driver's headrest, complaining about all sorts of things at school. The amount of stored-up anxiety he had through the day came out in the next hour or so at home. We did achieve success with this child through using an antidepressant as well as Ritalin and engaging in psychotherapy to overcome anxieties.

Dealing with home dumping

Home dumping is very difficult to deal with. There are four useful steps:

▶ You could help your ADD kid to become more assertive at school and deal with their problems there.

▶ Obtain a careful diagnosis. Many of these kids are misdiagnosed or missed as ADD sufferers at school even though they may test out in formal diagnostic and psychometric testing as actually having ADD.

▶ Look at school behaviour through close consultation with the teacher and other school welfare staff. Often kids like this need to reduce self-imposed expectations at school.

▶ Parents with a kid who is home dumping will often need

professional psychiatric or psychological help to actually deal with the anxieties in a more solution-based approach.

► OTHER ANXIETY THERAPY

There are many well-publicised and very successful strategies for dealing with Anxiety Disordered kids. Strategies such as systematic desensitisation, positive focusing, relaxation tapes, suggestive hypnosis, massage and similar tactics have also proved successful with Anxious ADD kids. Any means of relaxing these kids and thus reducing their hyper-reactivity is worthwhile.

Passive-resistant anxiety

If Conduct Disordered ADD kids are difficult to deal with, then passive resistant or passively non-compliant ADD kids with anxieties are usually more frustrating. At times they are the most difficult ADD kids. Anxious ADD kids who are passively resistant, for example those who just sit and refuse to comply, can be extremely frustrating. How can you deal with the kid who simply sits and says 'Yes, I will do it' but then does not move? How can you be effectively angry with the kid who appears to take in the messages, seems to pay attention but then simply does not comply or make any effort?

Even in therapy I have personally found this group much more difficult to deal with. They will promise all sorts of improvements in therapy, but then will not carry them through. Similarly they can sometimes just stubbornly refuse to answer questions, particularly if I touch on a sensitive topic. For parents, it becomes very hard to discipline this type of kid because what is it that they are actually doing wrong? It is not that they are yelling at you, being rude or swearing: they are simply not talking. If we scream at them for not answering, because they are anxious they simply become more anxious. Any strategy takes time and may be only gradually successful.

Talking for the passive-resistant

You may have discovered you can give your passive-resistant ADD kid two choices but she will not make a choice. One way to deal with no talking or making no choice is to begin talking for your child. The following dialogue may illustrate this point better.

> 'John, it is 5.00 p. m. Can you get in the bath?'
> 'Yes, Mum.'
> But John does not move.
> 'John, I asked you to get into the bath.'
> John looks up and nods but still does not move.
> 'John, the choice is bath and get to play the computer or no bath or TV. And computers are off until dinner-time.'
> John looks up. 'Okay' (but John still does not move).
> 'John, by not moving you are telling me that you want the computer turned off and telling me that you want the TV off also, or you can get up and hop into the bath which means that you get extra computer time tonight. Don't move and you are telling me that you want both TV and computer off.'
> John looks up and says 'Don't hassle me.'
> 'John, this is the third time I have spoken. You chose not to answer or move, therefore you told me the choice was computer off and no TV.'

You can see that basically I took over the role of John's voice. In doing so I took away the power of his non-compliance. It is the only effective method I have found to keep a non-compliant ADD kid moving. There are similar terms that we can use in this situation, such as 'Your behaviour says that this consequence will happen; by not complying you are deciding that this consequence will happen.'

In summary:

Dealing with Anxious ADD requires patience, small steps and lots of reassurance. These kids often need very clear recognition of ability and gains made in the past. Parents need to be aware progress is gradual. In spite of stalls, eventual success is certainly possible. Anxious ADD kids will often need psychotherapy, as well as support from more traditional anxiety and stress reduction or relaxation work.

$\mathcal{S}$ELF-ESTEEM

— chapter 11 —

I have often thought that ADD could have been named the 'low self-esteem disorder'. I have yet to meet an ADD kid who does not have low self-esteem. They lack confidence, have a poor academic self-image and are self-critical and pessimistic. This negative image is often mixed with a non-caring, don't-worry-about-the-consequences, live-life-by-the-minute attitude. This sometimes masks the fact that underneath the brazen exterior and tough shield is a scared little kid.

Self-esteem could be described as risk successfully ventured and gained. ADD kids take the risks but rarely gain the success.

▶ *TWO FACES OF LOW SELF-ESTEEM*

There are generally two types of ADD kids with low self-esteem. The most easily recognised and more common group are those whose low self-esteem is very obvious. These kids are very negative about themselves, they distrust their own ability, often put themselves down and have very little confidence, which seems to stretch across many boundaries, such as sport, academic life, social engagements, and so on.

The other group is a little more complex. They have a very brash and confident exterior which is in fact a cover for low self-esteem.

These kids often have the gift of the gab and may well go on to be excellent salesmen, presenters or promoters, but are at extremely high risk of developing addictive disorders such as alcoholism or workaholism, or less often at risk of suicide. Because of their convincing brashness and apparent confidence they are very often missed. Because of their outlandish behaviour they fail to be noted and treated and their low self-esteem is never truly understood.

► NATURALLY NEGATIVE

'That's great work, James.'
'No it's not, Mum, it's really messy and dumb.'

I have yet to meet an ADD kid who is not naturally negative. Natural negativity refers to an ADD child's ability to take what is an apparently positive situation and turn it into one that's negative. If you try to praise them they will often turn it around to 'But I am hopeless at that.' If you make mention of a positive feature, such as 'your beautiful hair', they will immediately turn this to 'my huge hips'.

Typical kids will most often describe positive features in a picture, whereas ADD kids have an amazing ability to find and discuss the most negative death-oriented, gory or sad images. I have casually tried showing kids several positive cartoons with one negative one. Whereas typical kids talk about the fun cartoons, ADD kids often prefer to talk about the negative cartoon. I do not believe that their negativity is always caused by parents, but rather it is almost an automatic response.

When positives backfire

It is a common occurrence for parents to be told by welfare workers that they should overcome their ADD child's low self-esteem by being more positive, for example telling them when they are good. This is also termed 'making affirmation statements' or 'giving unconditional positive regard'. While such statements have the potential to be successful, they can also seriously backfire.

Parents have been blamed for not being positive enough, but they are aware that the more positive they are, the more negative conclusions occur. They complain that more fights ensued when they tried to be positive. This may in fact be true. The difficulty is that most ADD kids have the potential to turn positive statements to negatives. A mum might say to an ADD kid 'That's good homework.' The kid will impulsively respond 'No, it's not. It's really messy. I'm the dumbest in the class.' Mum tried very hard to build the child's self-esteem but in fact it has backfired into a negative situation.

A golden rule is to avoid making broad positive statements. Rather, make a very specific statement.

Be specific

If you are going to praise an ADD kid or try to build self-esteem by being positive, you need to concentrate on very small details, ideas or concepts. Try to avoid using broad generalisations; replace them with very specific, precise praise. For example, rather than saying 'That's good work' you might say 'Gee, I can see you have really tried hard to keep this picture neat.' Try to avoid saying 'You're working well' but replace it with 'You are doing a great job of making a neat heading. Mrs Carter will be pleased.' Similarly, if an ADD kid has behaved himself well tell him exactly what he has done, such as 'You really helped by cleaning out the dishwasher. Now we have more time to play out the back.' Avoid general statements like 'You're a good boy.'

You will note that we not only specified what behaviour was appropriate, but also showed the kid how it worked out well for them. Try to concentrate on praising behaviour or effort that is not debatable. If you comment on a whole project there is great scope for an ADD kid to find errors or problems. If the writing is neat just concentrate on this. As an alternative, if you praise a whole topic finish with specific praise: 'That's a great project. I especially like the neat writing.'

Focus on gains, not the total goal

'But I don't want to wait. I've been doing it for hours (really ten minutes). I'm hopeless, I can't do it. This thing's stupid.' Sound familiar?

Most ADD kids are impulsive and insatiable, therefore they want to achieve the total goal. They are not willing to work at tasks slowly and gradually. When they have not reached the goal quickly they believe they have failed. To overcome this problem we try to constantly recognise small gains they have made, rather than the total goal.

Let us take the example of Nathan, the teenager who was trying to make the school athletic team. Even when he was starting to improve and had cut some thirty seconds off his time, he responded to my suggestion that he was doing very well by saying 'No, I'm not. I am really hopeless. I have done nothing. I will never make the time.' Again we needed to go back and recognise the small gains that he had made, to recognise each step along the way, rather than concentrating on the total goal. To achieve this we went over the record of his improvement in times, to demonstrate that he could actually achieve his goal.

Most ADD kids are so impulsive that they want only the total goal, so we overcome this by mapping out a self-esteem chart of each little achievement, marking off by very obvious visual means how they are getting there. Similarly, if they become overwhelmed by a large project, break it into small pieces. Try to avoid focusing on the whole project, but work on one piece at a time, noting each small part finished and recognising each as an achievement when completed.

► LIGHT AT THE END OF THE TUNNEL

Living in the world of ADD is like being stuck at the end of a long dark tunnel. People don't understand you, nothing is easy and the solution is hard to see. It is little wonder then that ADD kids often feel trapped. To overcome this I try to find a light at the end of the dark tunnel. This will never be a huge leap. Rather I try to find any small achievement to build on. We can look on the few times that an ADD kid has controlled his temper, for example, as the first few steps towards a new emerging light.

The same premise is true for you as parents, often expecting too much of yourselves and having very poor parental self-esteem. If you can improve a little at a time you too will find the light at the end of the tunnel. The fact that you are looking through this book to find better ways to deal with your kid is the first small step. Further, you are a highly motivated parent trying for your kid. The light is getting brighter. Don't worry just yet about reaching the end of the tunnel: just focus on the light slowly getting brighter.

► LEARNING STYLES AND PRAISE

ADD kids have different learning styles:

- ► through a hands-on approach
- ► through verbal instructions
- ► through visual demonstration.

It is possible by consulting an educational psychologist or other experienced specialist in the field that you can determine your child's learning style. It is by means of their particular learning style that the ADD kid is most likely to absorb and accept praise.

If you have a typical ADD boy, for example, with auditory-verbal and language processing problems, he will rarely process and remember what he hears. Therefore giving him verbal praise such as 'You are a good boy, you are doing well' is very unlikely to succeed in building self-esteem. The message will merely float by without being absorbed. Rather you need to *show* him precisely what he did well, for example moving a pen along a line of writing and saying 'This is really neat writing. Look how you've kept on the line.' Support this with a cuddle and praise while pointing to the neat work. You might even write a little note to the teacher about how Sam is trying to be neat.

For the kids who learn only through a hands-on approach, demonstrate their good work or improvement. With one boy who felt he wasn't achieving we had a grid marked across my desk in chalk marks for each gain. As we discussed gains we moved a very small car across one grid mark. I wanted him to become aware physically of how he had improved, although he could not actually understand when I first talked with him about the improvements he had made.

Even those ADD kids who learn through auditory-verbal channels need self-esteem messages repeated. Although they learn through what they hear, they will not always process the information the first time they hear it.

We can develop self-esteem better by praising and building confidence through the learning style that suits your ADD kid.

▶ *APPROVAL AND AFFIRMATION*
Restore 'I' statements

You will remember in the basic Four Step procedure that we tried to remove 'I' statements, such as 'I am disappointed in how you behaved' or 'I am upset that you are disrupting the family.' The idea then was to make your ADD kid more responsible for his own behaviour and to own his problems. The opposite rule applies when we are dealing with low self-esteem in an ADD kid. Rather than removing 'I' statements for bad behaviour we make many positive 'I' statements.

Your ADD kid must understand that you approve of their behaviour. Therefore we put the 'I' statements back in for any positive behaviour. 'I am very proud of you because you have improved your marks by three in this exam' is appropriate, just as 'I was really pleased with how you shared nicely with Tom' is positive. Your ADD kid needs to know that when they are behaving well we are very involved in their lives, rather than being detached or bored when they are acting inappropriately. In this way we feed good behaviour and avoid feeding the ADD problem. We feed their insatiability for warmth, recognition and approval when they are good, but remove it when they are bad. Again natural rewards often work better than artificial systems. A good example is verbal praise such as 'I am very proud of you for sharing' tied into a cuddle and a little extra playtime.

Reaffirming messages to themselves

Parents of ADD kids have long been told to give their kids affirmation statements. An even more effective means of raising their self-esteem is to try to encourage them to make positive comments about themselves. Therefore we would add to a statement such as 'I am really pleased with how neatly you are writing' an ending such as 'Tell me what you are most pleased with about your work today.' This is a difficult task but aimed at getting ADD kids to make positive comments about their own ability.

Some ADD kids will turn this strategy into a negative. If your child does this, it is important to dismiss this statement by saying 'No, not bad things, what I really need to know is what you think is good about it.' Go over again what you think is good, such as the writing being really neat, then try again to find a small feature for your child to comment on positively.

Putting emotion back

When we are trying to raise self-esteem, we need also to put back parental emotion and interest. So as not to feed ADD attention-seeking behaviour, in the basic Four Step procedure I suggest you use a boring, low, monotonous voice for bad behaviour. When you are trying to build self-esteem you need to make sure that you are enthusiastic, warm and genuine. A boring or passing comment will prove very ineffective with ADD kids, who are more perceptive that many other kids. They may even turn it into a negative, such as 'You don't really care about me.' Rather we need to be involved and enthusiastic.

A *word of warning:* ADD kids can become overexcited or hyper-react with too much stimulation. Therefore be enthusiastic, warm and positive but be brief. A small amount of praise is all that is required. Overdoing it can hype up your kid too much.

Letting others know

ADD kids expect their parents to love them, be proud of them and praise them. As a result, your kid might respond with 'Oh, you are just saying that because you're my mum.' Again very well-intentioned attempts to raise self-esteem may fail or even backfire.

One way to overcome this is to let others know of your recognition and approval. You can make the praise more formal or pass the message to someone else. As an example, if you were trying to build Kim's esteem, when making a phone call to Grandma you would clearly state how proud you are of Kim's sharing when Kim is within earshot. Similarly when Dad comes home you can make a real point by marching Kim up and saying in front of Dad the specific things you are proud of, such as Kim sharing with her sister. The aim is that Kim hears you conveying the message to Dad.

Another useful strategy is to keep a written record, such as writing positive little notes. ADD kids appear to accept this more formal manner of recording self-esteem messages.

The power of the note

I even found that notes in one case helped to prevent a suicide. This particular ADD kid, whom I had not seen for more than a year, had become withdrawn and suicidal. Years before, I had encouraged his mother to write little notes to him that she was to stick under his pillow whenever he had done anything she was proud of or thought was worthwhile, to build his self-esteem. This boy had never mentioned these notes or even recognised that they existed. However, he had become so depressed that he contemplated suicide and was walking to the edge of a cliff. He was seen by a helpful gent who walked towards him to talk him down. Before the man had reached the top of the cliff this boy had begun to climb back down and had obviously decided not to commit suicide. During a conversation later that day he opened his wallet and there hidden in the back section was a huge pile of these notes. He explained that he had got as far as the cliff,

opened his wallet to look at them and simply could not go through with it.
Although he had never admitted that the notes were effective they had, in
fact, a very positive outcome.

► AVOID FEELINGS:
FOCUS ON SOLUTIONS

ADD kids with low self-esteem are hypersensitive and hyper-reactive.
Recent neurology studies and brain scans seem to confirm what parents
have told us for a long time, that their ADD kids over-react to
everything: food, noise, windy days, criticism, irritation, teasing, etc.
We must be careful then not to focus too much on feelings when an
ADD kid is upset or they will become more distraught, at times
hysterical. Therefore try to avoid using phrases such as 'Do you feel sad
about that? It must make you feel terrible; tell me how you feel' which
will only promote distress and over-reactions.

Try to focus on solutions, letting your child know we can help him
overcome the problem. For example, if your ADD kid cries that his friend
hates him, try to focus on a solution about how we can make up with the
friend tomorrow. ADD kids do not see the sequence of events necessary to
solve problems. Try to teach them the precise and sequential steps toward
solution, rather than concentrating on bad feelings.

Trade-offs

'Did you have fun in school today?'
'No. Mr Smith was cranky, Anna hates me, I'm really dumb, no-one
likes me.'

As we have established, ADD kids are so naturally negative that any
question you ask can be turned into a negative comment. A very simple
comment can open up a series of complaints about all the negative
experiences they have had that day. This is particularly true for the
more anxious or depressed ADD kids.

A way to overcome this is to work on 'trade-offs'. The rule is that we
will in fact listen to their negative problems, but only after they have
traded off a positive comment first. For example, if your child comes out
of school complaining they have had a really bad day, say 'Okay, I will
listen to what went wrong but only after you trad- off and first tell me
two good things that happened.' If your child claims you are not
listening or caring, stick to a bland approach: 'I do care, I will listen to

the problem, but only after you tell me two good things.' Once he or she has discussed the two good things, it is important to go back to the bad thing that concerned them first. Again, however, when doing this try to find a way to solve the problem, rather than just discussing how bad they feel about it.

After-school questions

'How was school today, dear?'

'Uh huh.'

'What did you do today?'

'Nuff, huh.'

'Did you have fun?'

'Ahh, hmmm, neerrr.'

I am sure all kids are secretly taught how to speak orang-utan language. How else can we explain the above conversation? In fact, part of the problem is ADD itself. ADD kids have very poor sequential recall; that is, the ability to recall information in a set sequence. The other part of the problem is that the question is not specific enough.

We can help solve these problems with a single approach; that is, asking very specific questions that follow a sequence. For example, you should ask questions such as 'Did Mrs Smith have you for computers today?' followed by 'What program did you use today on the computer?' then 'Did you enjoy it?' etc. This means that you have to know what activities are in each school day. Ask teachers for a day program or work schedules. Your kids will believe you are more interested if you are aware computers is each Thursday, rather than asking a boring 'mum question' like 'How was school today?'

With teenagers, you need to be careful of prying too much. ADD teenagers want you to be involved, but not to invade their privacy and independence. Ask as many questions as they are comfortable with, but don't push for answers until they are forced to reject you. Still look at their timetable and be aware of what subjects they have day by day. Try to find when they feel it is comfortable to talk. This may not be straight after school.

Success Books

ADD kids often have very negative self-images, which they can produce at any time to defeat your efforts to raise their self-esteem. One way to overcome this is to gradually build up a Success Book. This means keeping a photo album or scrapbook of any of your ADD kid's small achievements.

Don't hold out for the one merit certificate that your child might receive each term. A Success Book is effective only if it is constantly updated. Try to keep a record of any little thing they do well.

The Success Book — James

James does well at school and his teacher makes a positive comment. You put in your own small note: 'Mrs Smith was very pleased with James today.'

Becky cooperates well at a party. Insert the invitation with a note: 'Becky shared very well at Melissa's party.'

Your child receives a reward, such as a sticker or stamp at school. Obviously you include this.

Your kid is rewarded with a treat, such as going to McDonald's for good behaviour. Keep a small piece of McDonald's wrapper and mark next to it why the reward was given.

When your ADD child comes in and says that they are hopeless and nothing is good, you can get out the book and say 'Well hang on, what about this whole book of awards and improvements? How can you be no good?'

► SPORT AND OTHER ACTIVITIES

Sport or similar activities can help ADD kids to gain confidence and self-esteem and develop a sense of responsibility, as well as improve gross motor skills and growth. Not all activities need to be formalised sport. Riding a bike, climbing trees, skateboarding, rollerblading, building and constructing are examples of good activities. ADD children leave school feeling like caged lions. They need activities to let out pent-up energy and to feel good about themselves. ADD children who have been active often sleep better as well. As parents are aware, however, many ADD children are fairly awkward and uncoordinated or have only very particular interests. It is a pity that their levels of stamina and energy cannot always be channelled in the right directions or into appropriate fields. A small ADD group, often the more hyperactive, are in fact very talented at sport.

Even given awkwardness or difficulty in fitting into team sports, it is still important that we persevere and find success with sport or similar activities. We can look at anything from more formal activities such as baseball, cricket and football to more individual sports such as swimming, rowing, karate, tennis and golf and even to other pursuits such as scouts, drama groups, and so on. The aim is to get your child into some form of activity where they can receive some support, recognition and guidance from others outside the family. It is often a good outlet for their frustrations and a way to express themselves.

Young ADD children and team sports

'How did he go at Rugby, darling?'

'I'm never doing that again. I played for Australia and my son sits under the goalpost making mud pies.'

This is a true story, but a common problem for many families. As a general rule, I have found that young ADD children do not fit well into team sports. While participating in team sport might be a long-term goal the majority of ADD children find it too difficult to manage. If you imagine a poorly coordinated ADD child, who is distractible, restless and has a short attention span, is it any wonder then that he is the one who is sitting up at the end of the field playing in the dirt? I have coached several sporting teams. In football the ADD kid is the one who gets the ball but runs the wrong way. Then when everyone screams he becomes too upset, drops the ball and runs off the field in tears.

Similarly I have tried to hide an ADD kid in the baseball outfield. It is amazing how, just when the ball is hit in the air, the ADD kid in my team happens to be sitting on the ground, chewing a mitt and chasing a caterpillar. Unfortunately this can lead to distress for all. We don't want kids to fail in their own eyes or their mates'. Therefore early on I prefer to place ADD children in more individual sports or pursuits such as tae kwon do where they are not forced to fit in with a team and maintain attention span. Try your child in team sports but don't let them fail week after week.

Learning difficulties reach the sporting field

Learning difficulties are not isolated to the classroom. They affect play, social skills and sporting ability. For example, disorganised ADD children can have difficulty processing a lot of information. It is extremely difficult for a seven-year-old to process factors such as three or four children running at them, the slope of the ground, a football bouncing in several directions, people yelling at them and the need to make a quick decision such as where are the goals. It is not surprising then that they kick the ball backwards. More individual sports involve more steady activity and less information to process.

There are, however, exceptions to this rule. A small number of ADD children are very active, sporting and well coordinated. In fact almost any sport seems to suit them. These children are very fortunate as they often have higher self-esteem and confidence. Even though they can be terrible readers and socially awkward, their sport is the one area where they can actually fit in, gain recognition and believe in themselves.

Fourteen tries

Even though I have said I would never give up on ADD children I had almost given up on this kid. With his parents we began by trying to find a sport or activity that would suit him. We went through cricket, baseball, T-ball, soccer, league, AFL, drama class, cartooning, etc. In fact we tried thirteen activities. Somewhere in the back of my mind I believed that if we got to unlucky thirteen, that would turn out to be the lucky sport for him. Needless to say, the thirteenth sport also failed.

I have never yet understood how an ADD kid could be good at chess but, regardless, this child's fourteenth sport of choice was chess, which his grandfather taught him. He became so good at chess that he went on to be the school's chess champion. As he began to beat the champions of other private schools his status within the school rose. He was actually brought down to assemblies and treated as being very important because he had won the school competition. He brought delight to the school when he challenged the teachers and was able to beat all but one. There is little doubt that most of the school saw him as a great cult figure once he could say that he was smarter than most of the teachers in the school. So, while I had almost given up on this kid, his parents' perseverance to the fourteenth try actually saw him have success. You may argue that sport and chess are not the same thing but it was chess that built the child's self-esteem.

Recognising small gains

When dealing with your ADD child try to avoid large goals or gains. For example, I have seen a parent promise his ADD kid that if he scores a try in football he will get one dollar. The chances of success are unlikely, which leads to compounding difficulties. Look rather at smaller goals and gains. I worked with an ADD kid playing soccer. Rather than rewarding a goal, we decided that if he actually ran at another kid and challenged him for the ball his father would yell praise and count one point. If in a game he reached ten points then he received one dollar to spend at the club canteen after soccer.

ADD children get distracted by bigger goals and other factors. They do not process verbal praise well, so quick or occasional amounts of verbal praise would be ineffective. Rather try to keep some form of records, such as a weekly chart of the number of tackles made, a record sheet of belts gained at karate, a badge chart for scouts awards, or improvement in tennis games.

A success story

When I first saw Jason he was an attractive-looking but slightly thin lad. His elder brother had always been a star and was considerably bigger and more popular. Jason had tried many different activities with little success. Then he decided he was going to prove to all he was capable by making it to the school's elite rowing team.

Initially his progress was slow. Despite effort Jason needed constant reassurance not to give up. I regularly had to reinforce my belief in him. Despite criticism we stuck at it. When he didn't think he could make the qualifying time we had to go over every little gain to keep him motivated. As Jason improved he began to work very hard himself. His father became proud of his effort. His darling mum loved him even more. Though there were battles Jason kept at it until he made one of the junior rowing teams.

Jason was not ready to give up. Despite his size and others' disbelief we decided he could make the elite first eight the next year, even though he wasn't in his final year. Jason worked harder and harder. He surprised everyone by making the first eight the next year and kept his place despite challenges.

Many other things happened in this process. On the negative side we did battle at times with his becoming a little obsessive about training and healthy diets. But this was far outweighed by the positives. Jason went from a thin kid to a muscular young man the girls loved. His status in the school changed remarkably. He was now a valued student rather than a troublesome one of low ability. Teachers began to see him in a different light. Jason began to believe in himself to the point where he beat some of his learning weaknesses. He saw for the first time that through effort came reward. He worked and improved his grades, and received his first very positive school report.

Jason's family had always accepted him but now had more reason to admire him, not so much for sporting success but for showing determination and willingness to stick at difficult tasks and improve. He went from feeling that he was a nobody to believing he was somebody, not just a class rower but a champion young man who had beaten many of ADD's adversities. Rarely have I been so proud as I was being involved with Jason. Congratulations, friend!

In summary:

Low self-esteem is a common feature of ADD. It is sometimes masked by a don't-care exterior. A particular difficulty is that ADD kids can turn almost any positive into a negative. They distrust their own ability and need help to recognise every gain, no matter how apparently minor. Building self-esteem is extremely difficult. However, if we keep at it, ADD kids can eventually get to like themselves, believe in their own ability and have real confidence.

$\mathscr{S}$OCIAL PROBLEMS

—— chapter ——

ADD kids often experience very significant problems with social interaction. This is a very neglected area of ADD behaviour. The particular social problems of ADD kids include:

▶ impulsive behaviour and poor awareness of consequences that can lead to specific problems

▶ organisational difficulties that mean ADD kids often fail to put together all the separate factors that are relevant in a social situation, resulting in social failure

▶ immaturity that sees them struggling to relate to peers their own age; they may prefer to play with older or younger kids

▶ hyper-reactivity, which means that they they can misinterpret or over-react in social situations.

As a result ADD kids can display many inappropriate behaviours such as:

▶ bursting into games

▶ having trouble waiting their turn

▶ demanding unfair advantages

▶ being dominating and suffocating in friendships

▶ having trouble keeping friendships

▶ telling family secrets to everyone

▶ discussing inappropriate topics

▶ acting 'over the top' in social situations (e.g. at parties)

▶ withdrawing when unsure

▶ interacting poorly with peers of their own age.

▶ ADD KIDS IN SOCIAL SITUATIONS

Acting without thinking

'I'm sorry Mrs Smith, Scott didn't mean to hit her with the bat. He just never thinks before he acts.' Mums and dads of ADD kids become experts at making apologies.

ADD kids act without thinking and certainly with little regard for the consequences of their behaviour. For example, Scott grabs the baseball bat and takes practice swings, unaware who is behind him. This is rarely deliberately malicious behaviour. If they want to partake in a game they will rarely ask first but merely take the leader's role. In many activities they assume that they can have first turn.

In many social situations, part of the total answer to impulsivity problems is to have good structure and organisation. The more consistent and firm the rules, the less chance there is that the kids will break these rules. It also helps to prepare for social situations, rather than hoping that the worst will not occur. Try to go back through a sequence of behaviours to look at the cause of problems, not the result, and to prepare for another such event. It is also helpful to use very distracting reminders to help ADD kids to remember what their behaviour should be. These strategies are explained more fully later in this chapter.

Hyper-reactivity and over-arousal

One group of ADD kids (often the more hyperactive with other behaviour problems) are often hyper-reactive in social situations. They can be over-aroused, either becoming overly stimulated or actively seeking too much stimulation themselves. They will not accept 'boring' play, but will seek out more dangerous and thrilling challenges. For example, parents of young ADD kids sometimes blame the food at parties for behaviour. But, on checking carefully, we find they began mucking up even before the food arrived. The real reason for misbehaviour is that they become aroused with all the stimulation available, and thus can't control their impulses. The junk food later only makes it worse. They often cannot curb their impulsiveness in this situation and so they cause problems for themselves, their friends and their families. This group does not inhibit their behaviour. They miss social warning signals from peers, and rather storm over problems. Their poor sequencing skills and memory mean that they don't learn from their mistakes.

One answer is to limit the time in which they can become over-aroused by having quiet times away from the party. Further, it is wise to act before your child becomes so overstimulated that calming down is no longer possible.

Disorganisation and sequencing in social situations

Another group of ADD kids (often the inattentive, learning disabled, disorganised) tend to be very unsure, anxious, initially withdrawn and demanding in social situations. They can be very touchy, emotional and nervous. They refuse to take social risks, rather, for example, withdrawing to the safety of the computer. This group fails to see the links, organisation and sequences necessary in social situations. They don't see what fits with what or easily realise what they are expected to do. They may be struggling to see common factors in new situations. As a result they experience them as totally new, rather than adapting from past social learning. They may not see that their behaviour will lead to a series of negative consequences. Their poor memory and sequencing weaknesses mean they can't easily remember how they solved social problems in the past. They may misinterpret tone in voice or non-verbal language, for example believing others are being more critical than they really are.

This group often withdraws or sits aside until they can work out how to interact. They may lack the language skills to keep up verbally and thus remain quiet or make inappropriate or out-of-context comments, appearing silly in front of peers. They are often very outspoken at home, but shy socially until they are used to the situation.

Poor attention to detail

Many ADD children also pay poor attention to detail in social situations, failing to concentrate or pay attention to all factors. The result is that they miss very important signals. A simple example is that an ADD kid may miss the tone in another child's voice, when they are trying to let the ADD kid know that they are feeling overwhelmed. They miss the signs suggesting that they back off.

ADD kids may operate from a single stimulus. For instance, they may simply perceive that someone is angry from their facial expression, reacting to this detail alone, not paying attention to other factors such as what is actually being said to them, who has authority in the situation, whether it is appropriate here to swear back or what other options are available to them.

► *A SIMPLE DESCRIPTION*

A typical case often involves an ADD kid who took other kids' toys at pre-school, cried and fought with playmates, was only ever invited to a few parties, became too hyped up at sport for the coach to handle and broke Grandma's most valuable vase when charging through her house. These kids are so aroused and active that they break the bounds of what is normal behaviour. They don't seem to pay attention to the details of what others are doing or what behavioural expectations are. Pity their poor parents!

Social disaster

Mum has left Nathan at his first birthday party in two years. Nathan's mum senses something is wrong when another mum storms past giving her an icy glare as she walks in to collect Nathan. Then the party mother lets out a great sigh of relief as Mum enters. Nathan's mum turns the corner to find Nathan with sauce all over his best shirt, chocolate 'make-up' mixed with tears running down his face, isolated from the others, feeling rejected, angry and hurt but not realising that his behaviour led to the problems. ADD kids have learnt to manage parties, but only with great effort and understanding.

ADD kids don't learn like sponges

Most typical kids, without ADD, learn social skills by osmosis. They are like sponges; they naturally soak it all up without effort. Non-ADD kids observe social interaction, grasping the concepts and rules, which they then take in naturally without teaching. Wouldn't it be nice if ADD kids managed this feat?

ADD kids are more like a dried-out car chamois than a sponge. Drop a sponge in a bucket of water and it soaks the water up and retains it for a long time. Dip a dried chamois in water and it barely soaks up anything at all. Only after you dip it in several times does it soak up any water, and then after you leave it for a while it quickly dries out again.

Unfortunately many ADD kids with learning difficulties are the same. They don't naturally pick up social concepts. They need constant exposure to social learning, and refreshing every so often. The only way they will actually learn social rules or behaviours is if they are taught over and over.

► SOCIALISATION DISORDERS

A Socialisation Disorder is a form of Co-morbid Disorder with ADD, much the same as Oppositional Defiance Disorder can be a Co-morbid Disorder. Generally a kid is classed as having a Socialisation Disorder when their social skills are so deficient that it interferes significantly with their daily functioning. For example, a boy who very occasionally has a scuffle in the playground is fairly normal. But when a child is constantly sad, angry, bossy and withdrawn and cannot maintain friendships the child may have a Socialisation Disorder. Similarly if a child is constantly teased, rejected or attacked and can't stop over-reacting to this teasing, problems are recognised as needing attention. A child who is overly aggressive and hurtful to others and simply never fits into social situations may also be seen as having a Socialisation Disorder.

Language-based Socialisation Disorder

Occasionally very aggressive, reactive and emotional ADD kids who have been diagnosed as having a conduct problem in fact have a language-based Socialisation Disorder. This is not true for all conduct problems. This small group of ADD kids usually have severe receptive and expressive language problems. As a result they struggle to cope verbally if teased or rejected. They cover these difficulties by being physically aggressive, for example by hitting out in the playground. When called to the principal's office they rarely can explain themselves, and therefore become more upset and angry.

Brash cover

A very small group of kids with socialisation and ADD problems, more often in teenage years, cover their poor social skills with a boastful brashness. They can appear quite confident, often taking excessive risks or being bullies. Underneath this brashness can be very insecure, troubled souls. They may cover this with fanciful tales, amazing stories and boasts about their own abilities. This group is very much at risk.

The vicious circle

Unfortunately kids with social skill problems fall into a vicious cycle that feeds on itself. For example, an ADD girl, Sally, may be overly impulsive and unaware of consequences. This leads to her being bossy or demanding in games, and other kids become very intolerant towards her. Sally acts back aggressively, bringing further rejection on herself. As she feels more rejected she tries harder and harder to control the game. The more she tries to control the game the more she is rejected. As she is rejected she becomes increasingly hurt and upset, which leads to more difficult behaviour. As a result the other kids are unlikely to invite Sally to play, which makes her more determined to control the next game.

In many similar ways ADD kids create a vicious circle for themselves, which is then reinforced by peers, who don't understand their ADD. The other kids are unable to cope with the ADD kids' many social and behaviour problems.

Reverse role-play

I came up with the idea of reverse role-play many years ago when working with an ADD kid who refused to see the need to play fair. Rather he wanted only to satisfy his insatiable needs. I deliberately brought in a Nintendo GameBoy to a session. I explained we weren't talking today but playing for six minutes (cheers of delight and 'Ian, can't we play for the whole time?'). I said we could have three minutes each, me first. To show him the reverse side I kept going past my three minutes, despite his pleas. Only then could I get him to see how his mate might feel and why he would storm home, refusing to ask my ADD kid back to play. Talking wasn't enough: he had to experience it.

Similarly, with another kid who demanded extra turns in back-yard cricket, I began a card game. However, I made funny rules such as: I was only out every second time and I could pick up two cards, not one. Again, he had to experience the reverse side. His parents had talked to him, but like many ADD kids with language difficulties he had tuned out. He learnt only through practical experience. ADD kids like inventive games to solve problems rather than too much talking!

▶ *LOOKING AT ALTERNATIVES*

Someone else's fault

Rarely do ADD kids realise, see or accept the sequence of events that lead to problems. For example, Wayne may have been sent to the principal's office for fighting. He will complain that the other kid hit him. He will not remember or accept that he took this child's pencil in class without asking, threw it away in the playground and called him names like 'Tech-head'. All Wayne sees is the final step, when the other kid confronted him and hit him.

ADD kids can, through forgetting, be unaware of everything but the last step in a sequence of events. However, they also can be brilliant in taking the focus away from themselves and blaming everyone else for their problems. This requires a very obvious sequential approach (steps often written out) to social skills training. ADD kids need to be taken back to the very first instance and shown how each step contributed, with the focus taken off the final step.

This sequential approach is the first step in helping ADD kids to own their problems by seeing the only solution is to change the first behaviour, not to blame someone else at the conclusion. With patience and time we can help them to realise that the final outcome is not changeable; what is changeable is the sequence of steps that led to this outcome.

Sequential plans look very much like flow diagrams; for example:

1.................................2.................................
3.................................4.................................
5.................................6.................................
No asking.............took pen.................................
threw away.............called names.................................
chased.................got hit.................................

Wayne, we can begin by changing 1 and 2!

Changing friends

ADD kids with social problems rarely have close long-term friendships. They either destroy friendships with their domination and demanding nature or move on because they are bored with any better-quality friends. We try to teach them different behaviour that leads to different consequences. However, we need to work just one step at a time.

For example, a kid who demands to be king in handball, to have extra turns and who refuses to be out can be taught the consequences of this behaviour. We would begin by setting a plan in which he receives high-level rewards if he agrees with the rule that squares are decided by who is there first, not by the bossiest person.

Similarly, a young teenager who demands longer time on the computer than his friend needs some governing. We explain that we trust him to share. If, however, he doesn't share then we have the right to govern the situation. As such, we might use a ten-minute clock to divide turns. Refusal to play by the clock means the computer goes off. Even though this might cause some embarrassment, unless the teenager learns to share he will never maintain friends. He will simply believe his mate is just a jerk for going home early. Again in therapy I would map out in order the consequences of not sharing turns and of demanding extra time.

Dominate and smother

ADD kids tend to struggle to make and keep friends. Unfortunately when they finally make a friendship they can become demanding in the relationship and tend to smother the other kid. Holly is an ADD girl who has had very few friendships and certainly no long-term close friends. When Holly finally developed a new friendship at school it quickly became intense. Through fear of losing her new friend, Holly began demanding that she play with her alone and with no-one else. Holly became hurt, rejected and angry when her new friend chose to play with someone else for one day. Holly had demanded all her new friend's time, until she felt so smothered that she refused to play with Holly at all. Holly could see only that her new friend was being mean.

To overcome this kind of problem we need to begin by showing ADD kids all the separate factors that make up behaviour. Often this involves some counselling or individual therapy. In a therapy situation I might explain what messages a child can give back, down to fine detail such as frowns, pleas and voice tones. We need to map out how each behaviour is leading to the next, perhaps on a flow chart or in a practical demonstration so that they can see how their behaviour is leading to the final outcome.

Teaching alternatives

ADD kids will not automatically know alternative ways of acting. They need to be shown. Again a flow chart or practical model, which shows them what will happen by choosing this alternative method of behaving, can be helpful. Each step needs to be mapped out, not just discussed with the child or teenager. Remember to reward them, as this is a very difficult task for an ADD kid to undertake.

Recognition and praise

Because ADD kids do not maintain relationships for very long they get very little practice in what appropriate or friendly play involves. Even when they play better they are often unsure whether they are doing the right thing. They need to be taught simple social rules or expected behaviours. More importantly, as ADD kids behave more appropriately in social situations, they need high levels of recognition and praise. This encourages them to keep going and reaffirms that they are doing the right thing.

Expect small failures, remember overall gains

Even as ADD kids improve socially they will still make mistakes. It is very much three steps forward, one back. Don't become distraught and concentrate only on the backward step. ADD kids tend to remember only the last thing that happens. Recognise the setback, but begin to plan how to go forward again. Often at these times I go back and list all the successes on one side of a set of balance scales and the few misses on the other side. They will see the overall gain, rather than wanting to give up.

Another way of showing ADD kids that they are concentrating on the few social failures rather than the many successes is to play the $20 for $1 game. Ask your child if he will give you $20 for $1. When he says no, explain that this is how he cheats himself when he looks at his own life. He trades off twenty good improvements for one bad mistake he made socially. Tell him he can continue to do this only if he gives you $20 for his $1.

▶ *INDISCREET BEHAVIOUR*

LOTs OOPs

LOTs OOPs stands for Lots Of Thoughts, Out One Pops. ADD children's brains have thoughts bouncing around all the time. The difficulty is that they don't govern these thoughts, which usually escape from the mouth with little awareness of whether it is polite, hurtful or the right thing to say. ADD kids are very prone to embarrassing themselves or their parents. They constantly have to say 'Oops, I'm sorry.' For example, ADD kids are renowned for telling family secrets at parties.

Obviously we need to be a little more discreet about what we say and do in front of ADD kids. If you do decide to discuss sensitive issues with them, set rules before you begin about where it is appropriate to discuss this topic. Finish the conversation with another reminder that this is a private conversation and not to be repeated. Ask your ADD kid to repeat where and when it is okay to discuss this topic and where and when it is not.

ADD and tough questions

Has your seven-year-old darling come home with one of these questions?
'Mum, why do big girls have periods?'
'Mum, what is anal rape?'

These may be extreme examples, but they are questions parents have rung me about, frantic for advice. Many normal kids ask similar tough questions. The difference is that ADD kids ask them more frequently, and won't give up until every question is fully answered. Often the questions are out of balance with their maturity levels, so how much can we tell them?

ADD kids generally are very perceptive so, depending on age, you are probably better telling them the truth. They will get the information anyway, but this information is often distorted. We are better informing them properly.

With younger kids try to keep explanations simple. For example, one of the answers above could be 'It means that a man holds a woman down and forces her to have sex. But it is strange sex in the bottom. The woman doesn't want to, but the man makes her.' Not only did we make this explanation, we discussed at length how wrong rape is and that it means going to jail.

Unfortunately ADD kids are preoccupied with death, knives, guns, crime and so on. At any opportune time it is worthwhile reinforcing the consequences of such behaviour. Again, we need to begin and end such a discussion with the warning that it is not appropriate to discuss this in the school playground.

ADD kids are troubled about the world; generally it is confusing for them. If you start early being honest with your kids, they are more likely to come to you at a more difficult time. It is a good idea to use aids, such as books and pamphlets, when you explain. It helps ADD kids grasp difficult concepts.

ADD kids will have an insatiable desire to know more, so you will need to limit your number of answers. For example, say 'I will answer only three questions on this topic. Then I am happy to talk about other things, but that is all on this topic.' Be firm then. If necessary explain that repeated questioning will lead to a negative consequence. Remember that as adults we need to set standards, not be governed by an insatiable, irrational eight-year-old's demands.

A word of warning: ADD kids can be hyper-reactive in these situations, so you might need to go over issues several times to ensure they get the message clearly, rather than distorting it because they are being giggly and silly.

▶ *FOCUSING AND JUMPING ON THE GOOD*

ADD kids will not always do everything right. To encourage them we need to identify any small improvement and focus on it in a positive manner as soon as it occurs. As well as looking at social errors we need to sequentially examine successes and praise every small gain. Children will not be motivated or improve if we only pick on their negatives. It also helps them be more sure what is expected.

▶ *FAMILY FUNCTIONS AND OUTINGS*

Do you fret and panic when the invitation to the family barbecue arrives? If so, then you are like most ADD families, because it is a time when many of the family get together to impart their professional wisdom as to what is wrong with your child and in fact how they could manage to deal with him or her much better.

One way to cope is to ignore your child's behaviour, hoping he won't be too bad. Unfortunately you finally decide you can no longer ignore it, your child is so hyped that no reasonable outcome is possible. Another way to cope is to arrive determined and positive but make a rapid retreat as soon as trouble starts. Another way to cope is to withdraw from social occasions.

While it is tempting and seemingly easier, it is important not to totally withdraw from social occasions. While I understand parents' reluctance to go out and be socially embarrassed, unless we provide LEARNING opportunities for ADD kids they will never master social behaviour.

It is wise to limit the time that you would be in a social situation. For example, being at a family barbecue for eight hours will likely lead to problems. Rarely would a young ADD kid cope with this extremely long time. Whether you have to make an excuse or whether you just say that a few hours is as much as your kid can cope with, limit the actual time.

Choose which are likely disasters and avoid them. Use your parental judgement to decide which outings an ADD kid can manage and which they can't. Go to the outings you can manage successfully and avoid the others. With teenagers, I believe we can expect a little more. But remember all teenagers think going out with Mum and Dad is uncool.

Children in adult settings

Rarely would an ADD kid cope over a long period in an adult environment. They have a high need for attention, an insatiable demand for stimulation and little patience. While the relatives might not think it is appropriate, it is better to bring the favourite toy or game, so your kid can quietly sit and entertain himself for brief periods rather than have him destroy the whole social setting.

Parents of young ADD kids cannot expect their kids to play independently for long periods. Equally though, you should not give in to constant demands for all your attention. You do have a right to talk to adults sometimes. Normally I suggest parents set very definite boundaries of when they will and won't be involved. For example, show your young ADD kid a clock. Explain quickly that you will talk from 10.15 a.m. until 10.30 a.m. When the big hand reaches the six you will play with her for ten minutes. Continue to set on and off attention time.

Teenagers and adult settings

Teenagers also have difficulties in adult social settings. Again, let them have some freedom even though other adults without ADD kids may feel it is inappropriate. For example, if it is to be a long party, arrange for your ADD teenager to be able to watch a video after several hours. If your teenager says he can't cope without taking his Walkman, negotiate with him to talk to the relatives for the first hour. After that he can plug his earphones in and wander on his own a bit.

Many ADD teenagers delight in entertaining and leading younger kids. Sometimes allowing them a little responsibility will prove very effective. For example, one of the most difficult ADD teenagers I ever dealt with was given this opportunity at a party. She did such a good job a pre-school director at the party offered her some work experience. From this eventually came a job. I'm sure this saved a potential street kid. Do try to trust your ADD kid's better skills sometimes.

Don't give in to sudden demands to go home right now because they are bored. Rather prepare by setting definite boundaries before getting out of the car, for example saying 'We won't be leaving before 4 p.m.' Try to set consequences before you depart from home, such as 'Waiting until 4 p.m. without arguing means you can have your choice of TV shows tonight and an extra half-hour before bedtime, but arguing means no computer or TV when you get home.'

Removing ADD kids from the audience

Do you feel you can't punish him when your mum is watching, because she'd have a fit? Many parents of ADD kids feel the same way.

ADD kids make it worse because they are very perceptive that parents tend to act differently in front of a crowd. Whenever you need to discipline an ADD kid in a public setting it is important that you remove them from the audience. If you need to talk to your child, quickly remove him to one side, out of the crowd's view. For example, if your ADD boy is beginning to do laps around Grandma's coffee table, don't whisper or hope he won't be too bad. Go to him as soon as he begins behaving badly, remove him to the kitchen and discuss what is appropriate behaviour, what rewards he will get for this and how he will be removed to a Time Out area if he does not comply.

If your ADD daughter is silly in the pool, don't try talking in the pool area; remove her for a brief moment to the side of the pool, explain the rules, then let her return. In most social situations it is important to get in early before the behaviour becomes so excessive that it is uncontrollable. As with other strategies it is important that there are very clear consequences mapped out and definite boundaries. Explain these apart from an audience.

► *LIMIT TIME FOR FRIENDS' VISITS*

With young ADD kids who have very poor social skills, limit time in any difficult social situation. For example, rarely would we invite a young ADD child to have a friend over from early in the morning until late the next afternoon. Rather we might invite a friend late in the afternoon to sleep over and have him return home early in the morning. In this way we would limit the chance of difficulties and not push the child past what is reasonable.

With socially troubled pre-schoolers and early school starters we might limit time even more. For example, we might invite a friend over to play for half an hour, rather than the usual two or three hours in the afternoon. In this way your child slowly learns social skills and is not overwhelmed by the amount of time and effort they have to put into behaving appropriately. As success occurs you can gradually increase time.

ADD kids will impulsively demand more, but not be aware of the consequences of their demands. Use your parental judgement to know what is right and enforce it. If they argue remain firm: 'Half an hour or nothing. It is now your choice. Arguing gets you nothing. Agree and you decide your friend can come over for half an hour.'

Even ADD teenagers can struggle to cope with social situations for extensive periods. We need to reduce the amount of time friends will be in heavy face-to-face confrontation. Try to reduce periods by arranging time when focus is directed elsewhere. We might structure a night to allow your ADD teenager and friend a few hours isolated together, but then set a rule that they will watch a video for a while. The aim is to let your ADD teenager come and go from the interaction with ease.

► *ENCOURAGE THE SOCIALLY TIMID TO TAKE RISKS*

In contrast to hyperactive ADD kids anxious, overly passive and disorganised ADD kids are sometimes prone to withdraw from social situations. They believe they can't cope, or they fear failure. To avoid embarrassment or failure they may deliberately deny social opportunities or fail to take up invitations. The more they withdraw the more they over-internalise their feelings, escape to fantasy worlds and risk becoming more depressed and anxious. They almost stew on their problems to the point that they cannot get out of them. For example, it is not wise to allow your ADD kid to withdraw and play computers all day. This allows him to escape reality and be too comfortable hiding away.

We need to provide rewards and support to take social risks, but also to make it difficult for the timid to remain comfortable at home. I believe we should encourage and push ADD kids gently, for example by suggesting your kid can play with the computer, but only after he has attended a social group (scouts, martial arts, a tennis lesson, inviting a mate over, etc.). We need to praise and reward effort in going, such as having favourite lasagne for dinner for going to scouts. If they choose not to attend then we need to remain firm and withdraw a privilege. For example, state 'You chose not to go to scouts, you chose no computer today.' Don't own the problem. Answer comments like 'You suck, you are really mean' with 'It is not really up to me. You choose to go, you get lasagne and computers; you decide not to go, you decide no computers.'

ADD kids' anger may disguise your ADD kid's feeling that he can't make social approaches. Don't expect your ADD kid to pick up the phone and invite a friend over. Begin in small steps. The first thing we want to achieve is getting the friend over. Begin by making the call yourself. Once he has established a friendship, gradually withdraw support until he can make the call himself. Before the call, practise what he is going to say so that he doesn't get stuck on the phone.

► *LIMITING TIME TO PLAY AND INVITATIONS*

At the other end of the spectrum are the more active, insatiable ADD kids who want someone over all the time. We need to limit this time, especially during the week. One way to achieve this is to set rules, such as Tuesday and Friday are visiting friends' days only. Insatiable demands are met with 'I'm sorry, but rules are we have someone to play Tuesday or Friday, not today.' By having a firm rule there is less to argue with. Don't get diverted into lateral arguments, stick to the rule. If you remain firm your kid will eventually grasp asking on Thursdays never works.

▶ PREPARATION FOR SOCIAL SITUATIONS

Many ADD kids encounter each social situation as a new learning event. They either forget what happened last time or fail to see the similarities in social situations and struggle to adjust from one occasion to the next. It is important that you explain to ADD kids what is expected. For example, if you are going to Grandma's place, re-establish the rules about not touching Grandma's valuable ornaments. Further, set out what will happen if your child does touch and what recognition they will get for not touching.

If your child is going to a friend's place, try to prepare briefly what is expected, the rules they need to follow and how they will manage it. Even with small events, try to prepare. For example, if we are working with a kid on sharing in the back-yard cricket, before the game begins quickly prepare what the rules are, what will happen if he does or doesn't share. The aim is not to wait until the problem occurs, which it surely will, but to prepare, build success and avoid social failures.

Other ways to act

Try to avoid criticising your ADD child too often for any social errors: they will hyper-react and problems will increase. Remember errors may not be deliberate, rather the result of failure to remember or the result of impulsiveness. Try to remember to use a firm, monotonous voice to reinforce the rules and choices. Encourage other ways to act. For example, 'One turn out each. If you choose to argue you are in Time Out on the verandah. If you take turns, then I can stay and play another ten minutes.'

If the situation failed several times and back-yard cricket was abandoned try to resolve the problem later. Wait until calm has restored, then help your kid to look at problems in a different light. Again this might involve a flow chart, showing one flow pattern that led to no cricket, and another that could have led to equal shares and more cricket. Keep explanations brief, otherwise they will tune out.

Interrupting others

I wonder if some ADD kids have in-built sensors to determine when Mum has just begun talking to Dad, so they can immediately interrupt. Besides impulsiveness, interruptions are partially due to ADD kids' fear that unless they interrupt now they will forget what they want to say, or lose thoughts, and then feel very defeated.

While it is unfair to simply expect your kid to wait, it is also inappropriate that he or she should always interrupt.

One technique I have used is to teach a 'target word' system. The idea is that your ADD child doesn't interrupt fully, but gives you a target word to remember, then waits. This word expresses the main idea of what your child wanted to talk about. Alternatively, train your child to write down on a piece of paper one or two words about what she wants to say. Once it is her turn she can have her problem noted or dealt with. Obviously any waiting needs to be highly rewarded in terms of both praise and positive rewards. You need to explain this system and practise it several times. Try to give it a name that can be briefly referred to, such as 'Target Word'.

▶ BULLYING

Bullying other kids

While ADD kids can be the victims of teasing they can also delight in having power over others. Bullying needs to be dealt with in a firm, consistent and strict manner, using immediate consequences. (The Four Step procedure is too slow to use for bullying.) Normally simple rules apply, such as bullying means automatically out for five minutes. For example, at home: 'You chose to bully him, you chose to be out straight away.' At school mild bullying immediately leads to removal from the playground for ten minutes, to be sat against the wall away from others' play. More severe bullying that hurts other kids may need more severe discipline. However, it should be dealt with quickly. Interviewing and disciplining several days later is not effective, as an ADD child will likely have forgotten the events.

Being bullied by others

Some, but not all, ADD kids are over-reactive or timid, thus becoming clear victims for teasing. The normal strategy of telling a kid to just ignore the bullying is likely to be unsuccessful, as most ADD kids are too verbally and physically responsive or too hyper-reactive to cover their feelings. In fact ADD kids often show an overly dramatic response, which encourages the bully to attack them more.

We need to teach them very quick verbal responses for bullies, then a technique of walking away from the conflict. In this way we are trying to encourage your child to quickly and briefly say something back to the bully, then walk or look away as though they weren't affected. We often teach ADD kids to also keep a mental score in their heads for each time they beat the bullying.

Your ADD child will often need to practise with quick responses, saying them over and over again at home until they are confident. Whatever your ADD child says back should not be aggressive or negative to other kids. Rather it needs to be very brief and quickly delivered, without too many words that will be forgotten. If the bullying doesn't stop, contact the school. Bullies will stop if caught out often enough. Examples of what they can say include 'That's original!'; 'Feeling bad?'; 'Need to show off?'; 'Is this supposed to impress everyone?'

▶ INAPPROPRIATE SOCIAL BEHAVIOUR

Fighting, biting and hitting

Some young ADD kids display sudden aggressive behaviour (as do some teenagers). Aggression needs to be dealt with very swiftly and directly. In this setting we would not use the Four Step procedure, but rather more immediate outs. Particularly in pre-schools we often use a rule such as 'Biting is out.' Immediately a kid bites he is removed without discussion to a Time Out chair. The less that is said at this time the better. We don't want to feed attention-seeking behaviour.

If the kid disagrees with the punishment, be repetitive; for example, simply saying over and over 'You bit. No, biting is out.'

Swearing

It is true that generally most kids swear more now. Swearing is often an impulsive behaviour, linked to frustration and aggression. Unless we teach ADD kids to curb swearing they will do it in the most embarrassing or inappropriate situations. Swearing can lead to long-term problems, such as teenagers swearing at teachers and being suspended or adults swearing at bosses and getting the sack. It is the high frequency of swearing and the situations in which ADD kids swear that cause most problems.

As swearing is so often impulsive you need to use a very quick reminder, such as the warning 'Swearing is out.' I would suggest one very brief, interrupting warning, then an automatic out: 'You kept swearing, you chose out.' Don't just expect your ADD kid to remember not to swear, but provide a distraction that reminds him not to swear.

Teenage swearing and abuse

Working on stopping swearing in childhood prevents verbal abuse of parents during teenage years. It is difficult but not impossible to prevent teenage swearing and abuse even if the swearing has been allowed for many years. Equally, if you swear a lot as parents, you cannot expect an impulsive ADD teenager to curb swearing.

When many ADD teenagers swear they are angry and possibly looking for a fight. Try not to buy into the fight by demanding aggressively that your teenager doesn't swear at you. Stay calm and firmly state 'Swearing is not okay, but I am willing to listen if you speak reasonably.' Try to buy a little time out of the heat of the situation and attempt to talk elsewhere; for example, 'Jason, abusing me is not okay. I won't accept that, but if you want to talk reasonably I will listen. I'm going to take my coffee to the back porch. You come out in a minute if you want to talk quietly.'

Sometimes we add an immediate incentive for ADD teenagers, such as 'Tell you what, I'll even listen for five minutes without saying a word, so you can say what you want.' The aim is to avoid backing an aggressive ADD teenager into a corner.

If the abuse continues try to set a limit. As in other strategies the third time a behaviour occurs a consequence must follow. At Step 1 suggest talking outside. At Step 2 restate that swearing is not okay, suggest talking calmly outside but also state further abuse will mean a definite consequence. Let your teenager know a third occasion of swearing means a definite consequence, such as loss of skateboard, computer ban, refusal to wash favourite clothes, withdrawal of Mum's taxi service that afternoon, and so on.

Visual or auditory distractions as reminders

ADD kids rarely transfer what they are taught in clinics or at home into real life. Once distracted by other events they often forget their aim to control bad behaviour. A way to overcome their forgetful nature is to provide constant reminder systems:

▶ switching the watch to the other hand to help a forgetful ADD teenager to remember detention

▶ having kids wear particular jewellery or objects to remind them of what we are working on; for instance, helping an ADD kid not to swear by having him wear a brightly coloured friendship bracelet that he constantly sees as a reminder not to swear

▶ encouraging an aggressive kid not to hit by having a daily sticker on the back of his hand for a month, until the aggression is curbed.

Remember also to reward control of socially impulsive behaviour.
Even with ADD adults we have used similar reminder systems:

▶ An ADD dad I saw had difficulty coming home and remaining calm. Although he hated getting angry he often stormed into the house and at the first whisper of trouble yelled and screamed at his kids. We found a simple solution of placing a bright red sticker on his steering wheel and one on his car keys. They reminded him to go in calm and try to find something positive to look at.

▶ ADD mums complain that they cannot remember to be positive with their kids. We have placed small red dots on the kettle, favourite coffee cup, TV remote control, etc. When she finally reaches for a cup of coffee it is often the time when her ADD child is finally being quiet and well behaved, the best time to praise her kid for being good.

▶ *MISPERCEIVING NON-VERBAL LANGUAGE*

ADD kids are often oversensitive and hyper-reactive. This can lead to an overly emotional response or incorrect perception of non-verbal language. The most easily demonstrated example of this is the tone of voice. For example, ADD kids complain to their parents 'Stop screaming' when in fact the parent is just using a firm voice. Similarly they might perceive slight disapproval on a face as absolute rejection.

ADD kids also sometimes fail to recognise or absorb all factors that contribute to communication. For example, ADD kids often only hear the anger and hurt in an aggressive father's voice. They don't hear and process what their father is actually saying or understand his concern. Thus they react against the anger alone.

Many ADD kids also incorrectly perceive general social interactions. They may miss sarcasm or joking, taking it seriously. Some ADD kids cannot put together tone, body language, verbal information, and so on. This can lead them to misunderstanding a social encounter, for example thinking a hurt person is just acting and having fun.

In negative situations it is important to keep anger, rejection and hostility to a minimum. Try to be aware of tone, facial expressions, threatening hands, standing over kids aggressively, dominating terms, rejecting body position, etc. This is why, in the basic strategies, we concentrate on such features as non-emotional reactions and a monotonous voice. Remember that ADD kids may hear, feel, see and perceive a level of non-verbal language and language that is much more intense than actually exists.

► ATTRACTING OTHER DIFFICULT KIDS

I am amazed at the ability of ADD kids to attract either other ADD kids or kids with behaviour problems. It is almost as though they have magnets that search each other out. I have seen parents who plan to change their child's school to overcome friendships with less desirable kids. Rarely does this strategy work, for in fact in a few days they will seem to have found a similar group of friends.

Many years ago I went to the extent of preparing an ADD kid for a new school by making sure I had several good kids for him to associate with. The good kids were set to show him around for the first two days. Despite all my efforts he had managed to seek out the two other ADD kids by recess and already they had formed an explosive friendship.

► PREPARING FOR CHANGE

Most ADD kids have extreme difficulty in coping with changes in social environments. Therefore whenever you expect change to occur in their lives the more you can prepare them the better. For example, if an ADD teenager is going to go to a new school we would arrange for the teenager to be shown through the school two or three times. We would explain as much as possible of what will happen and what the routines will be. We also should show them clearly what the rules are and what will happen if they misbehave. We would try to give them some form of reminder such as noting in a school diary where the Year Adviser's office is, and what is outside this office that might remind them it is here and how to get there. We would have them write out several reserve timetables in case they lose the original. The more preparation the greater the chance of success.

Don't assume ADD kids will understand change through having previously been in similar circumstances. They often fail to make common associations. If the baby-sitter is to change explain why and how. At the beginning of each new school year many ADD students will take time to adjust and understand the new class system, teacher styles and teacher demands. It is better to prepare your kid for change than let them get into a crisis and then have to try to rescue them.

► *INSATIABLE TEENAGERS, TOUGH QUESTIONS AND SEXUALITY*

As well as tough questions, an often forgotten problem with ADD teenagers is the sexuality issue. ADD teenagers can have difficulty understanding the bounds of what is acceptable. Their impulsiveness can lead to problems. ADD girls can be easily led by impulsive feelings of love. The more aware that teenage ADD girls are of their bodies, their responsibilities, safe sex and their right to say no, then the better protected they are. ADD girls might demonstrate an insatiable curiosity about sexual matters, but it is often because they are confused, they have misheard information or they are bewildered by new feelings. They need caring guidance and reassurance.

Teenage ADD boys have similar levels of confusion and hear the same distorted messages. Unfortunately they are less likely to talk about it. Further, teenage ADD boys can face another problem. A small number of ADD teenagers I have seen have come very close to committing date rape. This problem has usually arisen when they have been sexually active with a girl. In the early stages the girl has been willing to engage in heavy petting or sexual foreplay, but not intercourse. Driven by their impulsiveness and insatiability they have struggled to accept the clear 'no' messages the girl gave. It is often not until their girlfriend screams that they actually become aware that they are doing the wrong thing. Parents or counsellors need to make very clear to ADD youths what is unacceptable force and the severe and serious consequences for continual sexual activity beyond what a girl permits.

Another difficulty is that ADD teenagers can be over-aroused, impulsively looking for reckless stimulation and satisfaction. The result of this is that they often break acceptable bounds. ADD youths often fail to see when their girlfriend is telling them to stop in a sexual encounter. Similarly, ADD teenagers can reject parents' rules regarding no sex because they have a desire to do what they want or to satisfy their insatiability and impulsiveness. ADD teenagers can also over-react to blocked sexual advances, misinterpreting them as rejection.

In more serious relationships, through early adulthood, ADD sufferers can face other problems such as over-rapid sexual intercourse. Partners often complain their ADD boyfriend is too aggressive and rapid, looking for immediate satisfaction and failing to take into account the needs of their partner. Alternatively some ADD sufferers have a tendency to become easily bored even in sexual encounters. They are prone to wanting to satisfy their own needs and then drift off elsewhere.

Even in non-sexual relationships partners complain that ADD sufferers will be very attentive but then become quickly bored. For example, girlfriends of ADD teenagers often complain that their boyfriend is either highly emotional or totally oblivious of their needs. Basically it is all on or all off.

In summary:

I believe that ADD kids have great social potential but need help and guidance to achieve it. while they have weaknesses in social skills they also have strengths. They can be very stimulating and full of fun. ADD kids are very good at adapting to playing with younger kids or conversing with adults. They can have an infectious energy and spontaneity. In later life, if they learn to control weakness they can be real 'people persons'. ADD kids rarely hold grudges. They are willing to try things. They are often fiercely loyal and protective of friends and the disabled.

HOLIDAYS, RESTAURANTS AND CARS

chapter (13)

A re you like most ADD parents who are desperate to get away on holidays and escape many of the difficulties that exist at home, but then find the holidays turn into a disaster? This is largely because ADD kids don't adjust to change, unknown circumstances or disordered routines. Most ADD kids respond far better in a well-structured, formal and ordered environment, and when they go on holidays this is not always possible. The fact that they are actually in a different setting means that immediately structure has been thrown out. I have met hundreds of ADD parents whose first two or three days of holidays are an absolute disaster, and who are amazed that their kids settle down after this.

►AVOIDING HOLIDAY DISASTER

Explain the new system

It is important when going on a holiday that you take the time beforehand to fully explain what exactly is going to happen. Show your child how the holiday will be arranged, what will happen and how everything will fit together. I have even gone as far as drawing maps, marking days off on calendars, using travel brochures and other aids extensively to demonstrate what will happen and where.

Many ADD kids have a very poor concept of time or sequence, so saying that we will be on holidays 'for a while' is fairly ineffective. Rather I suggest you begin with a calendar and cross off the days until you actually leave. Then begin another clear recording system so that they know how long they will be on holidays.

A word of warning: Don't give hypersensitive kids too much notice before leaving. Too much warning can lead to their becoming too anxious or distraught. A few days' notice is enough.

Show them the system and routines

When you actually arrive at the holiday spot, walk your ADD child around so that they understand how things will work, the structure they will follow and the sequence of events. ADD kids often become very distraught and distressed because they do not understand how all things will fit together. You cannot explain every detail and cover every possible event, but a good overview will reduce upset in the first few days. For instance, you might need to show your child where you will be eating breakfast, how lunch will be arranged, where the swimming pool is, and how to return to your room. For the latter, use very clear reminders via landmarks, for example turn left at the fire hydrant after leaving the pool.

On a daily basis it is worthwhile explaining as well as possible what will happen that day. As a general rule, loosely structured holidays when no-one knows what they are doing are not very successful with ADD kids and even teenagers. They seem to cope better when they know what the day will involve and plans have been well arranged and clearly demonstrated. This does not mean you need to run an army boot camp for a holiday, but a fairly firm daily plan seems to help ADD kids. It is also important again that ADD kids have an understanding of time and sequence during the holidays. At times having your child wear a watch or explaining that, after a certain event, this or that will happen next will help them cope with the day. If you are going to stay somewhere until 11 a.m., put a small mark on their watch at the eleven or write the number 11 on their hand, so that they don't keep coming back asking what time we are going.

As an alternative try to take in real time rather than chronological time: 'We will swim until morning tea, then go back to the motel' rather than 'We will swim for a few hours.' Relate real-time talk to things they understand: 'We will be at the pool for as long as the start of school until recess' rather than 'We will be at the pool for a short while.' Regardless of how thorough you are they will still probably ask you six thousand times during the day 'What time is it?' and 'What are we doing now (or next)?'

Explain new situations

Each time a new situation arises an ADD child's impulsiveness will overwhelm them. They will find it hard to resist rushing into the new adventure. You might know the rules of the buffet breakfast; they will just see the jam croissants and grab three. Each time you move to a new or different situation, briefly explain the rules and expected behaviour. Keep it simple and concise but don't trust that they will just know what is expected.

Friends on holidays

As in other social situations, ADD kids often lack all the social skills necessary to make and, more importantly, keep friends on holidays. It is important that you guide them in the early steps; don't rely on your child or teenager to be able to make friends easily. Be also aware that once they make a friend they are likely to overwhelm this friend and almost smother them. You need to govern this to some extent. Although it is a holiday and you want to escape the dramas it is worthwhile putting in a little effort early on. Try to make sure your ADD child is balancing his time between different people at a holiday location and not concentrating on one friendship to the point that the new friend quickly withdraws. It is also a good time to reassure ADD kids about sharing, fitting into games, not dominating play and being willing to follow appropriate rules and turns.

For some ADD kids holidays are a great and different experience. They have made friends more easily, because they are free of their bad reputation from home. This lets them develop better social skills and gives them more confidence when they return home to develop social relationships. It can be great practice for social success.

Types of holidays

Generally we have found that ADD kids do better on highly active, slightly more organised holidays. For example, ADD kids may cope well on a well-planned camping trip, where they are not bound into a motel. They seem to be more successful where there are many activities and they can roam the wide outdoors. They often successfully manage well-structured scout camps, where their leadership can come to the fore. I have also found that they cope better in resort-style accommodation, where there is a high number of organised activities during the day.

Holiday travel

It is important that ADD kids have plenty of stimulation on a holiday trip. Travel is like a classroom: if *we* don't provide enough stimulation, ADD kids will make it. You should avoid trying to restrict ADD kids too much. Wherever possible, use whatever mechanisms are available. This is a case of not listening to the dull theory books. Remember my main ADD premise of 'What works is what works; forget the theory.'

As an example, if you have an ADD child travelling on a plane, don't imagine that they are going to colour in for hours at a time. I have even suggested that parents buy a GameBoy or similar type of hand-held electronic game to keep their ADD child satisfied. Otherwise it is very likely that ADD kids will be unsociable and destroy the plane trip — not a great start to the holiday. It might be bribing but it works to get safely through the plane trip.

Short-term goals for travel

Long trips usually involve parents making countless threats that ADD kids quickly perceive are idle threats or not enforceable. As an alternative, try to break the trip into shorter periods, clearly defined by time or stops. Then set some goals and definite limits. For example, each time they go for five or ten minutes without trouble they earn one point. Ten points earns them a clearly visible reward. Also set a clear limit that has a definite boundary. For example, make up a five-bead string on leather for the rear-vision mirror. Tie a small knot in the middle over which the beads can just be moved. Each instance of bad behaviour is given one warning before one bead is moved over the knot. If five beads are moved over the knot the child will suffer a consequence such as only getting water instead of a milkshake at the next stop. Arguments are handled by keeping it to their choice: 'You chose to muck up. You lost five beads. You chose water.'

Plan a program

Many families of ADD kids are doubly affected as one parent also has
ADD symptoms. This parent loves to run the holiday by whatever
happens next, never thinking ahead. While this is lots of fun it leads to
ADD kids driving parents crazy: 'When are we going to Dreamworld?
Can we go today? Please, you promised.'

This can be a personal choice for you. If you don't mind lots of
questions, have a free and easy holiday. If you do, as far as possible plan
a holiday program. Sometimes I have even had parents make up a little
holiday calendar, such as Monday–beach; Tuesday–Dreamworld;
Wednesday–bike riding and swimming. Let your ADD child cross off
each day as it passes. His incessant questions are then met with a bland
'Check the calendar.' It is quite acceptable to change the program.
Remember though to warn your ADD child and map out briefly what
the new plans are.

Christmas

I particularly wanted to discuss Christmas as it is such a potentially
dangerous time for ADD kids and their families. ADD kids'
hyperactivity and hyper-reactivity can lead to massive problems.
There are some basic suggestions, such as keeping ADD kids well
rested through this period as best you can, talking about routines and
expected behaviour, and limiting time in hyper-stimulating
environments.

It is a good idea to prepare briefly for difficult situations. Don't
expect your ADD child to remember from last year. It is all new to
them. Don't hype them up too much with the excitement of Santa,
presents and activity. It is better to slightly play it all down. Try to keep
your ADD child away from too much junk food.

If things become too stimulating take a break to a more calming
environment. For example, go for a quiet walk down the street rather
than staying in among ten screaming and arguing relatives. Cooling
your child down in the bathroom with a cool washer might also work. If
you are at home a tepid bath sometimes works wonders.

On Christmas Day try to avoid too many surprises. Every child
needs a few but sometimes breaking presents into half-surprises and
half-already-known can reduce hyper-reactivity. Also be careful of
buying breakable toys. Most ADD kids will have them pulled apart
before lunch is served.

Christmas holidays

The person who decided we should have six or more weeks' holiday at Christmas never understood ADD kids. Most of them begin the first day of every holiday with a statement like 'I'm bored.' By the end of holidays most mums of ADD kids are ready for the insane asylum. It is a good idea to break up holidays by enrolling ADD kids in 'learn to' classes, tennis camps, sport and recreation camps, Outward Bound and similar activities. This reduces boredom, adds some structure and gives mums some rest and respite. If you have the opportunity to send an ADD child away to a caring relative for several days, take the opportunity. Other than this, day activities away from home help. My only other suggestion is pray for fine weather and count the days until they return to school.

▶ EATING OUT — IT CAN BE DONE

The almighty being who decided kids should have ADD must have known nothing about schools and restaurants. How else could you explain trying to make a wild, untamed force stay still in a confined place without enough stimulation? Restaurant visits, however, don't all need to be disasters. With a little planning and a tight structure we can be successful.

Planning restaurant visits

You should plan for a restaurant visit in three ways:

▶   Choose a suitable restaurant.

▶   Provide entertainment.

▶   Have a set behaviour procedure.

Is it reasonable to take an ADD child to an à la carte restaurant and expect them to follow the rules? While we might eventually teach ADD teenagers social skills, this is not the place to teach a seven-year-old ADD kid social graces. I advise parents to make a choice: select open, easy, family-style restaurants, such as Sizzlers, Pizza Hut, Family Restaurants, Steak Houses or similar, or go without the kids. If you are frazzled parents of an ADD child you probably need the respite from their constant behaviour. I have gone as far as writing a prescription for parents to go out to dinner alone. This is better than taking the kids to save the baby-sitting fee but having the whole evening ruined by your ADD child's activity and disobedience.

The second rule is to provide entertainment. Some dull theory books will tell you that it is rude for a child to draw or play puzzles at the table. I am sure these theorists never had an ADD child. This is another case of 'What works is what works.' Take along a small colouring pad, puzzles or similar activity. Then set some rules, such as the first fifteen minutes is for family talk, then allow your child to draw or play. This might be the only way you get to talk to your partner or spouse.

The third rule is to prepare a discipline program, explain it beforehand and stick to it consistently during each restaurant visit. One corner on the road from the restaurant, stop the car and very concisely explain three or four expected rules and what will happen if they are broken or if, alternatively, they are kept. Don't try to explain the rules on the way in or after you're seated; your ADD child will already be too distracted.

I normally use a basic procedure in restaurants, which can be adjusted to suit your family. We return to the basic Four Step procedure to some degree. Tell your child he has three clear chances, marked by three counters. Place the counters on the table. Give your child one warning for bad behaviour. A second warning then means one counter goes into your pocket. Each next occurrence of bad behaviour means another counter moves to your pocket. Each time your child misbehaves, identify the behaviour and state 'You choose to break the rule. That is one counter. Three counters gone means out.' There must be a firm rule that if all three counters are lost your child is removed outside for five minutes.

I discussed before about making a name for Time Out so it is transportable. If you are using 'the corner', then the corner now might become the bonnet of the car. If your child loses all three counters, normally you would sit on the bonnet of the car for five minutes. It is important to remove your child quickly from the audience of the restaurant crowd. Otherwise most ADD kids will perceive you are not acting normally and take this as an opportunity to muck up more.

Once the five minutes are up, don't begin lecturing; all is forgotten. Place the three counters on the table and begin again. For more obstinate kids you might need to do this several times over several restaurant visits until the message sinks in that the same thing will happen every time they misbehave.

I accept that this program sounds hard but I have used it myself with my own kids and very difficult kids in a Behaviour Disordered (BD) unit with some success. For example, the BD kids could earn the right to go to McDonald's for lunch on Fridays if they earned enough class tokens. The rules were they got a hamburger each to begin. Good behaviour at the restaurant meant they received a sundae after hamburgers. We used the same counter system. Three warnings meant you sat outside on the pole with Ian for five minutes. If you settled down at the pole you could still earn the sundae, but if you didn't, no big deal, just a cold burger and no treat. Some of the tougher kids made it to the pole five or six times before they learnt the system, but eventually learnt to play the game.

With most kids a separate reward system can be useful. For example, each five or so minutes they are good put a pen mark on one finger. If they fill up five fingers they can choose a dessert.

▶ CARS — *SAFETY AND SANITY*

Driving your ADD kids home from school or to Grandma's place was designed to test your parenting skills to the extreme. It is an unfair advantage to allow an ADD child to sit in the back of the car, where he can attack his little brother or say what he likes, while you have to drive, keeping your hands on the wheel and eyes on the road. At best you can reach round and try to swat his fast-moving legs. Making idle threats about what will happen when you finally get home will rarely be effective, as your ADD child only thinks about *now*. Again, we have had some success by developing a system that gives you back some control and provides definite limits.

Similar to holidays, we have used a token or counter system to set limits. For example, adjusting my suggestions one innovative mum placed three small Matchbox cars in the console. She conformed to our system of giving one warning, whereafter each instance of bad behaviour was handled with brief comment and loss of one car. If all three cars were lost there was no TV for fifteen minutes when her ADD child arrived home. However, if he was able to keep one car he was allowed to have fifteen minutes of Nintendo, which normally wasn't allowed.

I have varied this system at other times. One family had two ADD kids and a non-ADD child who was good at stirring up the other two. This family had a very definite afternoon structure, with play allowed from the time they got home until 4 p.m. If the family fought on the way home and used up all three counters Mum simply stopped the car and waited five minutes. Each stop used up a part of the thirty minutes of playtime. If they kept at least one counter they earned an extra ten minutes of playtime in the afternoon. This gave Mum back some control even though she was stuck in the front.

Separate and stimulate in cars

It is a good idea to separate ADD kids from others where possible, but don't disadvantage the others by always giving the ADD child the front seat. Having rules, such as going to the school one child is always in the front and coming home the other child is always in the front, can reduce arguments. If you have three kids, have one in the front and make the middle back seat off-limits.

Remember that ADD kids coming out of school are ready to burst. They have been confined at length and want to run wild, only they can't do this in the car. Therefore try to provide some stimulation, even allowing them to play games, listen to a radio or Walkman or a similar novelty.

Don't allow your ADD child to badger you or wear you down for treats, lollies or other surprises in the afternoon. Instead develop a set structure that is kept to consistently. For example, make treat day each Wednesday only. If your child hassles on other days keep to a bland, boring, repetitive line such as 'Sorry no treats today. Treat day is Wednesday.'

Saving unnecessary car trips

Many ADD parents make regular trips back to the school after hours, hoping the classroom isn't locked, to retrieve forgotten items. Otherwise parents of ADD kids have been known to buy five school hats at a bulk discount because they know their ADD child will lose them during the term anyway. This is never their fault, in their minds at least.

Problems of not packing bags, losing items and forgetting hats is a part of ADD. It is largely caused by their forgetfulness, sequencing and memory problems. Whereas more typical kids have an image of what their packed bag should look like, ADD kids don't follow a sequence of packing their bag or checking all items are in it. They are too impulsively driven to get out of school.

To save car trips you have two options. With young kids you are better to just take over the problem and check their bag each afternoon before leaving. This will save you some car trips. When they are a little older and you want to teach independence I suggest you develop a checking procedure. As an example we place a small, discreet checklist on a clip inside the child's school bag. Don't make this a written list, as they won't read it. Rather, make a small card with a drawing of items to be checked. Cover it in translucent coloured contact and clip it to the inside of your child's bag. It is there to distract them and remind them to check possessions. Later on remove the list and put a bright tag or toy figurine on the zipper of their bag. This tag serves as a reminder to check possessions.

In summary:

There are many other situations where ADD parents like you feel they need help. They are too numerous to describe. I suggest you take these basic rules and adapt them to each situation. Often you will be delighted with your own inventiveness and feel good about your own success.

CLASSROOM STRATEGIES

chapter 14

*I*n the past teachers have struggled to understand ADD and have rarely been fully or even adequately trained to manage ADD students. It is true that the education profession has been slow to accept ADD. However, there are other issues involved in this matter.

▶ *INADEQUATE TEACHER TRAINING*

Up to several years ago many of the positive, innovative teachers I met complained they had received no training or in-servicing at all in relation to ADD. Further, new teachers could not look to experienced teachers in the past, as they also had very little exposure to ADD. Like many parents, teachers were bewildered by a difficult behaviour and learning disorder, which did not respond to normal classroom management strategies. Teachers finishing university even now have limited training in how to manage students with ADD. There is a critical need for more diverse and intense teacher training in ADD management. Given that conservatively three to five per cent of all students have ADD, teachers must be trained to manage this significant group of needy students.

▶ *TEACHER ATTITUDES*

The other and more unfortunate side of the story is that there have been very negative, critical and ill-informed teachers, principals and education staff who have roundly criticised parents and made them feel very guilty about accepting what is necessary medical treatment. The fact is that ADD does exist and medication works with appropriately diagnosed ADD students. Furthermore, we should have concentrated our efforts on helping parents rather than criticising them. Teachers who accept medical treatment of asthma and diabetes but reject the need for medical treatment of ADD are derelict in their duty of care to do their best for students. Further, I am convinced that little good has come from negative attacks on parents. Very few parents will return home motivated to do better with their child if they have been abused as being useless or dysfunctional parents.

Try to work together now

It is as nonproductive for teachers to attack parents as it is for parents to be seriously critical of teachers in this day and age. Rarely will we achieve anything if we do not try to work together. If we maintain a very defensive approach little is likely to be achieved. The recent gains made in clinics across Australia have been built on goodwill and cooperation between parents, school and professionals.

▶ *ADD PARENT STRATEGIES APPLIED TO TEACHERS*

Teachers generally need as much support as parents. Many of the strategies and procedures that we have demonstrated for parents in earlier chapters also apply to teachers, classrooms and schools in general. There are, however, other issues that need discussing and these are illustrated in the following pages.

Over-diagnosis

Many years ago a small group of dedicated ADD professionals, including myself, fought against a doubting majority to have ADD accepted. It is hard to imagine that at that time we might have argued against accepting all ADD cases. However, this has occurred due to a very small number of cases of over-diagnosis damaging the cause of genuine ADD cases. In rare circumstances some teachers are being overwhelmed by sometimes having five or six ADD students in the one class. They accept that maybe three or four of these cases are genuine, but doubt the other one or two. Thorough and intense diagnosis is critical to avoid the many genuine ADD cases being damaged by very occasional cases of over-diagnosis.

Under-diagnosis

A far more significant problem is still under-diagnosis. Almost every week in my clinic I encounter a teenager with very clear ADD symptoms. Careful diagnosis confirms that the teenager suffers with ADD. They often are very frustrated, defeated and depressed. They regularly have severe learning difficulties, but have slipped through the system. Potentially the greatest danger is long-term ADD sufferers who remain undiagnosed.

▶ ADD IS NOT AN EXCUSE

While the great majority of ADD parents are dedicated and highly motivated, a very small minority see ADD as an excuse and rely solely on stimulant medication, such as Ritalin or Dexamphetamine, to solve problems. Taking a child to school, saying he has ADD and simply handing him over to the school, excusing all his behaviour thereafter, is highly irresponsible and will prove unsuccessful. Research has clearly shown that relying on medication alone does not lead to better long-term outcomes.

Students with ADD do suffer in school. To many ADD sufferers school is like ten years' hard labour. If we were in a job and failed daily, as ADD students often do at school, we would quit. ADD students don't have this option other than truanting or refusing school. We do need to understand their pain and help them to survive more easily. However, ADD should not be used as an excuse. Parents who state 'But he has ADD, he can't do that' will rarely build confidence and success in their children. Rather we should accept that some tasks are more difficult but work toward overcoming these. A students who uses ADD as an excuse should be calmly dealt with by stating ADD is not an excuse.

Own the problem

ADD is not an excuse in childhood, adolescence or adulthood. Rather the ADD sufferer needs to be dealt with firmly and calmly, and helped to *own the problem*. Success with ADD students in school comes through identifying problems, owning the behaviours and learning strategies to overcome the problem.

Alex

Alex, a high-school student I saw, had built up to thirty-eight detentions, under a school rule that every missed detention meant you owed an extra one. Alex was not deliberately missing detentions; in fact he would often remember half-way home after school, only then it was too late. Alex's mum wanted him excused because he had ADD. He could not be excused. While I agreed the detentions had become a little ridiculous, Alex and I owned the problem. We developed a simple technique. Each time Alex received a detention he simply moved his watch from his left hand to his right. As it was uncomfortable it reminded him to turn up for detention. Don't expect ADD students to own problems overnight, but we can help them to do it and to stop using ADD as an excuse.

▶ REASONABLE EXPECTATIONS

Students with ADD need very particular classroom environments and management strategies. There are very different schools and teaching styles, and the following suggestions are by no means a prescription that must be followed. I hope they might be adapted to an ADD student's current classroom environment and teaching programs where possible and within reason, given normal school strategies and policies.

As with parents, teachers should not expect immediate success or overnight wonders. If you are working with an ADD student, remember you are in this for the long haul. It is only reasonable to aim for year-long goals, not having everything right by next week. Set a plan for what you would like to achieve over the whole year.

Who has ADD in the class?

In most schools ADD is being accepted as a medical condition. Once this is achieved it is important that teachers are aware of which of their students has ADD. In the distant past I encouraged parents not to tell staff in some instances, because they would be criticised for drugging their kids, turning them into zombies, etc. However, as these bad days leave us we need to be well informed, and it is equally important that information is fed back to professionals. Teachers can also be a very valuable source of information, particularly in customising ADD students' medication.

Recently as I was giving a talk in a high school it became apparent the staff had no idea who had ADD. The principal took this as privileged information for himself and the school counsellor only. My talk became pointless: if staff didn't know who had ADD, how could they apply strategies? Equally, teachers need to know who does *not* have ADD. There are simply conduct disordered, emotionally disturbed and dysfunctional family cases for which ADD strategies would not be useful, or in fact inappropriate.

Horses for courses

Sometimes parents believe every teacher should be suited to ADD students. The reality is that ADD students very quickly decide whether or not they like a teacher, and they can be inflexible. Interestingly, they are most inflexible with inflexible teachers who aim to beat this ADD nonsense out of them. Similarly, ADD students will soon perceive when a teacher doesn't believe in ADD and will act up on them. A teacher who merely punishes and never rewards other than in exceptional circumstances will be quickly tested by an ADD student.

In general, ADD students do best with firm, highly structured but adaptable teachers who are consistent from day to day, keeping to routines. They like teachers who praise but equally set definite limits for their behaviour, not changing the rules daily. They operate best when the teacher has firm boundaries and they are clear about where these boundaries are.

A relaxed, over-flexible and laid-back or creative teacher may struggle to have success with an ADD student. As parents, try to choose the teacher who best suits ADD if this is possible. You have a right to politely approach the principal to stress your child's special needs. Don't accept that you have no say in the issue, but also realise that you cannot *demand* your choice of teacher.

▶ *FIRM*, STRUCTURED SCHOOL ENVIRONMENTS

ADD kids generally are confused by inconsistency, change or disorganised routines. They like things to be the same every day. They eventually accept reasonable but firm limits, where they are not forced to make decisions too often.

Too many choices

Many years ago I agreed to moving a teenager from a rather disorganised high school to a more formal private school. This teenager found it hard not to be influenced by peer pressure. For instance, he left home every morning with football socks in his bag to change into just to be cool. Then began a constant game of escaping detection at school. When I next saw him after the move one of his first comments was something like 'It's cool. You just have to wear black socks. I don't have to worry about getting busted any more.'

One-to-one is best

There is no doubt that in an optimal environment we would teach ADD students on a one-to-one basis. While this may be possible and definitely preferred in remedial tutoring lessons it is not possible at school. Many parents have campaigned hard and long for very small classes of solely ADD students. Putting eight ADD kids together can be disaster. If you find managing your ADD student difficult, imagine eight of them together all day. Try to avoid groups in tutoring, but in a large class the best compromise is a very structured, firm and consistent environment.

Reduce distractions

ADD students are too easily distracted and taken off-task. While removing distractions alone will not solve all problems, it does help to reduce disruptions. Most ADD students will benefit from being in the front row, with an uninterrupted view, away from windows and outside movement and separated from noisy kids. Try to make allowances for what most distracts each ADD student. For example, students with auditory processing difficulties are very easily distracted by noise. I would not place this student near a school aisle where people walk, doors bang, etc. Similarly, ADD students with visual processing problems are very easily distracted by movement. Keeping these students away from windows, flickering lights, moving trees outside, etc. will help.

While it might be tempting to dismiss a disruptive ADD student to the back of the room, it rarely proves effective. There are too many distractions between the student and the front of class, the blackboard and where most teaching occurs. Even for those teachers who move around the room, the front of the class is still the centre of most activity and therefore should be where the ADD student is. It is still most free of distractions, for example when copying from the board. Generally they have their back to most of the distractions in the classroom.

Seating position

Seating ADD kids by themselves is best in junior school years. While most ADD students will dislike this arrangement for a day or two they soon realise they are far less distracted and can work in peace. Later, when improvement is noted, I suggest placing them near a calm, helpful student but not next to another who is talkative or disruptive. If you have groups of tables I have still found it better to initially seat ADD kids by themselves. For example, in one class we have three ADD kids. There are five groups of five kids in learning groups, but then three separate tables spread evenly across the front.

In high school, I still try to bring ADD students to the front and centre of the class. Sometimes I have been able to convince reluctant students by keeping a record of class offences and detentions gained at the front or the back of the class. If they can see for themselves that it is better for them to sit in the front they are more likely to comply. However, most high-school ADD students want to be cool, and it is not cool to choose to sit at the front. They usually will not have the self-esteem to stand up to peer pressure and taunting that they are 'sucking up' if they choose to sit at the front.

As a teacher, try giving the ADD student the excuse that by being the 'baddy' they were moved to the front. Work with them, but let their mates believe you forced the move.

▶ *FILTERING DISTRACTIONS OR LACK OF STIMULATION?*

Early theories on ADD suggested that it was really a filtering disorder, that ADD students could not filter out distractions. The assumption thus was that if we removed all distractions the student would not suffer any concentration problems. It was then found that even if all distractions were removed and the work was boring the student could still be easily distracted. This early theory was dismissed in favour of a second: ADD was in fact a problem of lack of stimulation and interest.

It is my professional opinion that both theories hold some weight. I would suggest that while removing distractions does help, building interest helps equally. The most successful cases I have seen not only build interest but also make sure that distractions are reduced. The reducing of distractions also depends somewhat on learning style (see pages 203–6).

Regular frequent breaks

Once an ADD student loses concentration they will rarely return to working at an acceptable level for a very long period. It is like completely exhausting a battery. It takes much longer to recharge the battery than topping it up occasionally. ADD students need to have a structure of highly interesting and stimulating work with regular breaks every twenty to thirty minutes in primary school. I have found particularly that giving a student a five-minute break every twenty minutes or so means that over an hour more work is produced, even though the student may have had three breaks.

Stimulating interest

ADD is not just a filtering disorder (that is, an inability to filter out distractions). ADD students demand very high levels of stimulation. Wherever possible, then, try to keep work interesting and alive, for example by changing tone of voice, having visual stimuli rather than long talks, showing clear rewards for brief spells of on-task time and allowing study in some area of interest. An ADD student who is bored will be more easily distracted and thus create disruption, voluntarily or involuntarily.

Tune them in

All ADD students have a deficit in attention span. Despite the best teaching an ADD student will lose concentration. Therefore, when you really want to have an ADD student's attention you must tune them in first. Again this relies on learning styles. If a student learns best through auditory-verbal instruction using a brief tone or verbal message, such as 'Listening now', will help them tune in. A student who learns best through visual stimulation might need a tune-in card on his desk, a tap of a target behaviour card on his desk, or visual interference, such as waving a hand before his eyes. A student who learns well through kinaesthetic stimulation will respond best to a light tap, touching or motor movement within their personal space.

Don't try reasoning

'Son, pay attention to me; I'm trying to teach you something here about responsibility. Do you understand what I am saying son, etc. etc. etc.'

The only problem is this student's gaze is drifting out the window and despite your teaching skills he keeps going off at irrelevant tangents. Have you tried to reason at length and debate with an ADD student in class, to find you only end up defeated? It is as true for teachers as for parents that long-winded reasoning must be avoided with ADD kids. I have seen very bright, capable teachers destroyed by trying to debate with an ADD student. Long drawn-out reasoning also seriously disrupts the education of others, as it saps teacher time.

Reasoning may be feeding the ADD problem by directing too much attention to the ADD student. Some older ADD students, with oppositional and conduct problems, delight in upsetting teachers, seeing it as a victory. The basic ADD parent strategy that we should speak less and more concisely, and act more quickly, is also appropriate in the classroom.

▶ SELF-ESTEEM

Be discreet

It is very important wherever possible to ensure that an ADD student's self-esteem is not damaged in the classroom; for example, long-winded lecturing constantly attracts very negative attention to the ADD student. Because of their impulsiveness and explosive nature they are unlikely to accept this for long and will react to avoid any further embarrassment. Similarly when we use reward and rebuke systems, they should be as discreet as possible. This is even more true with high school students. Being cool is everything to a teenager, so bringing attention to their ADD problems will surely cause a greater level or escalation of problems.

For these reasons we often use systems such as cards, coins and so on, which can be managed in a much more discreet way; for example, a student who calls out far too often may be given five red tokens on his desk. Each time he calls out inappropriately a teacher simply removes one of the tokens. Once five have been removed for calling out impulsively the student then automatically does a five-minute Time Out period or has a five-minute loss of privileges. In this way we don't feed the attention-seeking and the student is not overly embarrassed for his behaviour.

A similar discreet method of raising awareness of 'off-task' behaviour is a red/green traffic-light card system. A red and green card is kept at the teacher's desk or on the student's desk. When the student is 'off-task' the card is flipped over to red and flipped to green when 'on-task'. 'On-task' green time is rewarded by blocks in a bucket, tokens or points. If the student remains on-task the green card is tapped and a point or block given. In this way we can build awareness of off-task behaviour but not destroy self-esteem by constant rebuke. This has sometimes been effective in high school.

Coded systems for high school

In high school we also use a coded recognition system. As a simple example, when one disruptive student is on-task the teacher merely taps his desk with a certain ring, clearly telling the student he is working well. This coded system is prearranged. The student discreetly records the number of taps of the ring, which are rewarded at the end of the lesson. Similarly, when the student is misbehaving, we try to keep discipline messages brief, for example a coded touch of the teacher's nose and one statement, such as 'Ben, calling out' rather than 'Ben, I've told you dozens of time about calling out in class' and so on.

Status in class

ADD students typically have poor status in the classroom. Sometimes the other students play at trying to catch the ADD student misbehaving. They delight in 'dobbing' on every little thing the ADD student does. Alternatively, ADD students may be seen by others as the reason the class gets into trouble or work is incomplete.

Sometimes we have changed this lack of status and acceptance by beginning a brief class status program. For example, a rule is made that each time the ADD student receives a five-minute reward through the magic-bucket system (see page 197) the class gets a point. When the class earns five points the whole class gets five minutes of game play. In this way the ADD student wins the class rewards. Other students now encourage the ADD student to be good rather than expecting misbehaviour.

A word of warning: Make sure the class reward is achievable. Don't set too high a level so that the class constantly criticises the ADD student for not achieving rewards.

► MANAGING APPROPRIATE AND INAPPROPRIATE BEHAVIOUR

Frequent and immediate rewards

It is very important that we use frequent rewards with ADD students. An ADD child cannot concentrate for a whole day or even for an hour for a single reward, for example when he is expected to concentrate from 9–10.30 a.m. for one 'smiley' stamp in his behaviour book. While this may be a strategy that other students can handle, an ADD student often cannot concentrate for more than ten to fifteen minutes. The result is that he goes into class trying to be good but by 9.15 a.m. has forgotten this. He then gets into trouble throughout the morning. As he is about to go to recess he is likely to remember his smiley stamp and expect it, based on his behaving for the last few minutes. He will have forgotten all the misdemeanours in between. The system fails because an ADD student cannot keep concentrating for ninety minutes for one reward. Therefore we need to replace this with a far more immediate reward system.

The magic-bucket system

The magic-bucket immediate reward system involves the student being set two or three goals, for example to stay seated and not call out. Every five to ten minutes that the student actually meets these two goals his achievement is recognised and a small block is dropped into a magic bucket on his desk. We do not wait ninety minutes to reward him. As soon as he has six blocks in his bucket he is given a reward, such as five minutes' free time on the computer. I am well aware that this means that he is distracted and off-task for five minutes but I have clearly found in many classes that this five-minute break is very effective and actually beneficial. Again, ADD students need constant breaks in concentration. Once fatigued past their concentration level, they will rarely return to reasonable levels of concentration.

Other immediate reward systems

When the novelty of the magic bucket has worn off and become boring, we have replaced it with a series of flip cards, beads on a knotted string, checker counters in a small tube, stamps to fill a small sheet of ten blank squares, small dot stickers to fill a happy face, marbles in a plastic tube and similar systems. With pre-school children we have even used lifting a child's fingers while they sit on the mat until a fully open hand gets a reward. The aim is to keep the rewards small, simple to give, able to be given frequently and fairly discreet. High-school teachers may need to use even more discreet systems, and high-school students will not accept magic systems.

The red card warning system

A different system should be developed for inappropriate behaviour. It is important that the student knows when he is behaving badly and what will happen. The warning system should be different from the reward system in that you should not take back blocks from the magic bucket for bad behaviour. A simple example is the three red card system. Each time the student behaves inappropriately the teacher leaves a red card on his desk. Three red cards automatically means five minutes' Time Out. Another system is three-strikes-out checkers. The student begins with three counters on the corner of her table. Each time she breaks one of the behaviours she is otherwise being rewarded for (for example, she calls out repeatedly) one token is removed. The teacher simply taps the 'calling out' card on her desk. If she loses three tokens then she receives five minutes' Time Out. This does not mean she loses her blocks as well. When she returns to her desk she keeps the blocks she had in the magic-bucket system as it is separate.

Consistent discipline and consequences

'But I didn't think I'd go to Level 5 and get suspended' or 'Everyone else did it. I didn't think Mr Samuels would mind.' Does this sound familiar?

Even though the ADD student misbehaved, he was not aware enough of the definite consequences for his behaviour. The more consistent the rules and the more consistent the consequences, the easier an ADD student will adapt. We try to establish very consistent and stable rules and consequences that are not affected by moods, emotions or outside events. For example, if an ADD student is to be given a number of warnings before he is sent outside the classroom, it should be clearly demonstrated how many warnings there will be. It is important that they know a consistent and routine number of warnings will be given. Remember that many ADD students have learning difficulties. A quick reference to consequences will not be absorbed.

Therefore consequences have to be clearly mapped out and demonstrated. If a student is near suspension, map out on a flow diagram where the student is up to and the next step. Get him to repeat what will happen.

► REDUCING DEMANDS ON TEACHER TIME

Many teachers complain that behaviour reward systems require far too much effort and time from teachers. I agree that extensive time sampling or behaviour recording systems are too involved and are difficult to work with ADD students. The aim of the magic bucket and similar systems is to reduce this problem. The teacher is able to move freely about the class, still teaching. If the ADD student is working well, the teacher merely touches the 'stay in seat' card on the student's desk, then takes a block from a pocket and puts it in the magic bucket. No extensive praise is recommended. If we were using a flip card system, the teacher would merely flip a card and praise briefly, but would not greatly interrupt teaching.

Better positive time than negative

It is important to mention that many ADD students will normally cause far more negative disturbance, taking more teacher time, than this positive reward system involves. I have found that the amount of negative disruption is greatly reduced with this system. Therefore, less time is spent overall with the ADD student and more of it is positive time.

► APPLYING LIMITS
Don't overdo praise

Many ADD students are oversensitive and over-reactive, sometimes hyper-reactive. For this reason it is wise not to overdo praise, as many ADD students will become overwhelmed and too hyped up. Their good behaviour can lead to silly behaviour after too much stimulating recognition. Try to give very brief praise and then encourage a quick return to work.

Definite limits for rewards

'But I just want to finish this level, Miss. It's not time up, anyway. Let me finish, Miss.'

In the magic-bucket system (see above), we might allow five minutes' free computer time for gaining ten blocks. To be successful any rewards or punishments must be tightly structured and be given for a fixed time period. When we first instituted the magic-bucket system we found that ADD students did not understand the time limits. Therefore, as with the home strategy, we used a cake timer next to the computer. When the student begins on the computer as a reward, the timer is set. As soon as the five minutes is up he must return to his seat. If he argues he is threatened with losing privileges for the next half hour unless he cooperates. Without a very tight structure like this rewards will not be successful. In other systems, for example if we reward with shots at the basketball hoop, ten is the maximum number of shots; taking more loses the basketball for a brief period.

ADD students have poor understanding of sequences and consequences. How often we hear ADD students say 'But I didn't think about it; I didn't think it would happen.' An ADD student should clearly know where he is heading and what will happen. If he is to be rewarded with five minutes' computer time he needs to know how the five minutes is measured and what will happen if he exceeds the limit. If he receives permission to play, he needs to know the boundaries for that behaviour and what will happen if he breaks the boundaries.

Don't assume ADD kids know behaviour will be rewarded. Many distrust the reward system. The more oppositional think it is a 'rip-off'. ADD students must be aware of exactly what is expected and what they will receive for meeting expectations.

▶ EQUALITY OF REWARDS

A criticism of the magic-bucket system is that other kids don't receive the same level of help. While I believe that all kids need rewards I also believe that other kids are happy with less frequent rewards and can wait a little longer for them than an ADD student. Further, other kids are capable of working on group goals, such as all helping an ADD student to behave better. It is possible to explain to them that by the ADD student being on this system everyone will benefit. Most other kids will accept this as long as they get their stars on the class wall chart, occasional stickers, merit certificates and the like. Lastly, but sadly, I believe that the other kids know that the ADD student is a pain at times and are happy to try something to counteract this.

Explaining to other kids

If we expect the other kids to help they must be aware of the class's aims and their own role. Most often I have asked the principal or similar figure to take the ADD student briefly while we explain to the rest of the class that we are introducing a new system to help 'John'. Their role is to help 'John' to be good so that the whole class benefits. Talk about the good things 'John' does as well as how they can help overcome any bad behaviour, for example by ignoring attention-seeking or class-clowning. Make sure that the rest of the class knows of their reward system so they don't feel too disadvantaged. This method of explanation is not appropriate in a high school, where more discreet systems are needed.

It is not appropriate to tell the class as a whole what the ADD student's problem is, to use diagnostic labels like ADD or to set them up for being teased by telling the class that they are on medication. Otherwise, very soon the ADD student will be teased in the playground for being on 'psycho pills'.

▶ POSITIVE ATTENTION

Obviously, ADD students can attract a high level of negative attention. Unfortunately, this also means that they rarely attract positive attention. Perhaps one of the saddest things I see with ADD students is how rarely they are rewarded in particular classrooms. While a number of teachers are very positive and constantly reward and recognise the ADD students in their classroom, regrettably the majority of ADD students receive few rewards and little recognition. A typical example is a student I saw recently. Over a whole year he had received only one minor merit note. Many other students had twenty gold stars, had reached their spelling master's badge, obtained their writer's licence and had both merit certificates and merit notes. This little ADD student had but one merit note for the whole year. It is impossible to believe that any student with this extremely low level of reward and recognition would have any motivation left.

As demonstrated in the magic-bucket system, the emphasis should be on small, highly frequent rewards, rather than a long wait for a reward once a month, once a term or even once a year. Students with ADD typically have very low self-esteem and thus need more awards, recognition and praise than normal students although their behaviour may not always have attracted it. I am not promoting Mars Bar philosophy, where all efforts receive token rewards or lollies. Genuine recognition, stamps, affection, notes home for good work and merits for completing work are very powerful motivations.

Meaningful rewards

It is important that the ADD student sees rewards as meaningful and worthwhile. Some very good immediate reward systems have failed simply because, while we thought the rewards were good, ADD students found them boring or worthless. That is why I have chosen more interesting and perhaps radical rewards like free computer time, shooting hoops outside, free drawing or craft time, being boss of the class briefly, or sport time for the class, and so on.

Novelty of rewards

Did you ever set up a behaviour-reward system that worked wonderfully for a week or two, only to find that mysteriously it became less effective and eventually became useless? It is likely that the rewards were no longer novel. Unless an ADD student has an extreme and persistent need, most rewards will eventually become boring. Therefore we need to rotate rewards or invent new magic-bucket systems and provide novel rewards and recognition, for example ten raffle tickets that buy five minutes' free time. Similarly you might need to set a reward menu, where rewards on the menu change.

▶ KEEP TASKS TO A MINIMUM

ADD students are quickly overwhelmed by too much information or too many expectations. They have greater ability to learn if they are presented with only one or two tasks and not confused by too many. For this reason it is wise to try to change only one or two behaviours at one time. For example, if we were using the magic-bucket system we might work on staying in place, not calling out and writing neatly. At least one of the three rewards should be easily obtainable. Be sure the reasons for the rewards are very specific; for example, avoid general and undefined behaviour aims such as 'being good'.

Simple class rules

Try to avoid long lists of written class rules. ADD students rarely read (if they can read) or pay attention to long written rules. A few broad, very simple rules are more effective. They may need to be kept near for referral. Often with ADD students on a behaviour system we draw rather than write out aims.

► LEARNING STYLES

Learning style refers to a student's ability to learn far more adequately through one form of instruction than another. ADD kids' learning styles are idiosyncratic. Parents during an assessment may comment, for example, 'She is great at drawing and craft, but just can't express herself. She gets stuck for words' or similarly 'He can watch me pull a toaster apart and then do it without help. How come he can't remember his maths tables?' The reason for this odd and unequal performance is that for most ADD students there is a preferred and more effective learning style.

The simplest example is that many boys with ADD have language-based learning difficulties. The result is that they learn very poorly through verbal instruction. However, they are often far more able to learn through practical demonstration or visual instruction; for example, they build complex Lego designs but their reading is very immature.

Differences in learning styles

Research to examine ability to learn in the normal population has shown that there are no significant differences in learning acquisition and memory recall based on teaching through a particular learning style. This is likely because the discrepancies between learning styles in the normal population are nowhere near as significant as in ADD students. Many ADD students show very marked discrepancies between learning abilities. The result is that they learn very well through one learning style but struggle severely to learn through another.

For example, an ADD student with auditory-verbal processing and sequencing difficulties will struggle severely to listen and stay on-task in an English lesson but may learn excellently in a woodwork class. As a result it is more important that we teach ADD students, where possible, through their most capable learning style.

Determining learning style

An intensive and professional psychometric assessment will determine the nature of a student's particular learning style. This should give parents and teachers significant benefits in knowing how to deal with an ADD student. A simple example is that an ADD student with visual processing problems will have difficulty copying from the board, drawing diagrams, keeping writing neat, etc. This student may need extra verbal instruction.

In contrast a student with auditory sequencing problems will have difficulty learning through verbal instruction. Therefore, if the teacher were to give a series of instructions such as 'Take your book out, put the margin on the left-hand side, write the date, use this heading and begin with this sentence' the student would be lost. However, if the student had a visual reference sheet to check these details from, he might well be able to complete the task successfully. Similarly, if he gets one instruction at a time he will cope. Alternatively, if he is shown what to do he will succeed.

Occasionally ADD students even get in trouble for trying to use their own learning style. The student above with auditory sequencing difficulties will not absorb the auditory-verbal instructions, and so will begin looking around to pick up visual cues as to what he is required to do. The student might then be told to get back to his work and stop looking around and copying others, which he needs to do to survive.

In contrast the student who learns better through auditory instruction, but has significant visual perceptual difficulties, will work differently. These are often the students with very poor handwriting, poor drawing skills, who have difficulty copying from the board, poor coordination, etc. In the case of these students copying homework from the board would be difficult. The homework might not be completed in time or incorrect homework might be written down. Similarly in a high-school class, a student would simply not be able to copy notes from the board within a set period. This student could be given a copy of teacher's notes, and he could be allowed to sit and listen, through which he learns best. He should not be kept in for being slow. This style of learner would not understand what he looks at but would benefit from extra verbal instruction.

In teaching ADD kids with visual processing difficulties, new visual material should be tied in with past learnt concepts. Material needs to be presented in a very organised and meaningful manner to show the relationships of its separate parts. Blackboard and handout work will be difficult and will need auditory or verbal reinforcement. They will tend to learn piece by piece, so concrete approaches will help in understanding. Large visual images will need to be broken up and given a specific method of attack. Activities need to be presented in clear, logical steps to help with attainment of goals. Discussion of the steps to goal achievement will help. Assistance may be required in organising and planning set work, otherwise the student may get lost in detail, ignoring the whole. Homework will need supervision to ensure all work is being covered, not one topic only.

Practical learners

A few ADD students learn poorly through both visual and verbal teaching, seeming only to learn through practical demonstration or a hands-on approach. Unfortunately many of these students will always struggle at school. However, because of their practical strengths they often go into trades, computers, artistic or similar careers and earn better money than many of their supposedly more capable peers. These kids often do better in art, technics, science practicals and similar subjects. Where possible they will benefit from practical demonstrations or being shown how to complete tasks. They work well with functional learning aids, such as pie charts or blocks to help maths understanding.

A whole-school approach

No teacher can totally and always cater to a student's individual learning style. However, with awareness and flexibility we have been able to help many ADD students learn more adequately. In one very small high school we have adopted this as a school ADD strategy. Even roll books are coded A, V or K (for auditory, visual or kinaesthetic) to help teachers remember how each ADD student learns best. High-school teachers could not be expected to remember all the ADD students' learning styles without some prompts.

Learning styles, school, work and later success

The learning styles and teaching methods used in schools are mostly those through which ADD students typically learn poorly. Thus school does not suit their learning style and in part this causes them to under-achieve. In contrast, the real world is far kinder to them. This is why, if we can get ADD students from six to eighteen years of age successfully, they often blossom to be great successes. History is full of such success stories of late-maturing bloomers. Remember both Albert Einstein and Winston Churchill were square pegs who failed to fit the round holes of school life.

▶ *TRANSFERRING THERAPY TO CLASS*

Ever tried having a long talk to your ADD child, during which she promises to be good and never to do it again? Only ten minutes later she has forgotten and impulsively made the same mistake, without even thinking about it. This is probably why the average ADD parent's most common complaint is 'If only she would stop and think.'

Imagine then being an ADD specialist who relies on talking to ADD students and hoping they will remember your talk when they re-enter the real world of school. The reality is that ADD children treat their therapists in the same way, telling them they will behave at school, but forgetting before they leave the building. This is not to say therapy cannot work.

An ADD student will listen attentively in therapy if they trust their therapist. A therapist can go through, at length, why remaining in their seat, staying on-task or similar behaviour would be to their own benefit. The student will leave the clinic significantly motivated for his or her own good. The difficulty is that a good part of this message is lost once the student leaves the clinic and is distracted by other events. It is very important that we have means of transferring skills from a therapy or clinic setting to a classroom. Thus we use prompts or reminders wherever possible in the classroom.

A simple example is to have a drawing on an ADD student's desk to remind him to stay in his seat. Although he may have been motivated first thing in the morning, ten minutes through the lesson he will have forgotten that he was working on staying in his seat. A simple and discreet drawing on the top of his desk (perhaps on cardboard and covered in clear 'contact') will constantly remind him of this.

We often tie this strategy in when using the magic-bucket system. For instance, each time the student stays in his seat the teacher taps the appropriate behaviour drawing on the desk, then drops a block in the bucket. The teacher does not even have to stop talking to the rest of the class to reward the student.

Reminders and social skills

I have worked with many students who have been subjected to teasing. I encourage them to wear a brightly coloured, trendy surf bracelet to remind them in the playground not to react to teasing. It is important that they have this kind of reminder to prompt them at a particular time. The activities of the playground distract them from remembering the appropriate skill to use when teased. This is very true for students who have social skill deficits. They need constant reminders of the skill that we are trying to build in, because their impulsiveness often overrules their willingness to develop better social skills.

Sometimes we have instituted teacher-controlled systems. For example, one aggressive lad is constantly reminded to be gentle in the playground through a raffle ticket system. Each recess or lunch he collects from his teacher two or three raffle tickets which he must give to the teacher on playground duty. Several times through the play period he must come back and collect a teacher-signed raffle ticket. This constantly reminds him to be gentle, not aggressive. At the end of lunch he trades in his raffle tickets for an immediate reward.

Prompts that suit learning styles

Reminder prompts to transfer therapy from the clinic to the classroom are more effective if they in fact suit a student's learning style. There are many commercial and privately made systems to support this. A very basic example is a student who was constantly out of his seat but had very good visual learning skills. I simply had a small red stripe placed along the left and right edges of his desk. Each time he impulsively went to move from his seat, the red stripe distracted his impulse, and helped him to remember to remain in his seat. Once again, we may sometimes use their distractibility to our benefit. With other students I have used small prompts such as dolls with brightly coloured hair as reminders, stickers on pencil cases, or rulers balanced on the desk edge and sticking out.

As a funny aside, only once has this system seemingly failed. I had provided the above strategy and initially the student responded well, staying in his seat even though he often made it half-way up. There was also a Tourette's Syndrome sufferer in the class, thus the teacher was well aware of tic behaviour. The teacher became suddenly concerned that our ADD student also had developed a tic, referring to the student's flicking of his head to the left. In fact, when we observed him he was constantly turning and returning after noticing the red stripe.

Similarly, with some students who have had good auditory-verbal skills but poor visual skills, I have had teachers use some form of tone to prompt or remind them. With one student this simply involved a tapping sound on the desk and a reminder of one target word, for example 'talking'. Sometimes we have used small tones such as a chime or pitch tone to attract attention briefly and discreetly.

A similar commercial product is the MotivAider, which has been used in the USA. The MotivAider has a small receiving earphone that fits in the student's ear. The teacher carries a stimulus box on which the teacher can push a button that produces a tone to remind the student that he is off-task and to return to what he is doing. While not cheap, this is a discreet tool that caters to the student's learning style.

High-school prompts — Mark

Trouble can start if a high-school student is openly embarrassed, so for them we have developed more discreet methods. With Mark, an aggressive student who liked calling out, we worked on not calling out or answering back. Rather than feeding attention-seeking, the teachers raised their hands when Mark called out and rolled a ring on their fingers. This was a coded message or prompt to Mark. If he complied, there was no discipline; if he continued, consequences were applied. Further, if Mark continued, the teachers made a small X on his desk in chalk as a reminder things were deteriorating. Three Xs meant Mark was removed outside to isolation for the remainder of the lesson. Equally if Mark was on-task the teachers would quietly place a hand flat on Mark's desk and make a ticking motion. Mark knew he was heading toward an A in his behaviour record, which he wanted to achieve. Either way Mark had a visual prompt that he was off- or on-task to meet goals.

Particularly with older ADD adolescents any obvious systems will cause upset and distress. We have used discreet card systems as an alternative or touching a certain item on the student's desk as a coded signal. The more discreetly coded the signal is, the more successful it is likely to be.

► GIVING INSTRUCTIONS

Repeating messages

Because so many ADD students, particularly males, have significant auditory-verbal learning difficulties it is necessary to repeat messages where possible. Many ADD students will feign understanding by nodding their head or appearing to be tuned in, but the reality is that they are not processing and absorbing information. Particularly in primary school, it is very important that messages be given several times, where this is possible. While this interrupts normal teaching it is better than having the student disrupt the class continually because he does not understand what is going on. It is a good idea also to give an expanded message to the class in general, then break this down to a very concise message for the ADD student, giving one or two instructions at a time. For example, try to avoid using long sentences such as 'Margin on the left and then write the date up here on the right.' It will be more appropriate, after having given a general class instruction, to tap the ADD student's book and state merely 'Margin here, date here, margin here, date here.' When this is completed, 'This heading here', etc.

Separate instructions

Instructions need to be given very clearly with very definite separation after each instruction. An ADD student should only be given a minimum number of brief instructions at one time, perhaps only two to three. When the student has understood and completed these, further instructions may be given. Going through 'first . . . next . . . last' will help. Checking that instructions have been understood may help if possible.

Give sequencing prompts

Seeing 'first . . . next . . . next . . . last' as a way to attack a task will not be obvious to an ADD student. Instructions may be given a number of times, but through no fault of theirs, the student will not be able to follow them. Pressure on the student to just learn to do it is not appropriate; rather he should be continually shown the steps that need to be taken.

In a large class this may be difficult. To relieve pressure on the teacher it is often helpful to set up a 'buddy system'. A capable and helpful peer in the class can sit next to the ADD student, help quietly, showing him what to do. It is advisable to rotate the system at least twice a year so as to not place too great a burden on one student. For many kids, this is the only way to survive.

Forgetting work

Often, learnt material is forgotten due to poor delayed memory recall. Thus, what an ADD student learns today may be forgotten tomorrow. The student may initially understand the task at hand, but after beginning, can lose track or be distracted and then forget what is to be done. Rather than punishing try to encourage the ADD student to find the way to completion, with gentle assistance. Despite having done it before, he will not necessarily remember all necessary steps, but with a few prompts many ADD students find they can recall. Without prompts they may well get ten out of ten when Mum practises spelling on Thursday night, but only five out of ten on Friday in the spelling test.

▶ SEPARATE REWARDS FROM PUNISHMENT

ADD children are very perceptive but often don't have the social skills to match this perception. The result is that if they believe they are being mistreated they will act in a very negative and reactive manner. For example, if we give a reward to an ADD student but then take it back, they will believe we are cheats and not to be trusted. They will then likely behave badly as a result.

Therefore we need to develop systems that have one set of very clear, highly positive rewards for good behaviour and a separate set of consistent, firm discipline measures for negative behaviour. It is important that the two measures are different and separate. It will not prove effective with an ADD student to have the same reward and punishment measures, for example giving tokens but taking them back for bad behaviour. Alternatively, for instance, appropriate behaviour may result in five minutes' free time on the computer or five minutes' extra play, but discipline would involve perhaps five minutes' Time Out or being restricted from completing an activity the student particularly likes.

The more Oppositional or Conduct Disordered an ADD student is the more critical it is that rewards and discipline are kept separate.

Oppositional and Conduct Disordered ADD students in particular want to control their own outcomes. If they believe that we control the system by being able to take away earned rewards, they will refuse to participate. For example, if we are using the magic-bucket system, it would be totally inappropriate to give five blocks and take two back for bad behaviour. The student may go as far as to deliberately manipulate you into taking all of the blocks so the system is ruined. Rather we would give magic-bucket blocks for good behaviour and have a separate red card warning system for poor behaviour, where three red cards means five minutes Time Out.

▶ RESPONSIBILITY AND LEADERSHIP

ADD students are rarely given the opportunity for leadership roles or responsible positions. Teachers may comment 'I couldn't possibly trust him with that.' However, I have had great success in giving ADD students limited amounts of responsibility that they can handle. For example, many ADD students are skilled with computers. Many I have worked with have become great computer monitors. We might let the student share duties with another responsible student during the lunch-break, so they don't become overwhelmed. We keep tight rules, such as any monitor errors or silliness leads to one day's suspension as computer monitor.

Helping other troubled souls

While ADD students might struggle to relate to peers their own age they are often very good at relating to younger students. This is a skill that we can use to their benefit. ADD students are very good at helping younger children with problems. A very obvious example of this was with an intensive reading scheme I was involved in many years ago. Older students who returned from the special IR reading unit were encouraged to go to the kindergarten or Year 1 class to help new readers who were struggling to read. In this way they were not embarrassed in their own class due to weaker reading skills, and they got a thrill from helping younger kids. The ADD students who undertook this scheme turned out to be most effective, supportive and successful, often more successful than the learning difficulty students who had no ADD.

▶ PROJECTS

Projects are very difficult tasks for ADD students to complete for a number of reasons:

▶ sequencing difficulties; they find it hard to organise their work and put together separate pieces to make a complete whole

▶ quite significant difficulties in researching material; although they can occasionally express themselves verbally, comprehending notes from boring written text and presenting these in a logical and formal style is very difficult

▶ forgetting what they have to do by the time they get home despite understanding what is required in a project in the classroom.

For these reasons it is important that any projects have very clear instructions and separate and logical steps to follow. Again it is a time when we must be aware of an ADD student's learning style. For instance, if the student is having visual practical difficulties but learns through auditory instruction they may need an extra five or ten minutes at lunch to have the examples explained over again. In contrast, if the student has poor auditory-verbal learning skills, then they need more diagrams, arrows and visual directions on the project for them to organise the work and put all their pieces together.

Projects do have the potential to be positive experiences for ADD students because they call for creative, artistic, lateral and interesting thoughts that can be well presented. However, the difficulty is organising the more formal tasks such as note-taking and actually writing the assignment out. This is a time when many parents do need to support their children as they will not necessarily see how to put a complete project together.

▶ HOMEWORK

Homework is perhaps the greatest struggle of all for parents who have ADD students. If we consider that most children do not like doing homework, ADD students resist more than most. A significant factor is that ADD students have great difficulty recalling specific information at a later time. Because of their distractibility and delayed memory weaknesses they forget what occurred in class. Trying to recall class examples becomes a meaningless exercise that night.

Again it is important that they have lots of prompts or guides to get through homework.

Homework organisation

ADD students do better with a well-organised homework environment. Try to remove distractions and loud noise. A quiet background noise often reduces awareness of normal household noise. Learning disabled ADD students need to be near Mum or Dad to ensure supervision and help. This might mean primary students using the dining-table while by high school they should be returning to their own desk. It is wise to set a definite homework time to avoid rushing. If homework is finished ahead of time they stay at the table and read or draw quietly. Try to keep pre-schoolers away as best you can.

The Magic Cup for sibling rivalry

'But Mum . . . Mum, how do you do this? Mum, you're not helping me, it's my turn . . . Mum, you always help him but don't help me . . . Nathan, you're a jerk, I hate you . . .' Familiar?

Homework time is a disaster if you have more than one child with needs. Try to develop a consistent rule as to whose turn it is next for help. The aim is to objectively divide your time and remove arguments. One way of doing this is to use the Magic Coffee Cup rule: whoever has the Magic Cup is the next to ask a question. If you need to ask a question of Mum, you have to pass the cup to your brother or sister first. You ask your question, and clearly it is then your brother or sister's turn to ask the next question.

Homework help

I am often asked by ADD mums if it is acceptable to help their children to complete homework. The reality is that with an ADD child you may have to pass your School Certificate again. While I don't recommend that you do the homework for your child, there are many instances, because of their poor recall, when an ADD student will simply not know how to do their homework and without a good deal of help will not survive.

The general rule I have applied is that we should treat it like baseball: let them have a few tries but don't damage self-esteem by making them strike out. We don't want your child to fail altogether, lose confidence, become frustrated and then throw a tantrum.

Try the three-strike rule, which is as follows. If your son is stuck with homework, ask him to try it again but stay close by. If he is still stuck then give him several prompts to help him in solving the problem. If, however, after this second try he is still struggling, don't allow him to fail. Therefore don't let him strike out, but solve the problem with him or for him, keeping his attention on the solution. The aim of homework should be to prevent further defeat, because they are constantly failing.

Helping them write

With older students and teenagers with handwriting difficulties it is acceptable to provide help in writing. ADD students will often write in infantile fashion, for example writing in very simple language. They do this to avoid making spelling mistakes or because they are slow. This can be overcome by Mum or Dad writing out as the child dictates. A golden rule though is not to correct their work or turn the assignment into your own. You might also refer to the computer comments later in this chapter.

Homework speed

It is important to look at the speed at which an ADD student is able to complete work. A great majority of ADD students process information at a slower rate. For instance it, will simply take them longer to write down their spelling words. Similarly it will take them longer to write out an essay or read a large amount of text. Therefore it is important that we consider reducing an ADD student's homework load. It is inappropriate to expect an ADD student with a reading rate maybe three or four years below his age level to complete the same number of texts, novels and so on that everyone else in the class reads. Similarly, if an ADD student is much slower in writing it may take that student an excessive time to write out twenty spelling words three times over. The aim of homework should not be to destroy the parent-child relationship. Homework should only be a support to class and for these reasons it is sometimes necessary to reduce an ADD student's load. This might mean, for instance, doing five mentals rather than twenty. Similarly with reading we need to compensate in whatever ways possible such as allowing the student to be read to, listening to books, being able to view videos, etc.

Limit the amount of information

ADD students are easily confused by too much information. Their short-term memory is like a small cup rather than the large vessel that other students have. When the cup becomes over-full two things happen. What is in the cup becomes confused and a large amount of information spills out and is lost. This is often how ADD children retain information, so we need to present it in small chunks, repeatedly given, until mastery is achieved. Further, remember ADD students forget learning. Their small cup may also have a small leak through which learnt information slowly drips away over time till recall is lost.

As ADD students are confused by too much information, again this suggests the need to reduce the homework load. For example, if we try to teach an ADD student fifteen new spelling words, often the number of words will simply confuse. However, if we were to teach just seven spelling words consistently over three nights, there would be a good chance that retention by then would be complete. On the other hand, if you try to teach them the fifteen words, at the end of the three nights we would be lucky if they remembered five. If you are not sure as a teacher ask an ADD mum how often she has achieved a perfect score on Thursday night only to see her child score less than fifty per cent correct the next day in the spelling test.

Take advances slowly

A fault in some tutoring programs is that when a gain is made there is too quick advancement to the next level. The ADD student becomes confused because they are exposed to far too much information in too short a time. Again their small cup is over-filled. If an ADD student begins to make some gains do not immediately step them up to the next level. Success today does not mean they have mastered the task; in fact it will likely be forgotten tomorrow. It is more important that we remain at that level for two or three days until we are sure that the student has mastered the work.

Copies of notes, diagrams

When homework is set, it is helpful if an ADD student actually writes it down or gets it in some written form, for example writing in a homework diary or perhaps having a copy of the teacher's notes. ADD students cannot rely on their weak memory to recall later what is expected. The homework must have very clear directions or indications as to how to complete the task. Many ADD students will not recall instructions that the teacher gave in class. Simply writing 'Do maths homework' will not be effective. An ADD student likely will not remember what maths was set to do or how to go about the task. Similarly making a comment in a homework book such as 'Write story for English' will not be appropriate, as the ADD student will probably forget what the topic is or how much is required and when it is due. This is more true for high school, where homework is not left on the blackboard for days to check. Therefore make sure that ADD students are writing down the homework and making clear notes on all requirements.

Getting homework to school

As a parent do you reach the end of the term only to find at the bottom of your child's bag pages of crumpled, messy homework sheets, completed but never handed in? The same homework you slaved for hours to get your ADD student to complete? While this is frustrating it is not deliberate. ADD students are simply so forgetful that they can complete homework but then forget to hand it in. They may be too distracted by play or simply forget. Don't excuse this behaviour. Rather teach them to own the problem by placing a bright, fluorescent homework folder on the top of the school bag. Thus, when they open their bag at school, the bright folder reminds them to hand it in.

▶ EXAMS AND UNDER-ACHIEVEMENT

ADD students in later primary school and high school often find comments in their report cards such as 'It would be helpful if Jenny studied more for exams.' It is true by this time of their academic careers that many ADD students lack motivation, partially a result of repeated failure. They do need help, support and structure to study successfully.

However, it is also very true that many ADD students will under-achieve in exams compared to class performance. ADD students may be more able to discuss topics in class or complete immediate tasks. As a result of delayed memory weaknesses they struggle to recall very specific information in exams. Exams seriously disadvantage ADD students as they tend to measure their weaknesses: their organised and sequential memory. It is regrettable that school exams rarely measure equally their strengths, such as lateral thinking, creative problem-solving, mechanical, practical or artistic ability and other more diverse talents.

Exam study

ADD students need special study environments. They will study better in short breaks, such as thirty minutes on, five minutes off. They are also very distractible. A few ADD students will prefer total quiet, but I have not always found this to be the best method. Total quiet means that distractions are more noticeable. ADD students will often be less distracted if there is a steady, quiet background noise, but not loud, head-banging music! Try to set tight rules, such as the radio can stay on if the volume stays at level two, but not level seven.

Active study

ADD students have very poor retention rates, especially if bored. They do not comprehend well what they read and they struggle to recall later. Simply reading will lead to boredom, distractibility and very little recall. Therefore study needs to be very active and structured. Try to encourage a student to read using a highlighter pen for significant passages. Encourage stopping at the end of each paragraph to make a few brief notes; otherwise a whole page will be read without comprehension, leading only to a need to reread. Try to keep notes very brief, using consistent abbreviations. Use highlighters, underlining, stars, etc. to indicate most important areas.

Each set of study notes needs to go into a subject study folder. As a parent or helpful teacher, don't rely on their organisational system; help them set one up. Otherwise you will go into their room to find a mass of dog-eared, messy notes spread throughout the room in no order at all. A good set of personal study notes is invaluable.

Reward study

ADD students find study hard, boring and meaningless. They are not good at working for long-term goals, such as success in exams that are weeks or months away. Rewarding your ADD student for effort is very worthwhile. Be sure not to invade their privacy, but it is acceptable to knock on the door and offer a drink and favourite biscuit as a way of saying you appreciate the effort they are making.

A *word of warning*: ADD students under pressure are very prone to caffeine abuse. They are terrible procrastinators. Where possible, help them to keep to a study program or routine.

► ESSAYS AND STRUCTURE

Similar to their problems with exams, many ADD students have difficulty with story assignments or essay writing. They have good creative thoughts and perceptive ideas, but they struggle to get these thoughts on paper. Often essays have comments such as 'Very good ideas, but this essay lacks structure, organisation and logical expression of themes. Sentence structure needs some work.'

As a result of sequencing difficulties ADD students struggle to string thoughts into a logically flowing sequence. They often have basic expressive language disorders. Lastly, they are distracted by their own creative thoughts. Thus, they may begin one sentence, but drift into another thought midway through that same sentence. ADD students fear that if they do not get the idea down right now they will forget it.

Computers help to overcome these problems by allowing drafting and simpler rewriting. ADD students need to be encouraged to build brief notes that can be converted into an essay plan. As the essay is written the plan is kept nearby. As each idea is completed it is ticked off on the plan to maintain sequence. Any interrupting or distracting ideas are written on a notepad, while the current sentence is completed.

Spell checkers

The use of a spell checker or computer will help to overcome spelling weaknesses. ADD students need to be taught how to use spell check programs, as at times their spelling is too wild for the computer to recognise a near alternative. ADD students need to be shown how to enter various alternatives to assist the computer search.

► COMPUTERS

Computers are such a wonder for ADD children that it is almost as if they were designed for them. They have been a great career choice for many ADD adults. Computers have supported many ADD students at home and school, significantly improving their performance and presentation. For many reasons I support the use of computers with ADD students.

Computers allow ADD students to write and present work in a much more appealing and precise manner. Often their poor, messy handwriting is overcome. I have also found that many ADD children can type more quickly than they can write. Computers allow ADD students to check their spelling more easily. Spelling, grammatical and sentence structure errors can be corrected without having to rewrite a whole passage.

Parent help with computers

A computer allows parents to help their ADD child to present their work in a better fashion. For example, an ADD child might dictate a story while the parent types on the computer. It is important you don't write the story for them. I believe it is acceptable to, in essence, effectively be your child's secretary, but not a corrective secretary. It is also acceptable as a parent to type your child's weekly spelling list into a software game, so they can work on it in a more enjoyable format.

Computers, stimulation and multi-sensory input

Computers also are suited to ADD students as they are a highly stimulating, multi-sensory tool. The latest multimedia computers with CD-ROM provide visual, practical and auditory stimulation at the one time. There is a good deal of research that suggests that ADD students learn much better through multi-sensory stimulation. Computers stimulate ADD students' interest. Their general willingness to complete work on computers is higher than for traditional learning techniques. For example, an ADD student might play a computer spelling game, but will resist writing out his spelling words three times. ADD kids' application to computers is also high, which leads to more motivation and success, thus giving them a greater sense of achievement.

Correcting and saving time with computers

Many ADD students process with difficulty. This means that they simply take longer to complete tasks, for example to copy notes from the school blackboard. Similarly, it may take an ADD student several times longer to write out a story. If an ADD student has to write a draft story or essay, then rewrite it with corrections, it will take them a very long time. This is simply unfair. However, a computer allows for corrections without the excessive time demanded to rewrite a whole piece.

Computers and self-esteem

Computers help ADD children's self-esteem. It can be devastating for an ADD child to spend half an hour writing out a story that then looks messy and is full of corrections, and later the teacher puts red marks all over it. Similarly a teenage student has a better chance of receiving a good mark if his essay is presented well, rather than having his self-esteem being damaged through lower marks. Hopefully, if an ADD student uses a computer a much neater and more presentable piece will be submitted, which the student can be proud of.

Computers in the classroom

Computers are entering the classroom at a rapid rate. It makes sense that ADD students have greater access to computers in the classroom. Parents cannot demand their child have a computer in the classroom, but some more progressive schools have negotiated to have a small laptop in some classes, particularly in high school.

An important note: It is unwise to go to this length until your child can type with some precision. Many computers have built-in self-teach typing programs.

I do not believe it is within the educational budget of most schools to provide such a high level of computer support to ADD kids generally. However, I have found many second-hand computer dealers will sell out-of-date 286 laptops for several hundred dollars. They last for several years, are closer to being within parents' budgets and are very suitable. I would not recommend purchasing an expensive laptop, as they may end up forgotten, lost or destroyed from rough, impulsive handling.

Computers and other provisions in exams

In examination situations, ADD students who have severe learning difficulties and who have become accustomed to using a computer and printer have been able to use computers successfully. It allows ADD students to present work more equal to their potential, rather than being disadvantaged by poor writing, spelling errors or slow speed. A recent development has been that computers are allowed in some states' formal Education Department examinations. In New South Wales, for example, the Board of Studies grants special examination provisions to all children with disabilities, not just ADD students. In fact allowances have been granted for varied special provisions, such as extra time, quiet settings, readers, writers, rest breaks, etc. Many other states have yet to negotiate and develop such allowances.

A *word of warning:* Quite justifiably, as a general rule, special provisions appear to be granted only to students with evidence of long-standing learning difficulties, well-documented cases and significant weaknesses. It is not an expectation that will be met automatically in every case.

► THE NINTENDO CLASSROOM

Parents and teachers often wonder why learning disabled ADD students struggle in the classroom but are experts on their Nintendo or Sega games. The reality is that Nintendo suits their learning style, is highly stimulating and very rewarding, and requires quick responses. Perhaps we can look at what makes up a Nintendo game and sum up classroom strategies at the same time. If we could incorporate the following Nintendo features in a classroom we might well design a near-perfect classroom. The only missing features would be intrinsic rewards, teacher warmth and understanding. Obviously we could not realistically expect such a wonderful classroom, but imagine one that included the following features:

- ► a system of clearly graduated steps between levels of learning
- ► each new level is only slightly more difficult, so kids are not overwhelmed
- ► stimulation through new material being slightly different, not boring work
- ► frequent and high levels of stimulation, with breaks in concentration
- ► rewards that are given immediately achievement is made, not delayed
- ► a high level of rewards that are achievable, provided regularly, and often
- ► rewards that don't over-excite kids, but require a quick return to work

- ▶ a clear relationship between behaviour and rewards
- ▶ a system of very clear and easily recognisable levels of achievement
- ▶ prompts that tell what comes next or is expected
- ▶ warnings of danger, either seen or heard, rather than reliance on memory
- ▶ a clear way to see where things are going
- ▶ rewards and punishment that are very consistent, not governed by emotional factors
- ▶ all that happens occurs in a set routine and structure
- ▶ if a mistake is made the child is not totally sacked
- ▶ repetitive mistakes are met by a slightly more severe punishment
- ▶ opportunity to make up for errors
- ▶ a mistake is met by quick loss but then the chance for achievement
- ▶ opportunity to save and record achievements
- ▶ self-esteem is boosted through achievement and recognition by peers
- ▶ a multi-sensory approach that relies on visual and practical skills.

In summary:

Teacher training in management of ADD students and professional acceptance of the disorder are vital to positive outcomes. The nature of school and classroom environments, as well as the learning task itself, places great strain on ADD kids' resources. Strategies designed for their special needs actually save teacher time and offset disruptions to other students.

MULTI-MODAL MANAGEMENT

chapter (15)

ADD was first discussed almost a century ago, using different terminology. Little was known about treatment then. A decade ago the primary treatment for ADD was stimulant medication, such as Ritalin and Dexamphetamine. Attempts to control hyperactivity, provide counselling, use diet cures and teach ADD kids to learn effectively met with limited success. The lack of success was largely due to our limited knowledge of the condition. Since then we have made rapid advances. We are now using medication more effectively and developing broad treatment packages for a wide range of problems associated with ADD. This broad-range treatment is referred to as multi-modal management of ADD.

A problem of ADD treatment in the distant past has been too great a reliance on stimulant drugs and thus not enough emphasis being given to multi-modal treatment. Research has clearly shown that when a child is treated only with stimulant drugs (such as Ritalin, Dexamphetamine or other drugs) the long-term outcomes for ADD children are not significantly better. There is often an initial gain but only minimal and not very significant long-term gains. However, the long-term outcomes for ADD children are much better when multi-modal treatment, often including the use of stimulant drugs, is undertaken.

Professionals who treat ADD responsibly and carefully are alarmed when ADD is described as a 'flavour of the month, trendy condition' which is straitjacketed by strong drugs. Rarely does this responsible group rely solely on stimulant medication. Furthermore, ADD is not a trendy condition. It is very similar to child abuse, in that both problems are seen far more often this decade simply because we are better at detecting and identifying them. ADD has always existed, but in past decades overactive kids left school illiterate, covered their problems through adult life and never reached their potential. No doubt the higher number of ADD kids identified in this decade has highlighted issues of diagnosis and treatment. The criticisms levelled at ADD can be answered through using multi-modal management, in terms of both modal diagnosis and modal treatment.

► THREATS TO ACCEPTANCE OF ADD

I believe a major threat to the long-term acceptance of ADD are professionals who are not thorough enough in making a diagnosis or fail to use multi-modal treatment plans. Further, those few parents who rely solely on medication or use ADD as an excuse or fail to consider all their child's needs, could well damage the overall acceptance of ADD.

The great majority of ADD children are well managed by professionals and parents who use multi-modal methods. But we must be determined not to allow isolated cases of over-prescription, over-diagnosis and poor treatment to occur, which could lead to criticism of ADD as a whole. What then is multi-modal management, diagnosis and treatment?

► DIAGNOSIS

Much of the debate over ADD has concentrated on the use or abuse of stimulant medication, such as Ritalin. The debate has paid little attention to the anecdotal records that show that few risks or side effects occur where ADD is carefully and appropriately diagnosed. A broad multi-modal diagnosis can greatly reduce the risks of side effects or incorrect use of drugs. A good diagnosis will almost always lead to good treatment and thus increase the likelihood of positive outcomes.

Quality of diagnosis

Making a diagnosis of ADD is not a simple matter. ADD is a complex disorder that has many variations. It can also mimic other disorders. While this book is a practical guide, it relies on the premise that ADD children need to be treated differently from other children. Further, I have discussed using different strategies to manage Co-morbid Disorders, such as Oppositional Defiance, Anxiety ADD and others. To undertake such individual and different therapy it is necessary to rely on a thorough and precise diagnosis. Given the availability of more scientific and diagnostic measures to assess ADD, parents can rightly demand more scientific, thorough and precise diagnosis than is offered by a fifteen-minute consultation by a busy professional.

Broad-based diagnosis

As different professionals often use slightly different techniques to assess ADD, not every diagnosis can possibly be the same. Just as there are many ways to assess a tumour, through a variety of scans and X-rays, there are several related ways to assess ADD. There is no one ultimate method of diagnosis. Regardless, the overall aim should be to develop a wide-ranging and thorough means of differential diagnosis.

A good diagnosis will aim to assess from a broad base: a number of informants, situations and observations. A brief impression in a single situation, such as a professional's clinic room, is not a broad diagnosis. A good part of diagnosis should involve listening to parents and gaining a good grasp of the history. The diagnosis should aim to separate ADD symptoms from other possible conditions, which can be similar. This method is referred to as making a differential diagnosis.

Differential diagnosis

A rigorous professional will ask wide-ranging questions, not just those relating to ADD symptoms, thus lessening the chance of an inaccurate diagnosis. They will also use several different assessment measures, both subjective and objective. In this way the professional will attempt to differentiate the symptoms of ADD from those of similar disorders, such as personality disorders, depression, anxiety, substance abuse, caffeine abuse, situational disorders, etc. It also helps to identify other Co-morbid Disorders, thus allowing more precise treatment.

Confusion with similar disorders

Some theorists have claimed that ADD can be easily mistaken for autism, epilepsy, depression, the effects of unresolved family conflicts, the effects of abuse, and other conditions. I do not believe that experienced clinicians have the difficulty theorists suggest they might. By applying a broad differential diagnosis similar disorders can be identified and confusion eliminated. Experienced clinicians, using objective measures, can be precise in making a diagnosis.

Not a single situational assessment

An ADD child should not be assessed solely on behaviour in a single situation. For example, an ADD child may behave in my clinic because he is in a one-to-one situation, receives frequent praise and reward, has no distractions and is with an experienced person. In contrast, a nervous child who is made to wait excessively in a boring waiting room while the doctor runs late may display uncharacteristic restless behaviour. Relying solely on such single situational assessments can contribute to a lesser level of accuracy in diagnosis.

Your child's ability to concentrate on the computer at home does not equate with remaining on-task in a large class full of distractions, where language skills are essential. Similarly, your teenager might concentrate well in the technics and art classes at school, but nowhere else. A rigorous assessment will rely on reports from several situations, such as home, school and social environments, as well as clinical assessment.

▶ DIAGNOSTIC MEASURES

A practical management book is not the appropriate place to discuss in detail all the diagnostic measures available to clinicians. The first step of diagnosis is for parents or teachers to look for symptoms consistent with ADD. The main symptoms to look for are inattention, impulsivity, possible hyperactivity and constant insatiability. They might appear as academic problems, learning difficulties or under-achievement at school, poor social skills or behaviour problems. It is then appropriate to refer the child for professional assessment. This might be conducted by a paediatrician, a psychiatrist or a psychologist, preferably a combination of these.

In brief, a preferred diagnostic model might include:

▶ Diagnostic and Statistical Manual (DSM-IV) criteria — a manual clinicians use

▶ a structured interview — an interview routine that asks not only ADD questions

▶ a patient history (from conception to present, family and relatives, developmental, medical, school, home, relationships, past assessments and therapy, success of help, etc.)

▶ a neurometric assessment (for example, a Q/EGG or a CPT or a TOVA)

▶ a psychometric and educational assessment (for example, a WISC-III or Binet–4, as well as assessment of reading, comprehension, spelling, mathematics,

▶ a learning difficulty and learning style assessment (for example, discrepancies between IQ and basic skills or specific skill areas such as memory, concentration, sequencing, etc.)

▶ a behaviour assessment, using questionnaires and behaviour rating forms (for example, to compare a child to children of similar age and sex)

▶ other information, such as school reports, observations, exams, examples of work, etc.

It is important to note that rarely are all of the above assessment measures administered when making a diagnosis. While many of the larger capital city specialist ADD centres use a similar method, not every other centre has access to all of the above measures. However, the reliability of diagnosis does increase by using a broader range of assessment measures.

Irregular patterns in IQ profiles

A profile of sub-tests completed in an IQ can be graphed. Most ADD children have very irregular and significantly different IQ profiles, their sub-test scores fluctuating greatly. Generally they are talented in one group of skills but deficient in other skills, in simple terms a seesaw effect. Often ADD children are assessed briefly on an IQ scale and their teacher or parents told that their IQ is average. This can be grossly misleading. The total IQ is calculated by averaging the sub-tests scores. In many ADD children the extreme highs and lows cancel each other out to produce an average result.

A better description might be that the child has great strengths and specific weaknesses that restrict brighter potential. Describing an irregular IQ profile as being an overall average is like describing a roller-coaster ride as average. An average ride is a cruise along a flat road with a few gentle curves. The 'roller-coaster' IQ profile is often reflective of many ADD children's lives and academic careers, full of highs and lows with little stability in between.

Multi-modal diagnostic assessment

A multi-modal diagnostic assessment should have several aims:

▶   to confirm that the child has ADD and rule out all other possible disorders

▶   to identify any other co-existing or Co-morbid Disorders, such as Oppositional Defiance, Anxiety, etc.

▶   to help in developing individual and specific plans of ways to best manage the ADD child.

In summary, a multi-modal diagnosis should primarily lead to a multi-modal treatment plan, which increases the likelihood of positive outcomes.

▶ MULTI-MODAL TREATMENT

To most effectively treat an ADD child a multi-modal treatment plan should be developed. This can include:

▶   stimulant drug therapy

▶   parent management training

▶   school management

▶   immediate behaviour modification

▶   individual counselling

▶   remedial work and specific therapy

▶ support network building
▶ self-esteem enhancement
▶ social skills training.

Other strategies might also be included in treatment of specific ADD cases.

Stimulant drug therapy

Drug therapy is used very successfully with many ADD children. Some children with very mild cases of ADD are able to cope without medication. Many ADD specialists, myself included, believe that many moderate and severe ADD sufferers have been prevented from reaching their full potential through the failure to prescribe medication.

Drug therapy is not solely a behaviour control measure. It does help the brain to send inhibition or control messages, which tend to govern impulsive or silly behaviour. Drug therapy also helps ADD children to learn from their mistakes and not repeat silly behaviour day after day. It helps them to be more aware of the consequences of their behaviour.

Drug therapy also helps with learning. It allows ADD children to concentrate more, remain on-task and block distractions. It helps them remember what is being taught. ADD kids on drug therapy are often more able to organise their world, work sequentially and present work more precisely. A particular benefit of drug therapy is increased retention from day to day. As an example, remedial therapists often report that children can remember remedial lessons from week to week, rather than having to go back to square one each week.

Perhaps the most telling evidence is to ask a parent of an ADD teenager what they noted when their child began drug therapy. A typical parent response might be 'We just had our first real parent-to-child talk in three years, then he went off happily and did his homework. I'm still in shock.'

There are excellent ADD texts available to describe the benefits and effects of ADD medication. These texts are more appropriate for dealing with medication issues than this practical management guide. Dr Christopher Green's book *Understanding ADD* and Dr Mark Selikowitz's book *All About ADD* are two highly recommended Australian texts.

The honeymoon period

Most ADD children will show an immediate and sometimes dramatic improvement when placed on drug therapy. Several months later, however, when no other multi-modal treatment has been undertaken, parents sometimes report that the drug is no longer working. Sometimes drug levels need minor adjustment at this time. It is more likely, though, that the drug is working but other problems are resurfacing. Stimulant drugs only bring a child back to a more level playing field; they do not fix all problems.

Let us imagine an ADD child with severe reading problems being prescribed Ritalin, with no help given for his reading problems. As he begins drug therapy he is in less trouble and can concentrate better. Thus an immediate boost to self-esteem and confidence occurs indirectly through taking Ritalin, as well as some retention of learning. However, if reading help is not provided he will still be embarrassed in class when he reads. He is then teased in the playground for being slow, and he retaliates. At this time parents may report the drug is not working. The case is rather that there has been a failure to direct attention to remedial and social problems.

Similarly, stimulant drugs will not correct ingrained bad behaviour. Also, drugs often cannot cover every hour of the day. There are periods when ADD kids do not receive medication, for example before it kicks in each morning or late at night. Further, medication does not stop all behaviour problems, impulsivity and hyper-reactivity. If as parents you do not learn how to deal with your child's unique behaviour, it is likely problems will resurface after the honeymoon period.

Parent management training

Primarily this book is about parent management training, the process of teaching the specific techniques used to manage a unique group of kids who have ADD. More often, parent training has been completed in clinics and welfare settings, where ADD specialists help parents develop strategies to deal with the unique and different behaviour ADD children display. The most important factor is that management strategies must be specific to ADD. We have discussed that some parents have struggled because traditional strategies were inappropriate. As an example, I recently saw some delightful parents who felt guilty that their ADD child was still aggressive in kindergarten, despite what was described as six months of aggressive play therapy. The difficulty was that the therapy lessons did not stay with their ADD child once he left the therapy room.

Recognising parent mistakes

Many parents of ADD children harbour guilt for their child's problems. They often compare themselves to friends who manage their children beautifully. The reality is that most often it is the demands, constancy and problems of ADD that lead to parents struggling with discipline, rather than bad parenting causing ADD.

It is important, however, that parents of ADD kids recognise what mistakes they make and try to correct these. For example, concentrating only on negative behaviour and failing to provide a balance of positives will not motivate change in your ADD child. Excusing your constant yelling because your child has ADD will not lead to success. Instead you need to gradually reduce yelling. Dad staying at work, rather than coming home to problems, will not lead to a good relationship between Dad and son that will build esteem and family responsibility. We need to get workaholic dads involved. Mums who are martyrs, for example criticising Dad each time he tries (with statements such as 'Hell, I'll do it myself, I can never trust you'), will contribute to family dysfunction, not build success.

Treating ADD is not just a matter of changing the child. Effort needs to be put into changing parents' understanding and management. For example, a mum I saw recently expected her ADD child to sit quietly in the car doing homework while she was at her aerobics class. This is totally unreasonable. Refusing to change your routines to support an ADD child will lead to disasters.

School management

School simply wasn't designed for ADD children. It requires all the skills they struggle with: concentration, memory, organisation, sequencing and good consequential behaviour in a tight environment. ADD children would much rather be outside running or challenging the fantasy world of computers than being cooped up in a highly distractible, demanding place bounded by four tight walls. Thus, don't permit a human behaviour expert tell you it is easy to manage an ADD child in school. We need to help schools develop realistic strategies to deal with ADD students.

As at home, ADD children require unique and individual management plans in school. Remember though that schools must meet the demands of all children. We must expect some extra help but not a totally individual program. Don't expect schools to own the problem or to excuse all behaviour because your child has ADD. The greatest successes have been achieved where school and home have developed consistent strategies, working in harmony.

Behaviour modification

It is necessary for ADD children to own their behaviour and change gradually. It is unreasonable to expect an ADD child to change overnight or 'just learn to behave like everyone else'. ADD children need very direct, highly intensive and immediate reward and punishment systems, to help them learn appropriate behaviour in a consistent routine. They will not learn by osmosis, by divine intervention or naturally. They need to be shown and reminded what to do. This can be supported by behaviour modification programs; but as I have demonstrated, programs that require concentrating on long-term goals, and delayed rewards, and which lack regular reminders or prompts, will rarely change ADD behaviour. More likely they will increase frustration. The greatest strength of behaviour modification programs is that they help break vicious cycles, causing a change and setting up new behaviour patterns. They are not as good at maintaining change.

Individual counselling

Many of the specialists who refer patients to my clinic ask how I manage to relate to ADD kids who are very difficult, the ADD kids some professionals have preferred not to work with and who are often objectionable and reluctant to engage in treatment. I too struggle with some ADD kids. What success I have I believe is due in part to the fact that I like ADD kids: I like their energy, activity, debating skills, creativity and insight. I believe they see a lot of themselves in me and see that possibly they too can be successful. They seem to like the fact that I don't control sessions or use in-depth analysis, but rather deal with solutions. I take as a great compliment a typical comment ADD kids have made to their parents: 'Ian knows how I feel and how I act. He knows what ADD is and he doesn't beat me up.'

ADD children can respond excellently to counselling or psychotherapy. Many ADD children and adults need psychotherapy for co-existing or Co-morbid Disorders. A therapist can be a confidant who understands their moods, feelings and inadequacies, and can guide them in realising success and avoiding typical ADD traps. A positive therapist can be a very significant adult in an ADD child or teenager's life.

A *word of warning*: Make sure the therapist likes kids, and even more that the therapist likes ADD kids. Most ADD children are very perceptive. If they sense anxiety, rejection or disapproval they will often hyper-react, dismissing the therapist very quickly. The therapist also needs to be loose and light. ADD children will rarely respond in boring, dull or confined settings.

A *second word of warning*: Therapy needs to be transferred from the clinic setting to real life. ADD children may listen intently but forget the minute they leave the room. There must be some form of reminder. Therapy should often involve written contracts or reminder sheets because ADD kids and their parents often forget what was said. Don't trust the weak memories of ADD children. Therapy should not promise quick solutions as there are no magic cures for ADD.

Therapy should reassure

The therapist needs to understand ADD. ADD children, and particularly teenagers, need reassurance that they are not crazy. The therapist needs to have faith in the ADD child, rather than criticising. Few people trust ADD children. The therapist should show how ADD kids can be successful and that futures can be bright.

Be careful of a therapist who begins owning problems. This can occur, as ADD children are very good at blaming others.

Don't talk about ADD kids in front of them

As a personal style, I rarely talk to parents in front of their ADD kids in the early stages of treatment. While it is better to conduct a family therapy session with a dysfunctional family, I believe family therapy has too great a potential to backfire early in ADD treatment. When the family uses this chance to tell someone about all their ADD kid's bad behaviour, the child perceives this as a massive attack. I have seen ADD kids make their parents pay for weeks after such open sessions.

Some parents, when forced to speak in front of their child, may choose not to paint the full picture because they are afraid of the child's likely adverse response. Thus they unintentionally mislead the therapist, who thinks the child really hasn't got a problem.

I also believe many ADD kids, especially teenagers, need privacy in which to discuss their problems, given their hyper-reactivity. Many of my teenagers have commented they wouldn't have seen me otherwise. Not all therapists, however, will adopt this style. As a parent you must decide what you are comfortable with. If you are not comfortable with the setting you do have a right to say so.

Remedial work and specific therapy

Helping overcome learning difficulties is critical in the management of an ADD child. Unless they begin to develop academic confidence, to believe they can succeed at school or even just to read, ADD kids will never develop good self-esteem or cope easily with life. It is little wonder that many untreated ADD teenagers truant or refuse school, or put in little effort. If ADD kids cannot gain academic success and approval they may often seek approval from peers through negative or class-clown behaviour. A good remedial program will help an ADD kid to realise his true potential. A general rule is that ADD kids respond best in a one-to-one situation, as they often are too distracted and understimulated even in small groups.

Not all ADD kids need the same treatment. For example, a young child with sequencing, dominance and motor coordination problems might be better served by occupational therapy before beginning a reading program. In contrast, an upper primary school student who isn't reading may first need a concentrated reading program to build reading survival skills for secondary school.There are a wide variety of well-recognised and accepted remedial interventions, including specialist teachers in schools, special school units, private tutors, commercial and well-respected literacy programs (such as Lindamood, Visualising and Verbalising, Spalding Reading), speech therapy, occupational therapy, physiotherapy, gross motor exercises, self-esteem courses, social skills workshops and many others.

I have not provided in this practical management book methods of remedying learning difficulties. While I diagnose and plan remedial programs for many ADD kids, programming for learning difficulties is a complex field. A discussion of techniques for remedying ADD-related learning difficulties could fill a book on its own. I believe it would be irresponsible to discuss remedial strategies only briefly and as a result have parents head in the wrong direction.

A multi-modal diagnosis will identify exact problems and possibly also identify individual learning styles. From this diagnosis it is possible to select which remedial programs are most suitable. As with therapy, ADD kids must like the remedial specialist and the specialist must constantly reward and recognise effort or achievement. Remedial work should be almost as much a self-esteem exercise as a remedial program.

Beware of magic cures. The glossier the brochure and the more promises it makes of having the one and only cure for ADD, the more sceptical you need to be. Also beware of testimonials of others' successes. ADD children are all different. While one alternative therapy may have worked for one ADD child it may not work for your child. In fact, the experience of many other ADD specialists and myself is that many alternative cures work with only a very tiny percentage of all ADD children. Careful research has shown that many therapies claimed as cures for ADD in fact have no scientific base and when tested in controlled conditions had no significant effect or benefit. I have seen greater success from traditional remedial work. I have seen very isolated success with alternative therapies, but they are not suitable for most ADD kids.

I sympathise with parents seeking solutions; if I had an ADD child and was desperate to do whatever was possible to help I might also seek such help. But I have seen ADD children damaged from being dragged through dozens of therapies, with little or no benefit. These children never got to be just kids. If any group needs to come home, play, run and let off steam after the confines of school, it is ADD children.

Magic cures

I am reminded of a very highly motivated, caring mother who dumped $16 000 worth of receipts on my desk for her son, Matt. None of the therapies she had been through had clearly diagnosed ADD. They all promised cures for Matt's behaviour and reading problems. The result of a multi-modal diagnosis showed ADD, but it also showed that despite all the cures Matt was still reading five years below his age level, despite having been bounced to music, pulled, fed massive doses of vitamins, re-aligned, treated with corrective implements and given magic potions.

A brief word on diet

In the early days Feingold and others believed the cause of ADD was diet. The most recent research shows that while many parents felt diet was very significant in affecting their child's behaviour, careful testing did not reveal this to be the case overall. There does appear to be a very small group of ADD kids who are affected by diet. They benefit from careful diets and need continued dietary guidance. Most other ADD kids can be managed with sensible eating, without driving Mum and the rest of the family crazy by checking supermarket labels, eating bland foods and fighting over restrictions. A good book for parents with a diet-reactive child is *Different Kids* by Sue Dengate. Sue is an Australian mum who works hard in the ADD support field.

Support networks

ADD children need support in a wide variety of areas. Because of their learning difficulties and poor social skills they often fail to develop support networks. They are rarely elected class captain or given responsible leadership positions at school. Except for a few hyperactive kids, they are not often good team players, and miss out on sporting success and thus support. They don't have a wide group of friends (and if they do have friends those kids often tend to be other troubled or poorly behaved characters who provide little responsible and positive support). Their own behaviour often separates them from their families. As teenagers, impulsiveness, irresponsibility and even sexuality problems can destroy personal relationships.

It is important to build networks around a child in which they can gain support. In previous chapters we discussed social skills and sport as examples. Support networks might also be gained by achieving at scouts, becoming the computer monitor at school, having responsible jobs at home for which they gain attention and praise, looking after a pet (great therapy, too!), joining a club or other activities. In earlier chapters I illustrated success stories, such as a child gaining support through playing chess, achieving rowing success, or caring for another child. I believe ADD kids have great potential to develop unique successes.

Parent support groups

Across the world ADD parent and school support groups are becoming established. Parents of ADD kids can gain great benefit from support groups, not just through understanding but also through access to resources and training seminars.

Self-esteem development

As I discussed in Chapter 11, almost all ADD kids have low self-esteem and poor confidence. We need to help them to build confidence and belief in themselves, to overcome self-doubts, and to stop seeing themselves as stupid, dumb, crazy or hopeless. I also believe that by building self-esteem we can reduce the risks of ADD children and teenagers becoming involved in dangerous and damaging behaviours, such as substance abuse (drugs, alcohol, etc.), truancy, dropping out of school early and vandalism. The ADD teenagers I have seen with higher self-esteem also tend to be less oppositional and defiant.

Male role models

There are some very highly motivated dads of ADD kids, who perhaps understand ADD through their own troubles and provide great stimulation and guidance for their children. Unfortunately these dads are the exception rather than the rule. Most mums seem to carry the load. As a result ADD kids often seem to take much of what Mum does or says for granted. ADD mums' attempts to build self-esteem are often met with comments such as 'You're only saying that because you're my mum. Mums always say that stuff.' This may also be due to some ADD kids being in single-parent families and having primarily female teachers. Many of these kids have few male role models. The effect of a positive male then becomes greater.

I have seen the most dramatic changes in ADD kids when Dad became more involved. His involvement is a very important part of a multi-modal treatment plan. Dads do not need to spend hours with their child. A few minutes a night and some one-to-one time on the weekend has an amazing effect.

Other significant adults

Where Dad is unwilling or there is no dad, another significant adult can have a dramatic effect. This could be Grandpa, a sporting coach, an extra-special caring teacher, a family friend or a similar figure.

I am often asked in public lectures or seminars how I overcame sequencing and writing difficulties at school to now be reasonably successful and confident enough to speak in front of an audience of hundreds. While representing at sport certainly helped my self-esteem, I believe a significant adult changed my life. An English teacher heard me arguing with a school principal when I was once again in trouble. She had the insight to offer this rebellious lad the argumentative third speaker's spot in the school debating team. She believed in me despite the fact that my English essays were always full of great ideas but never structured or logical. She continued to encourage me, showing me I could be very talented in other areas and was bright, despite my writing and behaviour difficulties. She showed me my IQ and convinced me I was bright. She encouraged me when others constantly told me I was lazy and failing to reach my potential. She convinced me that I could make it to university, where I would find something I was really interested in and then I would achieve success. In fact she predicted I would change accepted thinking somehow because I always argued. She was right. I finished university with high distinctions. I'm sure Penny would be delighted to know I finally learnt to write, too.

Social skills training

Development of social skills is perhaps one of the most neglected areas of ADD management. It is to be hoped the need for social skills training might remain a high priority in parents' and teachers' minds rather than be lost among other concerns. In the early days of ADD we concentrated on behaviour and learning problems. We now have come to realise that it is poor social skills that often lead to great difficulties in childhood and even more dramatic and damaging problems in adolescence and adulthood. From the time they kick and bite at pre-school, fail to make it through birthday parties and destroy friendships, ADD children seem to be behind in social development. They may be caring, affectionate and protective with younger children and love animals but they don't cope well with peers and intense social situations. It is a problem that still exists when many of the other ADD problems are not as severe. I believe we need to give more attention to social skills training if we are to help ADD children become effective adults.

▶ BEING REALISTIC

The multi-modal strategies discussed are examples of what can be done with ADD children and teenagers. It is unrealistic to plan to carry out all of these at one time. In general, it is a good idea to be working on one or two areas at one time. The aim of multi-modal treatment is not to turn Mum into a six-day-a-week taxi service who is constantly doing something with her ADD child. Such a program will burn out both mother and child.

Respite

The demands of an ADD child or teenager are extreme. It is important that parents share the load, that one parent (usually Mum) does not end up doing ninety per cent of the work. Further, it is important that parents escape occasionally. This is a good time to test those grandparents who say they can manage the child. Call their bluff and take a weekend off. Saving an ADD child is not worthwhile if we destroy a marriage. Parents of ADD children need more time away from home stresses but generally take less.

In summary:

Dealing with ADD is very difficult. The problems of ADD children and teenagers will never be solved solely by applying any one treatment. It is not possible to do everything that's wonderful but greater success is realised through a multi-modal treatment plan.

Think of it as going on an overseas holiday. You are heading to unknown and strange territory, where everything you have always done may not work now. You would not just book an air fare to a country so different and expect a successful holiday. You would pay attention to all details, such as accommodation, transfers, meals and tours, and rely on guides who were experienced in the area.

If we follow this plan with ADD children we can realise great success. There are many cases of ADD children who have grown to achieve unexpected heights, with good multi-modal support from professionals, home and school. While you are heading to that unknown territory you might well discover you will achieve successes others couldn't. ADD kids can take you places and reward you in ways no other child can.

It is my choice to work with ADD kids and teenagers because I believe in their unique ability. Let's continue to look forward and develop more practical strategies and support for ADD kids. We can work together to perform little miracles. I wish parents well with these loveable rogues called ADD kids.

INDEX